I Am
from
HERE

I Am *from* HERE

Stories and Recipes FROM A Southern Chef

VISHWESH BHATT
with Sara Camp Milam
PHOTOGRAPHY BY ANGIE MOSIER

W. W. NORTON & COMPANY
Independent Publishers Since 1923

Printed in China
First Edition

For information about permission to reproduce selections from this book, write to Permissions, W. W. Norton & Company, Inc., 500 Fifth Avenue, New York, NY 10110

For information about special discounts for bulk purchases, please contact W. W. Norton Special Sales at specialsales@wwnorton.com or 800-233-4830

Manufacturing by RRD Asia
Book design by Ashley Tucker
Production manager: Anna Oler

ISBN 978-1-324-00606-0

W. W. Norton & Company, Inc.
500 Fifth Avenue, New York, N.Y. 10110
www.wwnorton.com

W. W. Norton & Company Ltd.
15 Carlisle Street, London W1D 3BS

1 2 3 4 5 6 7 8 9 0

CONTENTS

FOREWORD

There is no definitive answer to the question of what it takes to "become" a chef. If you put in the time and effort and complete a course of study at, say, medical school or law school, you will become a doctor or a lawyer, but by completing a course of study in cooking school, you are almost without exception *not* a chef.

I opened my first restaurant, City Grocery, in the spring of 1992 at twenty-six years old. With a sum total of eight years of cooking experience and a decent Southern résumé, I had absolutely no business opening a restaurant. I could run a kitchen, I could cook delicious food, but I was most definitely *not* a "chef."

Vish began dining at City Grocery shortly after we opened, frequently two to three nights a week. He ate meticulously, I noticed, as I would pass through the dining room—placing a bite of a single component of each dish on his fork, examining it and smelling it before placing it carefully in his mouth.

At first, we kept our distance. He would raise a fork when I passed. I would, on occasion, have a word with him, but not long, not wanting to interrupt the ritual of his meals. He was an even more regular presence in the bar upstairs and was always with a jovial crew, laughing and enjoying themselves. More times than I can count, an unexpected (and usually heavy-handed) pour of whiskey slid in front of me, accompanied by a handshake before he quickly scurried back to his friends.

But Vish soon kicked in the door to our friendship. He was fascinated with the restaurant, food, and operations. His thoughtful pours of whiskey turned into visits to the back door of the kitchen with a bottle of Burgundy, Champagne, or Scotch, and, eventually, into bites of his mother's cooking, to say "thank you" for a particularly enjoyable meal. Vish's mother cooked one night a week at the vegetarian café next door, and it was clear as crystal on his first delivery how proud he was of his mother's cooking.

Like many other chefs in the Western world, I suffered a tragic misunderstanding of Indian food, believing that the recipes the English stole during their colonial occupation and reimagined for the sadly bland palates of their countrymen back home were at all authentic. In 1994, I had no idea that a samosa even existed . . . much less that the addition of curry leaf and ajwain seed to mashed potatoes and peas could catapult those ingredients into transcendence. Though my greatest failing as a chef is that I am pathologically incapable of remembering meals and dishes, I do remember Vish bringing his mother's kachori and tamarind chutney by the back door of the restaurant to try. She left us far too early, but it is no secret to anyone who knows Vish at all that much of his cooking is dedicated to re-creating dishes she loved. To this day, her food and Vish's homages to it are some of the most explosive and moving dishes I have ever tasted.

In the mid-1990s, Vish decided that he would best advance his career by heading along to cooking school. After school, several jobs around the South, and a brief stint in ownership, Vish returned to Oxford in 2001. I knew from the moment he returned that we would open something to showcase his abilities.

Vish's time away had provided the experience needed to help me propel things forward confidently at City Grocery. His focus was firmly rooted in traditional French cooking, and his stoic discipline facilitated precise execution of everything he cooked. He was a quick study and a very firm hand.

Over the last twenty years, Vish and I have spent more time traveling together than most couples do. On these trips we would frequently descend into a conversation about finding a small spot for him to work on his food, Vish declaring that he would never be the cliché: a grinning Indian chef in a small Southern town hawking "curry" and tikka masala. He wanted to be taken seriously for the skills and techniques he had learned in Southern kitchens and through traditional education. In his mind, he was a Southern chef encased in the body of an Indian man.

I had traveled this murky path fifteen years earlier. I was assured in my abilities to please folks, but I had no idea what I was doing. By 1998, I had opened several restaurants in Oxford, and word was spreading nicely about what we were doing. I had begun to cook with confidence, and as a result found my path and my story.

Vish and I decided to open Snackbar in 2009, in a forlorn strip mall, half a mile up the main north/south corridor bisecting the Oxford square. The plan was to present a brasserie-style menu focused on classical French bistro items that addressed the unfortunate state of English pub food (interesting ideas for dishes, sadly executed by visionless English line cooks). It was a blast.

Over the course of eighteen months, we navigated the waters of cowritten menus: menus that he wrote and I edited heavily, menus he wrote less heavily, menus he wrote and I edited lightly—and, ultimately, a menu I could find nothing whatsoever to make a single note on . . . and, trust me, I tried.

Vish was cooking with confidence that would soon grow into joy. Unbeknownst to both of us, he had emerged from the chrysalis of his career. During this time, we had a conversation in which he lamented the loss of his mother, how he missed her food and was beginning to think about how it might fit into the landscape of Oxford. My advice was to never to suppress that feeling inside that inspires passion in you. I had been told by a very wise friend that the things he liked best that I cooked were the things I clearly spent the least amount of time thinking about.

Shortly thereafter, I was having dinner at the restaurant with a group of friends. We moved quickly into lively conversation, and I remember asking our server to please have Vish select what we would eat. The food began to arrive, and among the items were an okra chaat and a collard green saag. The flavors that roiled between those two dishes and the aromas that perfumed our booth were all anyone could talk about. I was swept away in a moment of professional bliss, tears rolling down my cheeks—right before my eyes, my friend was taking the step toward becoming chef.

The inability to contain that which drives your passion, and the ability to communicate that passion through food, is what marks the difference between an excellent cook and a chef. It was in this moment that people started to take notice of Snackbar and to become deeply interested in this Indian man in a small Southern town hawking the food that he loves.

Vishwesh Bhatt, is, simply put, one the finest chefs and finest humans I have ever had the pleasure of knowing. You now hold in your hands a roadmap to his heart, and indisputable proof that he is every bit the chef that anyone in our chosen line of work has ever risen to—and that is because he cooks entirely and unapologetically from his soul.

Thank you for this, my friend. I love you.

—John Currence, January 2022

INTRODUCTION

I want people to see me as I see myself: an immigrant, a son of immigrants, who chose to make the South his home, and in doing so became a Southern chef. I claim the American South, and this is my story.

I can't remember ever thinking to myself or telling anyone that I wanted to be a cook, and yet now that I look back, it seems that cooking and feeding people was what I was supposed to do all along.

I grew up in a very large family in the state of Gujarat, India. My mother was the oldest of eight children, and my father is the oldest of twelve. Both of my grandfathers were bureaucrats and were able to provide a reasonably good living for their families. Unfortunately, they both died early, leaving behind very little in terms of money for my grandmothers. Both women were strong, resourceful, and determined. They raised their broods to be successful and instilled in them a sense of family that has held us together for three generations. Since my parents were the oldest siblings in their respective families, they became de facto caretakers of their younger sisters and brothers, who came to live with us while they attended school in the city of Ahmedabad, where my father worked as a physicist.

I remember our house always being full. At one time, when I was six or seven, we had eleven people living in our three-bedroom flat. This meant that there was always a large crowd at the table and Mom, who was an excellent cook, was always busy in her kitchen. Each day for lunch, our biggest meal, Mom prepared a thali—a meal made up of many small dishes. There would usually be two lentil or bean dishes such as dal, at least two cooked vegetables, a raw vegetable like shredded carrots or sliced radishes, raita, something crispy like chickpea chips, and something sweet like semolina halvah or sweetened yogurt. She would put out pickles and chutneys for everyone to help themselves, and she would roll out fresh chapatis as everyone ate. After that, she'd turn around and make dinner—usually just one or two dishes. Everything we ate was vegetarian. She took pride in knowing that we ate well because she made nearly all of our food from scratch, by herself.

Being the youngest, I was home more than anyone else and always around my mother in the afternoons while she was cooking. In order to keep me occupied and out of her way as she worked through her long list of daily chores, Mom would give me tasks to do. At first, these were simple things like setting the table, handing her utensils, measuring a portion of rice into a pot, and so on. As time went on, the assignments got more involved. She would let me add salt to the dal, measure out spices for the stew, start yogurt for the following day, churn buttermilk, and eventually chop vegetables and put the pressure cooker on. Without knowing it at the time, I was learning how to cook—and really enjoying it.

My dad had a good job, but with so many mouths to feed, his salary didn't stretch far enough for us to have a lot of extras. We had neither a television nor a car. We didn't buy new clothes very often, and we didn't go on big vacations. Trips to the movie theater, for instance, were special events that included the whole family. During the holidays, we always went to one of my grandmothers' houses. Needless to say, we were a crowd. My mother, as usual, would be in charge of the kitchen, Dad would be responsible for getting groceries, and I would inevitably be in the middle of it all.

I loved going to the market with my father. I still do. When I was small, he would take me every Sunday to the main Municipal Vegetable Market in the old walled city of Ahmedabad, Gujarat's largest city. In those days, Ahmedabad was a progressive city; it had been so since its inception. That was the reason Gandhi had established his ashram and started his fight for India's independence from there. The merchants and mill owners who were the financial backbone of the city had invested in education and infrastructure. That was top among the many reasons young, talented professionals like my father had moved there.

Dad and I would ride the bus from the suburb where I grew up to the old city. We would carry empty canvas bags for groceries and talk on the ride in. We would talk about my school, or cricket, or politics, or a book that he was reading or one that he wanted me to read. As the bus wound its way through the city, he would point out some of the historic monuments left behind by the old rulers and show me the new ones, designed by the likes of Doshi, Le Corbusier, and Louis Kahn, that were springing up. As we crossed the Sabarmati River, he would talk about floods and famine and how the river affected the daily lives of the people who lived by it. Once we got to the market, he would talk to me about the vegetables and fruits we were going to buy. He would explain, very patiently, why we couldn't get mangoes at the market in October or why we should buy the small squashes that day because they wouldn't be around the following week. He would, as he still does, meticulously pick out okra one pod at a time, ask for fresh ginger from the back, ask which part of the district the guavas were from. Without fail, he would inquire about the vendors' families and how the rains had affected their crops. We would fill our sacks with produce, then repeat the process at the spice market, the dry goods market, and the grain market. Finally, we would sit and eat ice cream before hiring an auto rickshaw for the ride home. The rickshaw was my once-a-week luxury. It felt good to be chauffeured home.

I realized many years later that these weekly trips to the market with Dad had taught me about the seasonality of produce. They had taught me that there were real people growing the things we ate, and that it was hard work to do what they did. I had learned, without knowing it at the time, to respect farmers. And I had developed a knowledge of vegetables that serves me well to this day.

As soon as we returned home from the market on Sundays, my aunts and uncles would get to work on supper. Sundays, you see, were Mom's day off. The "kids" would put together a meal of various items, or sometimes a big pot of an experimental dish that they were very proud of. We would sit down and eat as a family—all of us. There would be talk of politics and history, cricket, the new play at Tagore Hall, the new exhibit at Hutheesing Gallery, an upcoming wedding or funeral. There was always music: a radio show or a jazz record or the new Beatles album, or just singing from various members of the family. We would always end the evening with devotionals that we sang as a family. It was, I suppose, our way of saying thanks for everything we had.

I tell you this not because I think we did anything special as a family, but to make you understand how meaningful cooking and sharing food are to me. I love to cook. I love to eat even more. But more than anything else, I love to share food. I am the happiest when I can sit down with friends and family at a meal. By extension, it makes me gratified to see a restaurant full of people enjoying the food that I have had a hand in making.

~~~

I haven't had to struggle as many other immigrants have had to. We moved to the United States when I was eighteen—my father had accepted a teaching position at the University of Texas–Austin. The next year, I began college at the University of Kentucky. After I graduated, I came to Oxford, Mississippi, to pursue a master's at the University of Mississippi. My parents were living there at the time, and my father was teaching physics. I was very fortunate to be in the right place at the right time when I got a job filling in for my mother, who made a weekly lunch thali at Harvest Café in Oxford—a progressive vegetarian restaurant, way ahead of its time. I did not know then that my love of cooking would quickly eclipse my interest in graduate school.

Later, wanting to formalize my training, I moved to Miami for culinary school. After graduation, I took a job in Denver. I kept an eye on opportunities in Mississippi, and before long I moved to Jackson. There, I met Teresa, a nurse. Soon, we were married. By the spring of 2002, we were back in Oxford. I returned to City Grocery, where I'd been working before I left for culinary school. I've been a part of City Grocery Restaurant Group (CGRG) ever since.

In 2009, we opened Snackbar. It has been my professional home for more than a decade. I'm proud that we have become a destination for the tourists, alumni, parents, and sports fans who visit Oxford and the university each year. I'm even more proud that we serve so many locals, our friends and regular customers, each week. They come for cocktails and oysters, for okra chaat in the summer, for fried chicken on Tuesdays, and for Friday night seafood stew brimming with fish from the Gulf of Mexico. They celebrate engagements and graduations and the simple pleasure of running into friends at the communal table that spans the length of the bar area. When the COVID-19 pandemic forced us to close our doors to in-person dining for three months in 2020, CGRG operations pivoted to offer take-out meals. Our regulars pulled up to the parking lot on those surreal spring evenings for yeast rolls by the dozen, enchilada casserole, and boil-in-bag chicken vindaloo. Staff donned masks and gloves and smiles to ferry each order to tables on the porch for a contactless hand-off. Customers ordered extras to stash in the freezer. They tipped more than they needed to. We stayed afloat.

Oxford is my home. I have spent more time here than anywhere else. I have grown up as a person and a chef in Oxford. John Currence, the CGRG team, and the people of Oxford have been very good to me. They have supported me wholeheartedly. Three decades later I am still here, doing what I absolutely love to do.

Cooking is my profession, of course. But it defines so much of who I am. It's how I interact with my family and friends. It's how I learn about cultures other than my own. It's how I make sense of the world and my place in it. A good many of the recipes in this book were born at Snackbar. Others I've adapted from my travels or from the cooks, professional and otherwise, who have marked my palate and my cuisine in some way. But most are the dishes of my everyday life. Like so many Southerners, Teresa and I love to entertain. The occasion can be as momentous as Thanksgiving or as quotidian as the harvest of backyard tomatoes begging to be sliced and shared. The four couples in our supper club take turns hosting one another for
~~~

monthly dinners. Many of my recipes serve eight. If I'm grilling a rack of ribs or frying catfish, I want to have friends over to share. I encourage you to do the same. That said, almost all of the recipes in these pages can be cut in half. And with the exception of fried foods, which are best served immediately, you can enjoy leftovers the next day.

~~~

Recently, someone important asked me if I consider myself a Southern chef. The answer is *absolutely yes.* I know that I wasn't born here, but this is where I have made my home, and this is where I make my living. My food, while very much influenced by my childhood in India, is my interpretation of the way we eat here in the American South. I use ingredients and techniques I have learned from Southern chefs. I grew up vegetarian, so everything I know about cooking meat or fish I learned from watching folks like John Currence, Ben Barker, and Ashley Christensen, some of the South's best chefs. They have patiently answered questions and have graciously taught me the difference between redfish and red snapper. They have generously shared their whiskey along with stories of their upbringings and their families. What I have learned from spending time with some of the best culinary minds in the country is that the traditions and values I was brought up with in Gujarat aren't that different from the ones they grew up with in places like North Carolina, Kentucky, Texas, and Louisiana.

When they talk about benne seed oil pressed in South Carolina, I am reminded of the times my grandmother would send me down to the local mill with the first sesame seeds of the season to get them pressed into oil. I remember the smell and taste of that freshly pressed warm oil. I remember how my grandmother would take the pomace left from pressing and cook it with jaggery to make halvah. When I hear the excitement in my fellow chefs' voices about sourcing raw milk, I remember the dairy farmer who would come to our house with his canister full of fresh buffalo milk, which my mother would boil to sterilize. When I hear two chefs discuss the virtues of Virginia peanuts over Georgia ones, I remember my father talking with his brothers about why he likes the peanuts from Bharuch more than the ones from Surendranagar. When there is a debate about Carolina Gold rice versus Louisiana Popcorn rice, I remember being taught by my mother that basmati rice is good for pilafs, but that the Sona Masoori varietal from the south of India is better for use in khichadi. I grew up eating okra, black-eyed peas, fresh tomatoes, and lima beans. I grew up drinking fresh sugarcane juice and "sun" tea over ice. Peanuts remain a staple in our kitchens. Cotton and tobacco fields still stretch to the horizon in many parts of Gujarat. As long as I've lived in the South, I've felt at home at the table and in the kitchen.

I want the food of my childhood, the flavors I grew up with, to become a part of the Southern culinary repertoire—just like tamales, lasagna, and kibbeh have become. I want to show that the ingredients of the modern Southern pantry were very much the ingredients of my mother's pantry as well. I want to tell you my Southern story the best way I know how: through my food.
~~~

BEFORE WE GET STARTED

Pantry, Equipment, and Techniques

Above all, I want you to cook from this book. My hope is that you'll bring what you know, whether it's a lot or a little, and learn something new in the process of reading and cooking these recipes. Maybe you've never begun a dish by blooming whole spices in oil, a technique that's second nature to home cooks across the Indian subcontinent. Maybe you haven't had the pleasure of eating catfish, a versatile, sustainable, and nutritious staple of the American South. Or perhaps deep-frying has always intimidated you. Here's your chance to try. And if you mess up, just laugh it off, invite your friends back over, and try again.

You can seamlessly halve many of the recipes that follow. If, on the other hand, you increase a recipe, don't automatically double the salt or pepper. Instead, begin with the amount called for, tasting and adding as you go along.

My cooking includes some spices and pantry staples that might be new to you, especially if your relationship to spices is limited, or if you live outside the American South. I want to introduce you to these ingredients and flavors with the hope that they become part of your own cuisine. You can find the vast majority of the ingredients for these recipes at your supermarket. A handful will require a trip to an international grocery store or an Indian market, or you can order them online.

In a pinch, don't let a missing ingredient stop you from trying a recipe. (Obviously, this applies to ingredients called for in small quantities—use your good judgment.) The resulting dish will have a slightly different flavor profile, but it can still be a success. The same goes for equipment. In most recipes, I suggest the best pot or pan for the task at hand. If it's not on your shelf, use what you have and cook on.

SPICES

In general, I recommend buying whole spices and grinding or crushing them yourself as you need them. They will retain their flavor and last longer than ground spices. More often than not, I begin by dry-toasting my spices. You'll see me use this technique over and over again, particularly with cumin and coriander seeds. I can't overstate what a remarkable difference this simple step makes. It provides a depth of flavor that makes bottled ground spices feel bad about themselves. You simply toast the seeds in a small, dry pan over medium heat until they become fragrant. Depending on the size of the whole spices and the strength of your stove's burners, this will usually take one to two minutes, but your nose is a more accurate guide than your timer. Shake the pan gently to toss the seeds so that they toast evenly. Remove the pan from the heat and, when the spices are cool enough to handle, grind them in a spice grinder or coffee grinder, or with a mortar and pestle. Set aside until the recipe calls for adding those spices to the dish. (In cases where texture makes a difference in the finished dish, I note whether the spices should be finely ground or coarsely crushed.)

Another technique you'll use often is blooming a spice, generally a whole seed, in oil. That means heating a neutral oil, adding the spice to the hot oil, and cooking very briefly (usually for less than a minute), until the spice becomes fragrant. With mustard seeds, the cue is that they'll start popping. With other spices, you'll smell the difference, and that's your signal to move on to the next step of the recipe. Resist the temptation to skip this step—you might save a bit of time, but you'll lose out on depth of flavor. And I don't recommend this technique with ground spices because they're likely to burn in the oil.

Below are a handful of the spices and spice blends I cook with most frequently.

Ajwain, sold in seed form, is also known as carom seed or bishop's weed. The flavor is a cross between thyme and oregano. You can find ajwain in an Indian market or online. In a pinch, you may omit it from recipes that call for small quantities, or sub in a bit of dried thyme.

Asafoetida (also spelled asafetida and also known as hing) is common throughout the cuisine of the Indian subcontinent. Made from the dried resin of the giant fennel plant, it is sold as a powder and has a nutty-umami flavor and a distinctive pungent scent. You can find it at an Indian market or order it online.

I cook with lots of **black pepper**. I usually begin with whole black peppercorns, which I toast in a dry skillet to wake up the flavors. I'll let them cool for a couple of minutes, then, depending on the texture I want in a dish, I'll crack, crush, or grind the peppercorns. If the recipe calls for cracked pepper, you can crack the peppercorns in a mortar and pestle or with a rolling pin or the back of a spoon. Keep going past cracked to get to crushed, and even further to get to ground. Of course, a pepper mill is the easiest way to make freshly ground pepper. If your pepper mill has a coarse grind setting, you can use that when crushed pepper is called for.

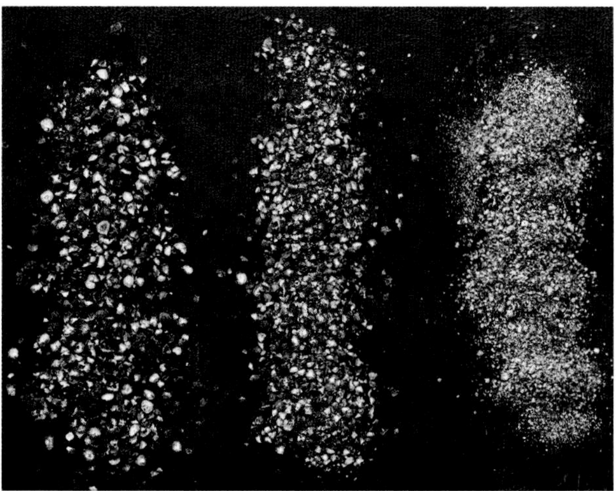

Cardamom pods come in green and black varieties. For the most part, I cook with green cardamom pods. Their aroma is much more intense than ground cardamom, with hints of citrus, mint, and spice. I use black cardamom, with its even stronger, smokier flavor, for garam masala.

Cayenne pepper is one of the few spices for which the ground variety is the default, and I use it frequently. If you are especially sensitive to heat, feel free to dial back the cayenne in any recipe that calls for it.

Chaat (also spelled chat) masala is a ground spice blend with fruity, tart, spicy, and funky notes, available online or at Indian markets. As the name implies, it is frequently sprinkled on chaat, the catch-all term for savory Indian snacks. I use MDH Chunky Chat Masala, which is inexpensive and widely available. I've included a recipe for chaat masala at the end of this section (page 8), but for most home cooks, it is more cost-effective to buy ready-made than to blend your own.

Coriander features heavily in Indian home cooking. I begin with whole seeds, which I usually toast and crush or grind, often with cumin, before proceeding with a recipe. (Fun fact: These are the seeds from which cilantro grows.) If your supermarket does not carry whole coriander seeds, you can find them at Indian grocery stores or other international markets.

Creole seasoning is a staple for home cooks in Louisiana, parts of Texas, and the Deep South. Tony Chachere's out of Opelousas, Louisiana, is the most popular and widely available brand. You can also make your own Creole seasoning blend (see page 8); you probably have most of the components on your shelf already.

Cumin is available at supermarkets in both ground and seed form. I almost always begin with whole seeds. If you use ground cumin, do yourself a favor and buy a new jar the next time you go to the grocery store. The flavor will not be as deep as the freshly toasted and ground seeds, but at least it will not be stale.

Curry powder is not actually a single spice, but a blend. The bottled versions sold by major brands in US supermarkets usually contain ground coriander, cumin, fenugreek, ginger, mustard, turmeric, and red chile, among other spices.

Fennel seeds have a floral, sweet, and refreshing aroma, with a hint of licorice.

Fenugreek seeds, bitter and citrusy, are popular in many Indian dishes. If you do not see them at your supermarket, you will find them at any Indian grocery store, where they may also be labeled methi seeds.

Garam masala, a blend of warm spices, is likely on the shelf with the bottled ground spices at your regular supermarket. If not, try an international or Indian market, or order it online. You can also make your own (see page 8) for maximum flavor and freshness—you probably have most of the components in your pantry already.

Kashmiri chili powder is available at Indian markets or online. It has a beautiful, bright red color and packs a bit less heat than cayenne. If you cannot find it, hot paprika is an acceptable but imperfect substitute. It will give you the red color, but not the same amount of heat.

Mustard seeds come in brown, yellow, and black. Use brown unless otherwise specified. Many Indian recipes begin with blooming mustard seeds in ghee or neutral oil to flavor the oil before proceeding with the rest of the dish.

I recommend buying **nutmeg** whole (the "nut" is actually the seed from a tropical evergreen tree) and grating it with a fine grating tool such as a Microplane zester when a recipe calls for it. It takes only a few extra seconds, and has so much more flavor than bottled ground nutmeg.

Paprika comes in sweet, hot, and smoked varieties. The sweet is the default. Use that one unless hot or smoked is called for.

Red pepper flakes, also labeled as crushed red pepper, appear frequently in my cooking. Feel free to dial these back a little if you prefer less heat.

Salt is always kosher salt. I use Morton's. I do not tend to use a great deal of salt, letting herbs and spices do most of the work of flavoring my food. When I believe a dish needs a certain amount of salt, the recipe will call for that amount. Overall, though, I recommend that you taste and season to your liking. You can always add salt, of course, but you can't take it away, so add it gradually, stirring and tasting, until you're happy with the way the dish tastes.

Star anise smells of licorice. Buy the whole pods.

Turmeric is a close cousin of ginger. The dried and ground root, from which the powdered spice is made, imparts dishes with a beautiful golden color.

Spice Blends

As a general rule, spice blends will retain the best flavor for one month when stored in an airtight plastic or glass container at room temperature. As you learn what you like, you can start experimenting with your own blends.

Chaat Masala

Makes about 1 cup

Black salt (sometimes labeled kala namak) is Himalayan pink salt that is heated and infused with herbs and spices, resulting in a deep, funky flavor. If you use regular kosher salt instead of black salt, the resulting blend will not taste like chaat masala. You can't fake the funk. Amchur is a powder made from dried green mangoes. It has a fruity-tart aroma. Both black salt and amchur are available at Indian grocery stores.

- 3 tablespoons cumin seeds
- 2 tablespoons black peppercorns
- ¾ teaspoon ajwain seeds
- ½ cup dried mint leaves
- ⅓ cup amchur (dried mango powder)
- 1 tablespoon ground ginger
- 1 tablespoon ground cayenne pepper
- 1¼ tablespoons black salt
- ½ teaspoon asafoetida

Toast the cumin seeds and black peppercorns in a small, dry skillet over medium heat, shaking the pan gently so that they toast evenly and do not burn. After 30 seconds, add the ajwain seeds (these are much smaller, so you want to be careful not to burn them). Toast until all are fragrant, about 1 minute. Remove from the heat. When cool enough to handle, grind all three together in a spice grinder or coffee grinder, or with a mortar and pestle. Combine with the mint leaves, amchur, ground ginger, cayenne, black salt, and asafoetida and stir to mix well. When completely cool, store in an airtight plastic or glass container at room temperature.

Snackbar Creole Seasoning

Makes about 1 cup

- ¼ cup paprika
- 2½ tablespoons salt
- 2½ tablespoons garlic powder
- 1½ tablespoons onion powder
- 1½ tablespoons ground cayenne pepper
- 1½ tablespoons dried oregano
- 1½ tablespoons dried thyme
- 1 tablespoon fennel seeds, crushed with a mortar and pestle
- 1 tablespoon red pepper flakes
- 1½ teaspoons dried dill (may be labeled dill weed)

Combine all the ingredients well and store in an airtight plastic or glass container at room temperature.

Vish's Garam Masala

Makes about ¾ cup

- ¼ cup coriander seeds
- 2 tablespoons cumin seeds
- 1 tablespoon black peppercorns
- 1 cinnamon stick
- 3 black cardamom pods
- 3 whole cloves
- 1 teaspoon black mustard seeds
- 1 teaspoon red pepper flakes

Toast all the ingredients together in a small, dry pan over medium heat until very fragrant, 1 to 2 minutes, shaking the pan gently so that they toast evenly and do not burn. Remove from the heat. When cool enough to handle, grind the mixture in a spice grinder or coffee grinder, or with a mortar and pestle. You may need to grind the mixture in two batches if your grinder is too small to accommodate everything at once. If that is the case, stir everything together after grinding to make sure the spices are evenly mixed. When completely cool, store in an airtight plastic or glass container at room temperature.

OILS AND FATS

When I call for a neutral oil, I'm probably using peanut or canola. I tend to use these interchangeably for most purposes, although peanut oil is my preference for deep-frying, and canola is my go-to for salad dressings. You can also use generic vegetable oil when a neutral oil is called for. If you choose to use olive oil in a dish that calls for neutral oil, be aware that the resulting flavor profile will be a little different. When a recipe begins by instructing you to bloom spices in oil, a neutral oil is especially important. In this case, you don't want to taste the oil itself—you want it to take on the flavor of the spices.

Several recipes in this book also call for ghee, a type of clarified butter that's a staple of the Indian pantry. Ghee is increasingly available in supermarkets, where it will be stocked either in the refrigerated dairy case near the butter or on the shelf with other oils. You can also make it yourself. When making your own ghee, begin with good-quality unsalted butter. I like to use cultured butter, which is widely available from brands like Vermont Creamery and Organic Valley. You'll cook it for longer than ordinary clarified butter, and the resulting flavor is deeper and nuttier. If you prefer a dish to be vegan, substitute a neutral oil when a recipe calls for ghee.

Ghee

Makes about 1 pound

Please note that these cooking times can vary significantly depending on factors such as the water content of your butter, the strength of your stove's burners, and the thickness of your pot or saucepan. Use your eyes, not a timer, as your guide.

2 pounds (8 sticks) unsalted butter, cut into 1-inch cubes

Place the butter in a heavy-bottomed pot or saucepan (a 2-quart pot is ideal) over medium heat. If you do not have a good pot with a heavy bottom, set your pot or saucepan in a skillet placed on the stove. This will protect the butter from burning. Cook, stirring occasionally, until the butter has completely melted and begins to bubble, about 4 minutes. Turn the heat to the lowest setting your stove allows and continue cooking. Watch the melted butter carefully. In another 5 to 6 minutes, you will notice the bubbles becoming smaller and foamier.

Using a wooden spoon, gently push the foam to the side of the pot. You will see that the melted butter is yellowish and opaque. Keep cooking and watching. After a few minutes, the foam will start to dissipate, and the butter will become golden and transparent.

Remove the pot from the heat. Let the butter sit for about 5 minutes to allow the milk solids to release the rest of their water and settle to the bottom of the pot. When the liquid is clear and golden, with grainy-looking, light brown sediment at the bottom of the pot, the ghee is ready.

Line a mesh strainer with a paper coffee filter. Pour the warm ghee through the strainer into a quart-size glass jar or a similar large container, preferably glass, with a tight-fitting lid. Allow the ghee to cool completely (it will become semi-solid) before capping the jar. You will end up with approximately 1 pound of ghee.

You may store the ghee at room temperature or in the refrigerator. It will keep for a month on your countertop or for 4 months in your refrigerator.

You can follow the same method starting with 1 pound of butter to make a smaller quantity of ghee, if you like. But since it has a long shelf life, I always cook 2 pounds of butter at a time and have no problem using every spoonful!

Do not throw away the toasty, buttery milk solids that are left behind. Spread them on toast while they are still warm and sprinkle with a generous pinch of sugar. They have a surprisingly delicious, toasty-tangy-buttery flavor.

DRY INGREDIENTS AND PANTRY STAPLES

Many recipes in this book call for **rice**. I generally use basmati because I like its aromatic quality. You may substitute any long-grain white rice. If you choose to use brown rice in a dish, know that the flavors will be slightly different and the cooking time will be longer.

Split pigeon peas appear in a couple of recipes. If you're shopping at an Indian or international market, you might see them labeled as toor dal. You can substitute a different split pea, bean, or lentil—mung (moong) dal, for example—if you prefer.

When a recipe calls for **fresh field peas**, I encourage you to seek them out. Otherwise, I prefer to cook with dried peas and beans. If you don't have time for the soaking that dried beans require, frozen is generally a better substitute than canned. However, there's an exception: Canned beans do tend to work well in soups and stews. (Rinse and drain them first, please.) The reason for this is that frozen beans yield less starch in cooking, so you'll lose that creamy mouthfeel that makes stewed beans so satisfying. The bottom line: Unless a recipe specifies otherwise, aim to use dried beans and peas, and set aside the time it takes to soak them before proceeding with the recipe.

Sorghum syrup is a traditional sweetener, especially in the Appalachian South. It has earthy, bright, and grassy notes as compared to cane syrup. I especially like Muddy Pond sorghum, made by the Guenther family in Monterey, Tennessee. If you cannot find sorghum syrup, cane syrup is the closest substitute, but maple syrup will also do. Speaking of sweeteners, it is worth seeking out **jaggery**, an unrefined palm or cane sugar, when a recipe calls for it. (In the US, this will almost certainly be cane jaggery.) But you may also substitute the same quantity of light brown sugar.

Chickpea flour is widely available at grocery stores thanks to increased demand for gluten-free alternatives to wheat flour. I love its nutty flavor. You may also see it labeled as garbanzo flour, or as besan or gram flour if you are shopping at an Indian market. If you see both coarse and fine options, buy the fine.

In my recipes, **coconut milk** is always full-fat and unsweetened. It's the heavy liquid that comes in a can (13.5 to 14 ounces), not the thin alternative milk (sold in cartons in the dairy aisle) that you would pour on cereal or add to coffee.

Creole mustard is my favorite kind of grainy mustard. The Zatarain's brand is widely available, but if you cannot find it, substitute any grainy mustard.

I cook with **homemade chicken stock**. Depending on what a recipe calls for or what else I am cooking, I'll make either Whole Chicken Stock (page 28) or, more often, Chicken Bone Stock (page 247). When the recipe calls for boiling a chicken, I like to use the resulting liquid as Whole Chicken Stock—there is too much flavor to throw away. Otherwise, I save cooked chicken bones and make Chicken Bone Stock for using in recipes. Both are seasoned but unsalted. If you buy chicken stock by the can or carton, be sure to choose an unsalted version.

For **hot sauce**, I use Tabasco or Louisiana, but you may use any bottled hot sauce you like.

My favorite **mayonnaise** is Duke's.

PRODUCE AND FRESH HERBS

Much of my cooking centers around fresh, seasonal, local produce—it's the main reason this book is organized by ingredient. That said, there are certain fresh ingredients I keep on hand, no matter the season, and despite the fact that they might not grow in Mississippi. These staples include green chiles, limes, lemons, fresh ginger, fresh garlic, cilantro, flat-leaf parsley (also called Italian parsley), and curry leaves.

When **cilantro** goes into a dish, I use the leaves and the tender part of the stems. For garnish, I use the leaves only.

Curry leaves are one of those ingredients that you won't miss until you've used it. Once you've smelled their singular aroma—nutty, citrusy, and herbaceous all at once—frying in ghee, there's no going back. You'll find them sold fresh, on the stem, at Indian markets (sometimes Caribbean ones, too). They are edible, so there's no need to remove them from the dish before serving. Omit them in a pinch. A sprig has 10 or 12 leaves.

HOT
SAUCE
TIM

Garlic should always be fresh, and the cloves are peeled before mincing or slicing.

Throughout the book, **ginger** is fresh unless ground ginger is specifically called for. Always peel fresh ginger before mincing, chopping, or slicing. If the precise volume measurement is important, the recipe will call for it. Otherwise, it will call for ginger root by the inch.

If a recipe calls for **green chiles**, serrano is my first choice, followed by jalapeño. (If you are using jalapeños, select ones that are on the smaller side.) I almost never remove the seeds from my peppers because I like the heat. If you prefer less heat, you should feel free to remove some or all of the seeds as well as the white pith/ribs any time a recipe calls for green chiles.

When cooking with fresh **tomatoes**, I rarely remove the seeds. In the few cases where I think it is preferable to seed the tomatoes, the recipe will call for it.

In most cases, I give market measurements and volume measurements for produce. In general, I encourage you not to waste. It is often fine to round a measurement up or down slightly in order to use a whole fruit or vegetable. Even though fruit sizes vary, you do not need to measure out the juice or zest of citrus (lemon, lime, orange) unless a precise amount is called for. But for reference, figure about 2 tablespoons of juice per lime.

EQUIPMENT

If you have an enameled cast-iron **Dutch oven**, you will return to it again and again, and a good-quality one will last for decades. I have these in various sizes, but the 5½-quart size is my workhorse. I use it so much at home that it lives on the stove—I never even put it away in a cabinet.

The other **pots and pans** I use frequently include a 2-quart pot with a lid for rice, a 10-inch skillet, and a nonstick skillet with tall sides and a lid. The small aluminum wok I use for stir-frying used to be my mother's, and it is as old as I am. I cook with wooden and silicone utensils because I don't like the sound of metal on metal and I don't want to scratch my pots and pans with metal tools.

A **food processor** and a **spice grinder** are probably my most-used tools. If you do not have a food processor, you can use a blender instead. A coffee grinder serves the same purpose as a spice grinder, or you can do as my mother did and crush or grind spices with a mortar and pestle. It's nice to have a **meat thermometer** for accuracy and food safety. Probe thermometers are easy to use and generally more accurate than the laser kind.

I love to **grill**. I use a Weber gas grill, but the grilling recipes in this book will work on any kind of outdoor grill, whether gas or charcoal. (When possible, I also provide alternative cooking methods if you do not have a grill.) I also give grill temperatures as an approximate range, knowing that grills vary widely in terms of how they register heat and how much control you have to begin with. Before grilling, always be sure to clean and oil your grates well to prevent food from sticking.

You might not know that you can also deep-fry in cast-iron or enameled cast-iron vessels placed directly on the grates of your grill. This is a great way to fry without causing your whole house to smell. However, don't ever deep-fry on a grill in the rain, as the oil will splatter and may burn you or catch something on fire.

SHOPPING LIST

If you are visiting an Indian grocery store to stock your pantry, especially if you've never visited one before, you're in luck: I made a shopping list for you. These are the ingredients that appear over and over in this book, specifically the ones that might not be available at your regular supermarket. Of course, I hope you'll pick up anything else that catches your eye. You might find some new favorites.

If you do not know of an Indian grocery store in your area, check the website of Patel Brothers (PatelBros.com), the largest Indian grocery chain in the

United States. They have locations from coast to coast, and there may be one near you. Of course, it's great to support small, family-owned markets, and some Indian restaurants have a small retail area with spices and pantry items. Many of these items are also available in the Indian or Asian sections at international supermarkets.

As you're browsing the aisle with dried beans, peas, and lentils, you will see that many of them are available in both whole and split forms. Usually the split form of a legume is called a dal (sometimes spelled daal), which is also a general term for cooked lentil dishes.

- Ajwain Seeds
- Amchur (may be spelled Amchoor)
- Asafoetida (may be spelled Asafetida, may be labeled Hing)
- Black Salt (may be labeled Kala Namak)
- Chaat (may be spelled Chat) Masala
- Chana Dal (may be labeled Split Desi Chickpeas or Split Gram)
- Chickpea Flour (may be labeled Besan or Gram Flour)
- Cardamom Pods, Green (You may also buy black cardamom pods if you want to blend your own garam masala.)
- Coriander Seeds
- Cumin Seeds
- Curry Leaves (These will be in the produce section. Back at your house, they will keep in the refrigerator for 5 days, so choose a recipe that calls for curry leaves—or a couple of those recipes—and have at it.)
- Fenugreek Seeds (may be labeled Methi)
- Garam Masala
- Ghee
- Kashmiri Chili Powder
- Madras Curry Powder
- Mustard Seed Oil
- Red Chori (whole, dried small red beans; may be labeled Desi Chori)
- Star Anise (whole pods)
- Tandoori Masala
- Toor Dal (split pigeon peas)
- Urad Dal (split black lentils)

ONLINE RESOURCES

Anson Mills (AnsonMills.com) of Columbia, South Carolina, sells a variety of heirloom grains and legumes. Best known for their Carolina Gold rice, they also offer a wide selection of corn products (grits, cornmeal, and polenta), flours, and Sea Island red peas.

Camellia Beans (CamelliaBrand.com) is best known for its red kidney beans, which feature in the classic New Orleans red beans and rice. They offer a variety of dried beans, peas, and lentils for mail order.

Original Grit Girl (GritGirl.net) is based right here in Oxford, Mississippi. These stone-ground grits are the ones I use at Snackbar and at home, and you can order them as well.

Rancho Gordo Beans (RanchoGordo.com) is another good source for beans, peas, dal, and other pantry items.

Simmons Farm-Raised Catfish (SimmonsCatfish.com) of Yazoo City, Mississippi, offers a variety of cuts for mail order. The 5- to 7-ounce fillets are perfectly sized for the recipes in the catfish chapter.

Spicewalla (SpicewallaBrand.com) was started by my friend Meherwan Irani, chef-owner of the Chai Pani restaurants in Asheville, North Carolina, and Decatur, Georgia. Spicewalla sells ground spices, whole seeds, and spice blends. If you're looking for a spice in one of my recipes that is not available at your regular grocery store, Spicewalla almost certainly carries it. Other good online spice resources include **Burlap & Barrel** (BurlapAndBarrel.com), **Diaspora** (DiasporaCo.com), and **La Boîte** (LaBoiteNY.com).

Two Brooks Farm (TwoBrooksFarm.com) uses sustainable methods to grow rice in the Mississippi Delta. You can order their rice and rice grits (aka middlins) online.

I Am *from* HERE

CHAPTER ONE

RICE

The story of rice is the story of human civilizations.

It is a story of all that is good about us, and all that is bad. Rice is a staple in the American South, where I now live, as well as in my native India. The grain has been a staple of kitchens in Louisiana and South Carolina for centuries. Today, as the US South diversifies and welcomes new Southerners from places like Latin America and Asia, rice is even more prevalent. I think of the coconut rice and peas at Nina Compton's Bywater American Bistro in New Orleans, or the bone marrow risotto with radish-top kimchi at Chris Shepherd's UB Preserv in Houston.

No matter where you live, once you start looking, you'll find rice everywhere. It is the centerpiece of iconic dishes all around the world. Spin the globe, and you'll find rice. Think of Persian biryani, Korean bibimbap, West African jollof, Spanish paella, Lowcountry purloo, Cajun jambalaya, British kedgeree, or Dutch-Indonesian rijsttafel. Rice dishes have evolved over centuries and across continents. If you believe, as I do, that every dish tells a story, rice is in a class of its own. Behind these dishes are stories of migration and diaspora; of conquest, resilience, and adaptation.

Thanks to dedicated scholars, farmers, and purveyors, centuries-old rice varietals that once faced extinction now appear on menus across the country. Mainstream publications like the *Wall Street Journal* have reported on heirloom rice farmers in Mississippi and Florida. What's even better is that we are now talking about the people behind the rice. We are starting to pay attention to the labor and sacrifices of farmers and seed savers. For hundreds of years, that wasn't the case. The enslaved men and women who worked on Lowcountry rice plantations brought with them sophisticated rice farming knowledge from their native Senegambia in West Africa. Their forced labor built the wealth of cities like Charleston, South Carolina. The story of rice isn't always a happy one, but it is a story that needs to be told and heard.

Virtually all of the rice dishes in this book are written and tested to work with inexpensive, commercially produced rice, but I also encourage you to try out new tastes and textures, and learn new stories, by seeking out locally produced or heirloom rice from small farms. I like to cook with Missimati, a sustainably farmed basmati-style rice from Two Brooks Farm in the Mississippi Delta. You might try Carolina Gold from Anson Mills, or its newer, aromatic varietal, Charleston Gold.*

Challenge yourself to cook rice dishes from many different cultures. Share them with your friends, and talk about the people and places those dishes come from. Think about how you can bring your own favorite ingredients and techniques, the ones that have been passed down to you and the ones you've picked up for yourself, to the recipes that follow. The last time I made jambalaya, an iconic Louisiana rice dish, I used lamb sausage instead of andouille and khada masala, a staple Indian spice blend that nods to my own roots. I think you will come to see, as I have, that rice is just one of the many things we have in common. And it's the perfect ingredient with which to begin.

---

* Fun fact: Anson Mills developed Charleston Gold with the help of Gurdev Khush, an Indian-American scientist who won the 1996 World Food Prize for his work fighting world hunger by means of rice production. It's yet another point of Indian-Southern connection, with rice as the conduit.

PERFECT RICE

If you're making rice for a crowd or a larger recipe, the method below works equally well with 2 cups rice, 4 cups water, and a more generous pinch (or two) of salt. I love eating just-cooked rice with a generous dollop of ghee or some grated Parmesan.

Makes 2 to 2⅓ cups cooked rice, depending on grain size

1 cup basmati rice (or your favorite long-grain white rice)
Salt

Place the rice in a strainer and gently rinse it under cold running water. This helps wash away any dirt and excess starch. Drain thoroughly.

Transfer the rice to a heavy-bottomed pot—a 2-quart pot is ideal. Add 2 cups water and a pinch of salt. Set the pot on the stove *without* turning on the heat for 15 minutes. You may skip this step if you are in a hurry, but the 15-minute soak will give you a fluffier result.

Turn the heat to medium-high and allow the water to come to a boil. As soon as the water starts to boil, turn the heat down to very low, cover the pot, and cook for 15 minutes. Do not take off the lid or be tempted to stir the rice during this time.

At the end of 15 minutes, turn off the heat, move the pot off the stove, and leave covered for 5 minutes to finish. Remove the lid, fluff the rice with a fork if you like, and serve.

KHICHADI SERVES 3 TO 4

In its simplest form, khichadi is a porridge-like dish made by cooking rice and lentils together. That's it! Cook one part rice and one part beans with water and a pinch of salt, and you will have made khichadi. It's that easy—but then again, the simplest dishes are never that easy. There are as many versions of khichadi as there are households, and if you tell anyone that yours is the definitive one, you are likely to start a fight.

As a matter of fact, my own parents were divided about what a "real" khichadi should have in it. The only reason we survived that rift as a family was that we ate the damn thing three times a week, alternating my mother's and father's preferred versions. This civil war has continued in my own household. You see, I learned how to make khichadi from my mother. It was the first dish she taught me to cook. Decades later, my wife honed her khichadi skills under my dad's tutelage. To this day, she will put her hands on her hips, jut her chin out, and tell me what's what if I dare suggest that she may want to ease off on the cloves.

In the spirit of peace, and to preserve harmony in our house, I offer my grandmother's recipe for khichadi. Toor dal (split pigeon peas) were my favorite growing up, so Grandma always used those when she made khichadi for me. Use any split bean/pea you like.

Remember that this is a dish you can personalize easily. Feel free to add and subtract ingredients as you like. Feel free to start your own domestic disputes. But above all, feel free to enjoy the process of feeding the people you love.

- 1 cup basmati rice
- 1 cup split pigeon peas (toor dal) or yellow lentils
- ½ teaspoon salt
- ¼ teaspoon ground turmeric
- 1 tablespoon ghee (store-bought or homemade, see page 9), plus more for serving (optional)
- ½ teaspoon brown mustard seeds
- 6 black peppercorns
- 2 whole cloves
- ½ small cinnamon stick
- ½ teaspoon cumin seeds
- ¼ teaspoon asafoetida
- Plain, full-fat yogurt (preferably Greek-style), for serving (optional)

NOTE: Basmati is a fragrant, long-grain rice that makes a relatively "dry" khichadi. Carolina Gold would work nicely as well. If you prefer a consistency more like risotto, use a starchy, short-grain rice.

Combine the rice and pigeon peas in a large strainer. Rinse thoroughly with cold water and remove any debris. Drain and put the rinsed rice-pea mixture in a heavy-bottomed pot. Cover the grains with 4 cups cold water. Add the salt and turmeric, stir, and allow to soak for 20 minutes.

Meanwhile, heat the ghee in a small skillet over medium heat until it is melted and fragrant. Add the mustard seeds and cook until they start popping, about 30 seconds. Add the rest of the spices to the hot ghee and swirl until everything is toasted and fragrant, 15 to 20 seconds. Be careful not to splatter yourself.

Pour the ghee and spices over the rice-pea mixture and bring to a boil over high heat. Once the mixture starts boiling, reduce the heat to low. Cover the pot, leaving a very small vent for the steam to escape so that the liquid does not bubble over.

Cook for 12 minutes, resisting the urge to lift the lid (or steam will escape and drop the temperature). When the timer goes off, check to see if the khichadi is done; if it's still slightly underdone or has excess liquid, give it another couple of minutes. When it's done, turn off the heat and allow the khichadi to steam for an additional 5 minutes.

Carefully remove the lid and fluff the khichadi with a fork. Spoon individual servings into shallow bowls and top with a drizzle of ghee or a dollop of yogurt, if desired.

VEGETABLE CONGEE WITH GINGER AND COCONUT SERVES 3 TO 4

It took me a long time to appreciate congee, a versatile rice porridge that is beloved across Asia. For years, I thought of congee as a sick food because my mother would feed me a simple, bland version when I was in bed with a stomach bug. (Of course, mothers are usually right, and it *did* make me feel better.)

One day, when I was a teenager, I walked into the kitchen to see Mom stirring a gently simmering pot. I could smell star anise, ginger, and coconut. Curry leaves and toasted black pepper, too. I asked her what she was making.

"Congee," she said.

That version was full of flavor and amazingly good. I helped myself to a second and then a third bowl, and I began to understand the versatility of that very simple dish. I have since made and served many different versions of my own—some with meat, some with kimchi, some with lobster broth. Yet my mother's recipe is the one I keep going back to.

1½ tablespoons ghee (store-bought or homemade, page 9)

½ teaspoon brown mustard seeds

½ teaspoon cumin seeds

1 small shallot, minced (about ¼ cup)

1 tablespoon minced ginger

¾ cup short-grain rice or rice middlins

¼ cup diced carrots (about 1 carrot)

⅓ cup diced cauliflower florets

¼ cup frozen green peas (no need to thaw)

¼ cup diced fresh tomato (½ small to medium tomato)

1 serrano or jalapeño chile, stemmed, seeded if desired, and minced

½ (14-ounce) can coconut milk

¼ teaspoon ground turmeric

2 tablespoons unsalted butter

2 tablespoons chopped fresh cilantro

Grated zest and juice of ½ lime

¾ teaspoon salt

1 teaspoon cracked black pepper (You want a texture that is coarser than ground. To achieve this texture, crack whole peppercorns with a rolling pin or the back of a spoon.)

¼ cup chopped roasted peanuts or cashews, for garnish

In a heavy-bottomed pot, heat the ghee over medium heat. When the ghee is hot and fragrant, add the mustard seeds and cook until they start popping, about 30 seconds. Add the cumin seeds. Cook and stir until the mixture is very fragrant. Stir in the shallot, followed by the ginger. Add the rice and cook until it is evenly coated in the ghee and slightly toasted, 5 to 6 minutes. The rice will begin to smell nutty. Add 3 cups water and bring the mixture to a boil, then reduce the heat to a simmer. Add the chopped vegetables, coconut milk, and turmeric. Simmer, stirring frequently, until the rice breaks down into a creamy porridge and the vegetables are cooked through, 35 to 40 minutes. As the congee thickens, it has a tendency to bubble and pop.

Once the rice is creamy, remove the pot from the heat and stir in the butter, cilantro, lime zest and juice, salt, and pepper. Taste and adjust the seasonings to your liking.

Serve hot in individual bowls. Garnish each serving with a sprinkle of chopped peanuts or cashews.

NOTE: The goal here is to cook the rice to mush. The recipe will not work with converted rice. If you use brown rice, it will take much longer. I recommend using your favorite white rice. You might also try rice middlins, sometimes called rice grits. These are broken grains, so they cook to a creamy texture that's perfect for this dish. (You'll learn more about rice grits later in this chapter.)

CITRUS-HERB RICE SALAD SERVES 8

By now, you know that I'm a believer in the versatility and the possibilities of rice. I've long suspected that I could use rice as the base for a salad, as a welcome alternative to pasta salad. We might not be accustomed to cold rice, but it's certainly not unheard of—think of dolmas, the rice-filled grape leaves of Greek and Lebanese cuisine. One summer, when I was searching for a dish to accompany seared scallops on the City Grocery lunch menu, I decided to test my hunch. My first attempt at rice salad was far from perfect. The texture underscored the oddness of cold rice rather than echoing the familiarity of an orzo salad. Happily, I solved the problem by adding some diced fresh vegetables and toasted, slivered almonds for crunch. Generous doses of citrus and fresh herbs lend brightness. The result is at once familiar and surprising.

Serve this dish as you would any grain-based summer salad, as a side dish on a lunch buffet or alongside grilled meat or seafood for an easy supper. If you like, you can use the leftover salad to make rice fritters, or try stir-frying it in a bit of neutral oil with an egg scrambled in.

FOR THE CITRUS DRESSING:

1 tablespoon rice wine vinegar

2 teaspoons fresh orange juice

2 teaspoons fresh lemon juice

1 teaspoon fresh lime juice

1 teaspoon brown sugar

2 tablespoons canola oil or shallot oil (from making Crispy Fried Shallots, page 28)

FOR THE RICE SALAD:

4 cups cooked and cooled long-grain white rice or wild rice blend

½ cup toasted slivered almonds

¼ cup grated carrot

¼ cup minced red onion

¼ cup peeled, seeded, and diced cucumber

¼ cup small-diced red or yellow bell pepper

¼ cup chopped fresh mint leaves

¼ cup chopped fresh basil leaves

2 tablespoons chopped fresh dill

Grated zest of 1 orange

Grated zest of 1 lemon

Grated zest of 1 lime

1 teaspoon salt

1 teaspoon freshly ground black pepper

First, make the citrus dressing: In a small bowl, whisk together the vinegar, citrus juices, and brown sugar until the sugar is dissolved. Whisk in the oil to emulsify the dressing. Set aside while you assemble the salad. (You can also make the dressing in advance and store it in the refrigerator for up to a week.)

To make the salad, in a large bowl, combine the rice, almonds, carrot, red onion, cucumber, bell pepper, mint, basil, dill, citrus zest, salt, and pepper.

Toss the rice salad with the citrus dressing. Serve at room temperature.

DIRTY RICE GRITS SERVES 4

I love to cook with Two Brooks Farm rice, sustainably raised by the Wagner family in the Mississippi Delta. A few years ago, Mike Wagner dropped off a couple of bags of his rice grits—a fortunate byproduct of the grains that are broken in processing—for me to try. I was talking with my sous chef Andy McCown about what we might do with them, when news broke that iconic Louisiana chef Paul Prudhomme had passed away. We decided right away that we should feature a dish on the menu that paid homage to Chef Prudhomme and his flagship French Quarter restaurant, K-Paul's Louisiana Kitchen. Since Prudhomme's blackened redfish took the nation by storm in the 1980s, I knew that we would serve redfish for certain. But what about accompaniments?

That was when Andy came up with the brilliant idea to make dirty rice grits. We used Chef Prudhomme's recipe for dirty rice, cooked with minced vegetables and chopped chicken livers, as an inspiration. Andy added a couple of brilliant touches—his addition of Italian sausage makes the finished product a bit brighter and less earthy than the classic Cajun dirty rice, and dry English mustard adds a pleasant heat. I think Chef Prudhomme would have been proud. I recommend serving this side dish with redfish, a slightly sweet fish in the drum family that's a Gulf Coast favorite, as we did that night.

1 teaspoon cumin seeds

2 tablespoons neutral oil, such as peanut or canola

½ cup ground hot Italian pork sausage

1 (6- to 8-inch) link smoked sausage, diced small

3 chicken livers, finely chopped

½ cup minced yellow onion

½ cup minced celery

½ cup diced green bell pepper

2 teaspoons minced garlic

2 scallions, thinly sliced (about ⅓ cup)

1 cup uncooked rice grits or arborio rice

2 tablespoons Creole seasoning (store-bought or homemade, page 8)

1 teaspoon dry English mustard, such as Colman's

½ cup dry white wine, such as sauvignon blanc or Chablis

4 cups Chicken Bone Stock (page 247) or store-bought unsalted chicken stock

2 bay leaves

2 tablespoons Worcestershire sauce

1 teaspoon hot sauce

3 tablespoons chopped fresh flat-leaf parsley

3 tablespoons unsalted butter

½ teaspoon salt, or to taste

½ teaspoon freshly ground black pepper, or to taste

Toast the cumin seeds in a small, dry pan over medium heat until fragrant, 1 to 2 minutes. Remove from the heat and, when cool enough to handle, grind in a spice grinder or coffee grinder, or with a mortar and pestle. Set aside.

In a large, heavy-bottomed pot or Dutch oven (nonstick if you have it), heat the oil over medium heat. Add the ground sausage and cook until the fat begins to render, about a minute and a half. Add the smoked sausage and chicken livers and cook until the livers are completely dry and cooked through, about 2 minutes. Add the onion, celery, and bell pepper and cook, stirring occasionally, until the vegetables have softened and the onion is golden brown, about 10 minutes. Add the garlic and scallions and cook until softened, 2 to 3 minutes.

Add the rice grits, Creole seasoning, and mustard and stir to combine well. Pour in the white wine and, using a wooden spoon, scrape up any bits that may have stuck to the bottom of the pan. Add the stock, bay leaves, cumin, Worcestershire, hot sauce, and parsley. Stir to combine. Raise the heat to medium-high and cook, stirring frequently, for 6 to 8 minutes. The rice grits have a tendency to bubble and pop, so be extremely careful to not burn yourself. After 6 minutes, begin checking the grits for doneness. You want a nice, smooth texture with a little bite. If the grits are crunchy, cook for a few more minutes.

When the grits are finished, turn off the heat, stir in the butter until it melts, and season with salt and pepper as needed. The grits are best served immediately. (Otherwise, you will want to add a little chicken stock as you reheat.)

RICE PILAF WITH CHICKEN, RAISINS, AND CASHEWS SERVES 8

My mother used to make rice pilaf with cashews, English peas, shallots, golden raisins, and saffron when the year's first aged Dehraduni basmati rice was available. Dehradun, located in the Himalayan foothills of northern India, is known for producing a superior basmati rice. It is then aged for two years, and the finished product is both more expensive and more flavorful than the rice we were accustomed to eating every day. Mom almost always paired this with her spicy tomato soup to make a light, simple meal. Every grain of rice would be perfectly cooked and would stand up separate from the other grains. She would bring the covered pot to the table and lift the lid. A cloud of steam would balloon up with the nutty aroma of basmati and the scent of cumin and saffron. She would garnish the top with shallots that had been fried in ghee until crispy and we would dig in. Even though this was just a pot of rice with a side of tomato soup, to us it was a special meal.

As the years went on and I traveled and ate rice dishes across India, I realized that pilafs held a similar pride of place in many homes and restaurants. The Hyderabadi biryani, which descends from a Persian dish, is probably the crown jewel of Indian pilaf repertoire. Another dish, the Parsi berry pulao, while invented in the kitchens of Mumbai's Irani cafés, is a direct descendent of the Irani jeweled rice. I make a point to have it every time I am in Mumbai. The version I like most—and I am about to offend some friends here, because folks can be fiercely loyal to their favorite cafés—is the chicken berry pulao from Britannia & Co. Restaurant in the Ballard Estate district.

After much tweaking, this rice pilaf does justice to my memory of my mother's simple, yet superlative, version. It is a meal all by itself.

- ¼ cup ghee (store-bought or homemade, page 9)
- 4 green cardamom pods
- 1 cinnamon stick
- 1 tablespoon cumin seeds
- 1 teaspoon caraway seeds
- ½ teaspoon ground turmeric
- 4 small shallots, thinly sliced (about 1 cup)
- 2 small carrots, peeled and grated (about ½ cup)
- ½ cup frozen green peas (no need to thaw)
- 1 cup roasted unsalted cashews, peanuts, or pistachios (optional)
- ½ cup golden raisins
- 3 cups basmati rice, rinsed under cold water and drained
- ½ teaspoon dried dill (may be labeled dill weed)
- 2 teaspoons garam masala (store-bought or homemade, page 8)
- 6 cups Whole Chicken Stock (page 28), plus chopped meat of chicken used to make stock
- 1 generous pinch saffron threads
- 1½ teaspoons salt, or to taste
- 2 teaspoons freshly ground black pepper, or to taste
- Chopped fresh cilantro, for garnish
- Crispy Fried Shallots (page 28), for garnish

NOTE: You will see that this rice pilaf calls for making Whole Chicken Stock (page 28). I do not know of a commercial stock that replicates the aromatics of this recipe. You could, in theory, do a shortcut version of this recipe by starting with a roast chicken and a carton of unsalted stock. But I promise you, the flavors will not be nearly as good. Instead, impress yourself—and your dinner companions—by making the stock from scratch. It might be the first time you've tried this, but I bet it won't be the last.

Heat the ghee in a large, heavy-bottomed pot or Dutch oven over medium-high heat. Once it starts to smoke, add the cardamom and cinnamon and cook for 1 minute, stirring. Stir in the cumin and caraway seeds and cook for 1 minute, or until fragrant. Add the turmeric and shallots and cook until the shallots start to turn golden brown and crisp on the edges, 10 to 12 minutes. Add the carrots, peas, and nuts (if using) and stir. Add the raisins, rice, dill, and garam masala. Gently stir everything until it is thoroughly combined.

RECIPE CONTINUES

Add the chicken stock, chopped chicken, and saffron and bring to a boil. Cover with a tight-fitting lid, lower the heat, and simmer for 12 to 15 minutes.

Turn off the heat and let the rice stand, covered, for 6 minutes to allow it to finish cooking and absorbing all the flavors. Do not lift the lid.

Season with salt and pepper and serve steaming hot, garnished with chopped cilantro and fried shallots.

WHOLE CHICKEN STOCK

MAKES ABOUT 1 GALLON (16 cups)

You can make this chicken stock for any recipe where you will go on to use the cooked chicken. For the purposes of stock, do not worry over the exact measurements of onion and carrot, nor the thickness of the slices. You will end up with more stock than you need for the rice pilaf. Use the rest in soup, or anywhere else you would use chicken stock. And of course, you can freeze it.

Note: If you want to make your own stock for a recipe that does not call for a cooked chicken, use the Chicken Bone Stock recipe (page 247).

1 (3½-pound) chicken, cut into eight pieces (see page 246)

1 cinnamon stick

5 star anise pods

10 black peppercorns

3 whole cloves

1-inch piece ginger, sliced

1 small onion, sliced

2 carrots, sliced

1 lemon, sliced

Put all the ingredients in a large stockpot. Add 1½ gallons cold water and bring to a boil over high heat. Reduce the heat and simmer for 45 minutes to 1 hour. Turn off the heat and allow the stock to cool completely. Strain the stock into a large storage container. Once the chicken is cool enough to handle, remove the meat from the bones, chop, and set aside. Discard the skin, bones, spices, vegetables, and lemon slices.

If you won't be using the stock immediately, be sure to cool it down to room temperature before refrigerating or freezing. The stock will keep in an airtight container in the refrigerator for up to 5 days or in the freezer for up to 1 month. I recommend dividing the stock into smaller portions for freezing (1 or 2 cups each) so that you can easily thaw and use only what you need for a recipe.

CRISPY FRIED SHALLOTS

MAKES ABOUT 1 CUP

2 cups very thinly sliced shallots (5 to 6 medium shallots)

3 cups canola oil or ghee

½ teaspoon salt

½ teaspoon freshly ground black pepper

Combine the shallots and cold oil in a heavy 3-quart saucepan and bring to a simmer over medium heat. Once the shallots start bubbling, increase the heat to medium-high and cook, stirring frequently, until the bubbles subside. (The bubbles are an indication of the water cooking out of the shallots.) This process takes about 20 minutes. Remove the shallots from the oil when they are golden brown and crispy. If the shallots begin to turn dark brown too fast, reduce the temperature of the oil to prevent burning.

Transfer the cooked shallots to a paper towel–lined plate or sheet pan, sprinkle with the salt and pepper, and allow to cool completely. Save the shallot-flavored oil for cooking or use it as the base for a salad dressing, such as the dressing for the Citrus-Herb Rice Salad (page 24).

HAM AND SUMMER VEGETABLE PURLOO

SERVES 4 TO 6

In 2003, when John Currence made me the lunch chef at City Grocery, he handed me two books with the directive to read them so that I would better understand the restaurant's mission. Those two books were *Bill Neal's Southern Cooking* (1985) and John Egerton's *Southern Food: At Home, on the Road, in History* (1987). They have remained at the top of my go-to pile of books ever since. You see, Currence began his cooking career at Crook's Corner in Chapel Hill, North Carolina, under Neal. Sadly, Neal and Egerton are no longer with us, and Crook's Corner closed in 2021, but their culinary and cultural influence on the Southern table remains.

While looking for menu inspiration in that summer of 2003, I came across Neal's recipe for okra and ham purloo. Purloo (also spelled pilau) from the South Carolina Lowcountry, just like its first cousin jambalaya from Louisiana, is a regional dish that draws on global influences. The culinary historian Karen Hess argued convincingly that South Carolina pilau descends from a Provençal dish of the same name, which in turn had its roots in Persia. But, added Hess, the centrality of rice in traditional Lowcountry cuisine also depended on the knowledge and labor of enslaved West Africans, both in the region's rice fields and in its kitchens.

I have continued to use Chef Neal's recipe as a template for my own cooking over the years, with some tweaks. The pork and okra are my constants. Neal recommends serving it as a main dish, as do I. (That said, some pickled shrimp on the side would be a fantastic accompaniment. See the recipe on page 204).

- 2 cups fresh shelled field peas, rinsed
- 1 small smoked ham hock
- 2 teaspoons olive oil
- 3 slices thick-cut smoked bacon, diced
- 1 cup diced yellow onion
- 1 cup diced red bell pepper
- 1 cup diced celery
- 2 tablespoons minced garlic
- 5 ripe medium tomatoes, cored, diced, and juices saved (If ripe tomatoes are not available, use a 14.5-ounce can plum tomatoes, crushed.)
- Salt
- 1 cup raw peanuts, skins removed
- 2 cups fresh corn kernels
- 2 cups thinly sliced fresh okra
- 2 bay leaves
- 4 cups Chicken Bone Stock (page 247) or store-bought unsalted chicken stock
- 2 cups basmati or other long-grain aromatic rice
- 1½ teaspoons freshly ground black pepper, or to taste
- ¼ cup chopped fresh flat-leaf parsley
- 2 tablespoons fresh thyme leaves

NOTE: If you do not have access to fresh field peas, you may substitute frozen. I suggest using the smallest fresh field peas you can find, such as lady peas, so that they don't overtake the rice. I've also made this purloo with purple hull peas as well as black-eyed peas.

Put the field peas and ham hock in a medium saucepan, cover with cold water, and bring to a boil. Reduce the heat to medium-low and simmer until the peas are just done, 25 to 30 minutes. Remove the pan from the heat and allow to cool. Drain the peas and set aside. Remove the skin from the ham hock and dice the meat; set aside.

Heat the olive oil and bacon in a large saucepan over medium heat and cook until the bacon is rendered and starts to crisp. Using a slotted spoon, transfer the bacon to a paper towel–lined plate and set aside.

Add the onion to the pan and cook until it starts to sweat, 8 to 10 minutes. Add the bell pepper and celery and cook until they are very soft, 5 to 7 minutes. Stir in the garlic and cook until it sweats, about 1 minute. Add the tomatoes with their juices and a pinch of salt and cook until the tomatoes start breaking down and releasing water, about 10 minutes.

Add the peanuts, corn, okra, and another pinch of salt and cook until the okra is just soft, 2 to 3 minutes. Be careful not to stir the okra too much or it will get slimy. Add the bay leaves, stock, rice, field peas, ham, and bacon. Stir gently and bring to a simmer. Add a pinch of salt and the pepper. Taste and add additional salt and/or pepper if necessary.

Cover and cook over low heat for 12 to 15 minutes, until the rice is cooked through and all the stock is absorbed. Turn off the heat and stir in the parsley and thyme. Cover again and let sit for 5 minutes before serving.

JAMBALAYA SERVES 8

Louisiana Creoles and Cajuns alike claim jambalaya as part of their respective cuisines. As anyone with a passing interest in food history knows, origin stories can't always be trusted. (In fact, they can *rarely* be trusted.) This is the case with jambalaya. It is said that jambalaya is a direct descendant of the Valencian and Provençal rice dishes that came to Louisiana with the Spanish and French settlers—think of paella. There is likely some truth to this. Yet for much of New Orleans's history, the African influence on Creole foodways wasn't given due credit alongside the Spanish and French. Given that history, not to mention the historic trade connections between southern France and Spain and parts of Africa, we can probably point to West African jollof rice as a jambalaya ancestor as well.

Perhaps fittingly, my own jambalaya borrows from many cooks and many recipes. I draw heavily from the ingredients and techniques of paella, including my use of clams, shrimp, sausage, and tomatoes. Native Louisianans might quibble with me, but making a dish your own is part of the beauty of cooking.

This is a great recipe to make for a crowd. But you could also cut it in half for a more intimate gathering.

1 pound littleneck or middleneck clams in their shells

Baking soda

3 tablespoons olive oil

1½ pounds andouille, chaurice, or similar spicy smoked sausage, sliced into half-moons or rounds

1 cup diced yellow onion

1 cup diced green bell pepper

1 cup diced celery

4 garlic cloves, thinly sliced

5 large ripe tomatoes, diced and juices saved

Salt

4 cups long-grain white rice

1 tablespoon Creole seasoning (store-bought or homemade, page 8)

2 teaspoons paprika

1 cup dry white wine, such as sauvignon blanc or Chablis

6 cups Shrimp Stock (page 31), warmed

¼ cup thinly sliced scallions

2 tablespoons fresh thyme leaves

1 pound large shrimp, peeled and deveined (save the shells to make the stock)

Freshly ground black pepper

2 tablespoons chopped fresh flat-leaf parsley, for garnish

Hot sauce, for serving

Rinse the clams under cold running water, then transfer to a large bowl. Cover them with cold water and add a pinch of baking soda. Let the clams soak for 10 to 15 minutes. You may see some bubbles released as the clams "burp." Rinse and drain them again to remove any sand.

In a Dutch oven or similar wide pot, heat the oil over medium heat until it begins to shimmer. Add the sausage and cook until browned; transfer to a plate and set aside. Add the onion to the same pot; lower the heat to medium and cook for 5 to 8 minutes. Add the bell pepper and celery and cook until they are very soft, about 10 minutes. Add the garlic, tomatoes with their juices, and a pinch of salt and cook until the tomatoes start releasing water, about 5 minutes. Add the rice, Creole seasoning, paprika, and wine. Stir gently to combine all the ingredients. Add the stock, turn up the heat, and bring to a boil. Stir in the scallions and thyme, turn the heat down to low, cover the pot, and cook for 10 minutes.

After 10 minutes, remove the lid, stir in the shrimp, sausage, and a pinch each of salt and pepper. Scatter the clams across the top and replace the lid. Cook over low heat for 8 to 10 minutes. Turn off the heat and leave the lid on for an additional 5 minutes to allow the shrimp to cook through and the clams to open.

Garnish each serving with a sprinkle of chopped parsley and serve with your favorite hot sauce.

SHRIMP STOCK

MAKES ABOUT 6 CUPS (If you end up with less than 6 cups, you can make up the difference with water in the jambalaya recipe.)

1½ cups shrimp shells (from 1 pound shrimp)

2 teaspoons black peppercorns

3 bay leaves

4 sprigs thyme

4 sprigs flat-leaf parsley

1 small tomato, roughly chopped

½ small yellow onion, sliced

2 celery stalks, chopped

½ cup dry white wine, such as sauvignon blanc or Chablis

Heat a Dutch oven or 5-quart saucepan over medium-high heat. Add the shrimp shells and toast them until they are no longer opaque and starting to turn pink, 1 to 1½ minutes. Add the peppercorns, bay leaves, thyme, parsley, tomato, onion, and celery and cook, stirring, for about 4 minutes, until the vegetables are slightly softened. Pour in the wine and cook for an additional 2 minutes, stirring and scraping up any cooked bits that have stuck to the bottom of the pot. When the wine has mostly evaporated, add 8 cups water. Bring everything to a boil, then turn down the heat to a low simmer. Simmer for 30 minutes.

Remove the pot from the heat and strain the stock through a fine-mesh strainer or a coffee filter. Discard the solids.

Use immediately or cool completely and freeze for later use.

RICE PAKORAS MAKES ABOUT 24 PAKORAS; SERVES 6 TO 8

Leftover rice is a fact of life for those of us who cook it regularly at home. The great thing about rice is that it is easy to repurpose, and there are scores of applications for leftovers. Pakoras are fritters that can be made with almost any vegetable. They are ubiquitous across India, most often as a street snack. Rice pakoras are something of an exception. As a way to use up leftover rice, they are the province of home cooks rather than street vendors. But often the most humble dishes are the ones we end up craving. Sometimes I will cook a pot of rice and let it cool just to make these spicy, savory fritters that were often my after-school snack. Serve them with Tomato-Coconut Chutney (page 99) for a snack, appetizer, or cocktail-party bite.

1 teaspoon coriander seeds

1 teaspoon cumin seeds

2 cups cooked rice (see page 18)

1 medium red onion, minced (about 1½ cups)

1 jalapeño chile, minced (about 3 tablespoons)

1-inch piece ginger, minced (1 heaping tablespoon)

2 teaspoons minced garlic

1½ teaspoons salt

1 teaspoon sugar

½ teaspoon ground cayenne pepper

½ teaspoon ground turmeric

Pinch asafoetida

¼ to ⅓ cup chickpea flour

½ cup chopped fresh cilantro, plus extra for garnish

½ teaspoon ajwain seeds or 1 tablespoon fresh thyme leaves

3 cups neutral oil, such as peanut or canola

Lime wedges, for serving

Tomato-Coconut Chutney (page 99), for serving (optional)

NOTE: You can make these pakoras with literally any kind of rice. The whole point is to use your leftovers. That said, I most often use a long-grain white rice such as basmati.

Toast the coriander seeds in a small, dry pan over medium heat for about 1 minute. Add the cumin seeds and toast, shaking the pan gently so that the seeds toast evenly and do not burn, until both spices are fragrant, about 1 more minute. Remove from the heat and, when cool enough to handle, grind in a spice grinder or coffee grinder, or with a mortar and pestle. Transfer the ground cumin and coriander to a large bowl.

Add the rice, red onion, jalapeño, ginger, garlic, salt, sugar, cayenne, turmeric, asafoetida, chickpea flour, cilantro, and ajwain seeds. Mix thoroughly with your hands to combine all the ingredients and distribute the spices throughout the mixture. This will also break up the rice, which will help the pakoras hold their shape.

Roll the rice mixture into balls about the size of a walnut. Wet your palms and fingertips with a bit of water to keep the rice from sticking to your hands as you form the balls. (Alternatively, you can use a 1-ounce cookie scoop.) Place the balls on a plate or sheet pan while you prepare the oil for frying.

Pour the oil into a large cast-iron skillet or Dutch oven and heat over medium-high heat. (Of course, if you have a dedicated deep fryer, this is the time to use it.) Use a thermometer to check the oil temperature. When it reaches 325°F to 350°F, gently drop a formed rice ball into the hot oil. If it sizzles and floats to the top, your oil is ready. If there is no sizzle and the rice ball sinks, wait a couple of minutes and try again.

Once the oil is ready, carefully fry the pakoras in batches, turning once, until the outside is golden brown and crispy, about a minute or less. Remove them from the hot oil with a slotted spoon and transfer to a paper towel–lined plate to drain.

When all of the pakoras are fried, transfer them to a serving platter, garnish with chopped cilantro, and serve with lime wedges and chutney, if desired.

SAVORY RICE PUDDING SERVES 4

I was a late convert to the combination of rice and cheese—it just wasn't something we ate growing up. The first time I tried a hot rice and cheese dish was in the mid-1980s. I was visiting friends in Zurich, Switzerland, and they served a baked rice casserole that was cheesy and divine. Since then I have had my fair share of Southern broccoli-rice casseroles and "Spanish" rice and even Rice-A-Roni with cheese, but I have never been able to get that first taste out of my mind. Eventually, I decided to make my own version. It is not quite as cheese-forward nor as heavy as the original Swiss dish. Instead, the fresh herbs and mascarpone made a light yet unctuous combination that I am sure you will like as much as I do.

3 large egg yolks

1½ cups heavy cream

½ cup mascarpone

⅓ cup grated Parmesan cheese

2 teaspoons hot sauce

2 teaspoons ghee (store-bought or homemade, page 9)

½ cup diced yellow onion

¼ cup diced celery

2 cups fresh or thawed frozen corn kernels

1 medium tomato, seeded and diced (about ¾ cup)

1 tablespoon chopped fresh dill

1 tablespoon chopped fresh basil

1 tablespoon chopped fresh flat-leaf parsley

2 cups cooked and cooled basmati rice (see page 18) or any white rice

1 teaspoon salt

½ teaspoon freshly ground black pepper

Preheat the oven to 350°F. Grease an 8-inch square baking pan or 2-quart casserole dish.

To make the custard mixture, whisk the egg yolks, heavy cream, mascarpone, Parmesan cheese, and hot sauce in a large bowl until the yolks are beaten and incorporated. Set aside.

Heat the ghee in a large skillet over medium-high heat. Add the onion, celery, and corn and cook until the onion is very soft, 5 to 6 minutes. Stir in the tomato, dill, basil, and parsley and mix well. Transfer the vegetable mixture to a large bowl. Add the rice, salt, pepper, and custard mixture and mix well.

Spoon the mixture into the prepared baking pan. Place the baking pan on a sheet pan and bake for 40 minutes, or until just set.

GROWN-UP STIR-FRIED RICE SERVES 6

A few years back, while I was visiting family in Ahmedabad, my father and I went to have tea with his neighbors. The Sastrys are from the South Indian state of Karnataka. While we were having tea and the usual cookies and other obligatory snacks and making small talk, their elementary school–aged children came home from school. Mrs. Sastry excused herself to make a snack for the children. I heard her chopping something in the kitchen and offered to help. She said no, so I asked if I could watch her as she put together this snack. She said yes.

She heated up a generous glug of ghee in a wok, then she added mustard seeds, sliced ginger, shallots, curry leaves, and some hot chiles. To this she added a handful of chopped, roasted peanuts, a generous pinch of masala powder, and a couple of cups of cooked rice—presumably leftover from lunch—and gave everything a good toss. She squeezed some fresh lemon juice on top and garnished it with chopped cilantro. She then put some in bowls for the kids, who sat down and ate it with glee.

Here was the grown-up, turbocharged version of the very simple after-school snack I had grown up eating. It took Mrs. Sastry all of ten minutes to put together, and it became the inspiration for a dish on the Snackbar menu, served alongside Collard-Wrapped Catfish (page 235).

It would also go well with Shrimp Recheado (page 221), Peanut Masala–Stuffed Baby Eggplant (page 112), or Braised Pork Shanks with Coconut Milk and Malabar Spice (page 283). Or simply top the rice with a fried egg for a savory breakfast or a late-night snack.

1 teaspoon plus 1 tablespoon ghee (store-bought or homemade, page 9), divided

1 teaspoon urad dal (split black lentils)

1 teaspoon chana dal (You may find this labeled as "split Desi chickpeas" or "split gram.")

5 tablespoons roasted peanuts, divided

½ teaspoon cumin seeds

2 teaspoons shredded dried unsweetened coconut

3 dried red chiles de árbol, stemmed

1 teaspoon brown mustard seeds

1 sprig curry leaves

2 shallots, thinly sliced

1 teaspoon minced ginger

1 serrano pepper, cut in half lengthwise

2 cups cooked and cooled long-grain white rice

1 teaspoon salt

Pinch sugar

Juice of 1 lemon

¼ cup chopped fresh cilantro, for garnish

Heat 1 teaspoon ghee in a skillet over medium heat. When the ghee is shimmering, add the urad dal, chana dal, 2 tablespoons peanuts, cumin seeds, coconut, and dried chiles. Stir and cook until everything is lightly toasted and fragrant, about 2 minutes. Remove from the heat and when cool enough to handle, grind in a spice grinder or coffee grinder, or with a mortar and pestle. Set this spice mix aside.

Heat the remaining 1 tablespoon ghee in a heavy-bottomed saucepan over medium heat until very fragrant. Add the mustard seeds and cook until they start popping, about 30 seconds. Add the curry leaves and stir. Add the shallots, ginger, serrano, and remaining 3 tablespoons peanuts and mix well. Cook until the shallots are soft, 3 to 5 minutes. Add the rice and the spice mix, stirring gently so as not to break the rice grains. Add the salt, sugar, and lemon juice. Cook, gently tossing everything together for 5 to 7 minutes, until the rice is heated through.

Garnish individual servings with a sprinkle of chopped cilantro.

MOM'S RICE "PUDDING" SERVES 8

This was the first (and, for the longest time, the only) dessert I could make. It has just three main ingredients: milk, sugar, and rice. That's why I call it "pudding" in quotes—it doesn't even require an egg-based custard, as most puddings do. My mother taught me that adding a pinch of saffron, a couple of pods of cardamom, and some almonds or pistachios to those three very basic ingredients and patiently stirring them so as not to scorch the milk makes for a rich and creamy dessert that could be eaten warm, as we often did when I was growing up, or chilled, as I almost always do now. This recipe makes a generous 8 servings. You could easily cut in half, but it's so creamy and comforting, I can't imagine why you would want to.

½ cup basmati, jasmine, or other long-grain aromatic rice, rinsed under cold running water for 2 minutes and drained

2 tablespoons ghee (store-bought or homemade, page 9)

8 cups whole milk

4 green cardamom pods

3 star anise pods

½ cup sugar

1 teaspoon saffron threads

3 tablespoons golden raisins

2 tablespoons toasted chopped pistachios, for garnish

2 tablespoons toasted slivered almonds, for garnish

Combine the rice with the ghee in a small bowl; set aside.

In a large, heavy-bottomed pot or Dutch oven, bring the milk to a boil over medium heat, stirring frequently. Once the milk has come to a boil, reduce the heat to low and continue to cook the milk, stirring constantly. Take care not to let it scorch. Add the cardamom and star anise pods; continue to stir and cook the milk.

Once the milk has started to thicken and is reduced by half, about 20 minutes, stir in the sugar and rice-ghee mixture. Continue to cook over very low heat until the rice is cooked all the way through, the sugar is completely dissolved, and the milk takes on a very light caramel color, 30 to 40 minutes. This requires constant stirring as you don't want the rice, milk, or sugar to scorch. You're aiming for a creamy-smooth consistency, almost like grits.

Once the rice is cooked, stir in the saffron and remove the pot from the heat. Stir in the raisins. If planning to serve chilled, allow the pudding to cool completely before refrigerating.

Garnish with chopped pistachios and slivered almonds before serving.

Store leftovers in an airtight container in the refrigerator for up to 2 days.

CHAPTER TWO

PEAS AND BEANS

When I was growing up, legumes were on my family's table in some shape or form at every meal.

We ate chickpeas, black-eyed peas, and lentils; adzuki, lima, and moong beans—and many more. When you don't eat meat, peas and beans are a filling and affordable source of protein. And they offer surprising variety.

My father would ask me as a child to bury eight or ten sprouted beans in a pot of dirt on the balcony of our flat. He would then ask me to water them every morning. Within a day or two, little green shoots would appear. As the days went by, they would grow into lanky vines that dad would train onto the clothesline. I would watch eagerly as the time passed and the first periwinkle flowers would appear, then turn into tiny bean pods. Finally, I would harvest the few beans that had survived my daily poking and prodding, and Mom would cook them and serve them to me. I always thought those were the tastiest of all the beans she ever made.

When we moved to France and then to Texas, the easy availability of dried beans was a godsend for my mother as she tried to keep our vegetarian family fed in places that were new to us. My mom took to Tex-Mex cooking very well. She adopted—and adapted—refried beans, salsas, and tacos into her ever-growing repertoire of recipes. She used the more familiar (to her) black-eyed peas and garbanzo beans instead of the Texas-standard pintos and omitted lard from her version of refried beans. Instead of salsa verde, she made tomatillo chutney. She had been rolling chapatis all her life and was able to pick up tortilla making without a hiccup.

"Kashmira's tacos," as my mother's black-eyed pea tacos became known to her friends, were the first dish Mom fed Teresa when I brought her to meet my parents. Teresa and I have continued to serve them to our friends and family throughout our twenty-year marriage.

Over the years, I have come to realize that peas and beans—collectively known in the South as "field peas" (in contrast to green "English peas")—are just as revered here as they are in India. At farmers' markets and on restaurant menus across the South, you'll find heirloom varietals with beautiful, evocative names: lady peas, crowders, rattlesnake beans, purple hulls. They begin conversations, debates, and seed swaps among chefs, gardeners, and home cooks. It always warms my heart when something as humble as a bean can connect people from various cultures.

SUCCOTASH SERVES 8

Depending on where you're from, summer in Mississippi might not be your idea of a good time. But hear me out. If you can get past the heat and humidity, there's much to love about this time of year. Local farms and backyard gardens are overflowing with tomatoes, okra, peas, peppers, squash, and corn. Blueberries arrive in early summer, and peaches follow. The University of Mississippi slows down, and the town along with it. I'm able to steal more time to sit on my porch swing with a glass of wine and contemplate all the beautiful summer produce. Succotash is the best way I know to take advantage of this bounty.

Succotash is a Southern summer staple. You'll find dozens of varieties in home kitchens, community cookbooks, and restaurant menus across the region. The constants are field peas—often butter beans—and corn. For me, tomatoes are essential, too. If you have trouble finding fresh peas, frozen ones are the next best alternative. They'll just need to cook longer, or you can blanch them first. Please avoid the canned variety. Once you've sought out the best fresh ingredients, this dish comes together easily. If succotash is familiar to you, you'll find that the warmth of the garam masala sets this version apart. Succotash plays nicely with just about any simply prepared meat. Try serving it as a side dish to accompany Grilled Pork Tenderloin with Tandoori Spices (page 273) or Cornmeal-Fried Catfish (page 229).

- 2 tablespoons olive oil
- ½ cup diced red onion
- ½ cup diced fennel bulb or celery
- 1½ teaspoons minced garlic
- ⅓ cup diced red bell pepper or sweet Italian pepper
- 4 cups fresh field peas
- 4 ears corn, husked and kernels cut off the cobs
- 1½ cups diced ripe tomatoes
- ¼ cup torn fresh basil leaves
- 1 tablespoon fresh thyme leaves
- 1 teaspoon garam masala (store-bought or homemade, page 8)
- 1 teaspoon salt, or to taste
- 1 teaspoon freshly ground black pepper, or to taste

Heat the oil in a Dutch oven or other large, heavy-bottomed pot over medium heat. When the oil begins to shimmer, add the onion, fennel, garlic, and bell pepper and cook just until soft, about 7 minutes. Add the peas, corn, and 1 cup water and bring to a boil. Give everything a good stir, then cover, reduce the heat to low, and simmer for 15 minutes, or until the peas are soft but not mushy.

Stir in the tomatoes, basil, thyme, garam masala, salt, and pepper. Cover and simmer for an additional 5 minutes, or until the tomatoes have released their juices and are warmed through. Taste before serving, adding more salt and pepper if desired. Leftovers will keep in the refrigerator for a couple of days; you can reheat them or serve at room temperature.

SUMMER PEA SALAD SERVES 6 TO 8

A few years ago, my friend Ashley Christensen, the chef and restaurateur behind Poole's Diner and several other establishments in Raleigh, North Carolina, made a midsummer visit to Oxford. She and John Currence went on a shopping spree at the local farmers' market and invited a handful of mutual friends to share the bounty at a dinner at John's house. The spread was a fever dream of summer produce: grilled okra, sliced heirloom tomatoes, squash casserole, and more. The showstopper: Ashley's field pea salad. She gently simmered purple hull, white acre, and lady peas with fresh thyme, garlic, bay leaves, and black pepper and served them at room temperature, dressed with a simple vinaigrette. When I tasted the dish, it was as if, for the first time, I was tasting the peas exactly as they were supposed to taste. The colors—shades of green, yellow, and cream, studded with bright-red cherry tomatoes—were just as beautiful. This is the magic that can happen when the best cooks use the best ingredients and then step out of the way.

I never asked Ashley for her recipe, but I have since created my own version of the dish. You may use one kind of field pea or combine multiple varieties, as Ashley did. If possible, let your local farmers' market be your guide. If you do choose an assortment, the peas should be of a consistent size (the smaller, the better) so that they cook evenly. Serve at room temperature for a simple summer lunch or, as Ashley and John did, as part of a peak-season vegetable supper to remember.

4 cups fresh small field peas, such as lady peas, white acre peas, or rice peas (Fresh is definitely best, but if you only have frozen peas, thaw them before proceeding with the recipe.)

2 tablespoons plus 1 teaspoon salt, divided

6 sprigs thyme plus ¼ cup fresh thyme leaves

2 bay leaves

1 serrano chile, cut in half lengthwise

3 garlic cloves, cut in half

½ cup minced fennel bulb or celery

½ cup minced shallot

½ cup halved cherry tomatoes

¼ cup chopped fresh flat-leaf parsley

⅓ cup fresh lemon juice

2 tablespoons good-quality extra virgin olive oil

1½ teaspoons sorghum or cane syrup

1 teaspoon hot sauce

1 teaspoon cracked black pepper, or to taste

Place the peas in a colander. Rinse well with cold running water and pick through for debris.

Transfer the rinsed field peas to a large stockpot. Add 8 cups cold water and 2 tablespoons salt and bring to a boil over medium-high heat. When the water boils, reduce the heat to a simmer and add the thyme sprigs, bay leaves, serrano chile, and garlic. Cook until the peas are tender but still hold their shape, about 20 minutes. Remove the pot from the heat and allow the peas to cool in their cooking liquid.

Drain the peas when they have cooled to room temperature; discard the thyme sprigs, bay leaves, serrano, and garlic.

Transfer the cooked, drained peas to a large bowl. Stir in the fennel, shallot, tomatoes, parsley, and thyme leaves. Whisk together the lemon juice, olive oil, sorghum, and hot sauce in a small bowl. Add to the pea mixture and toss to thoroughly coat the peas with dressing. Season with the remaining 1 teaspoon each salt and the black pepper; taste and adjust the seasoning if necessary before serving. Store any leftovers in an airtight container in the refrigerator. They will be just as good, if not better, the next day.

SUNDAY "EVERYTHING" DAL SERVES 4

To me, nothing says comfort food like a bowl of dal. No chapter on peas and beans would be complete without a recipe for my favorite dal.

Just in case you were under the impression that Mom did all the cooking while Dad sat around reading a newspaper and drinking tea, I'd like to set the record straight. My father was a very active participant in the kitchen, especially on weekends and holidays when he wasn't at his job. He started taking me to the markets to shop for food at a very early age. Almost everything I know about selecting and buying vegetables, I learned from him. At eighty-eight years old, he still cooks three meals for himself every day. While his repertoire may be limited, his imagination is limitless. One of our favorite dishes to cook together is this Sunday Dal, so named because when I was young it was only cooked on Sundays. Nowadays I call it Everything Dal—and I'm still most likely to cook it on a Sunday. This is a hearty, one-pot dish. The idea is very simple: You cook some dal of your choice in a big pot and throw in whatever vegetables you have on hand as the lentils cook. You can even add leftover cooked chicken—for instance, if you've roasted a chicken (see page 248) and have leftovers, shred or chop it and add it to the dal at the end. When we make this at home, Teresa and I like to eat it with some crusty bread and potato chips—yes, potato chips—crumbled on top for texture and that umami that comes from MSG. (Think of this addition almost as you would crackers on soup: a pleasantly salty crunch.) It's also a good dish to double for a potluck, especially if you're looking for a vegetarian-friendly option.

1 cup toor dal or moong dal (or other lentils or split peas)

½ small onion, minced (about ¾ cup)

2 tablespoons minced ginger

1 tablespoon minced garlic

1½ teaspoons salt

1 teaspoon ground turmeric

½ cup peeled and diced winter squash, such as butternut or acorn, or sweet potato

½ cup small cauliflower florets

2 medium tomatoes, diced (about 1½ cups)

¼ cup roasted peanuts

1 cup spinach or other greens (leaves and tender stems only)

4 tablespoons (½ stick) unsalted butter, plus more for serving (optional)

1 teaspoon brown mustard seeds

1 serrano pepper, cut in half lengthwise

2 teaspoons cumin seeds

3 whole cloves

½ cinnamon stick

½ teaspoon ground cayenne pepper

2 teaspoons garam masala (store-bought or homemade, page 8)

2 teaspoons fresh lemon juice

Cream, for serving (optional)

Fresh cilantro leaves, for garnish (optional)

Salted potato chips, for garnish

NOTES: My dad always makes this dal with water since he is vegetarian. But Chicken Bone Stock (page 247) is a delicious substitute that makes for a richer dal. Toor dal, or split pigeon peas, make for a meatier dish. Moong dal, or split mung beans, are lighter. Chose whichever dal you're in the mood for, or whatever you have in your pantry.

RECIPE CONTINUES

Rinse the lentils under cold running water to wash off any dirt and debris. Put them in a large, heavy-bottomed pot along with the onion, ginger, garlic, salt, and turmeric. Add 8 cups water and bring to a boil over high heat. Turn the heat down to a slow simmer. Skim off any foam that forms on top and stir the lentils occasionally to prevent scorching. In about 20 minutes the lentils will start to break down. Stir in the squash and cook for 5 to 6 minutes. Stir in the cauliflower and cook for 5 to 6 minutes. Stir in the tomatoes and cook for 5 to 6 minutes. Finally, stir in the peanuts and spinach. (Whatever vegetables you choose to use, add them from hardest to softest, cooking each one for 5 to 6 minutes before adding the next one.) Give everything a good stir.

In a small skillet, melt the butter over medium heat until it foams and smells nutty. Add the mustard seeds, wait 20 seconds, then add the serrano, cumin seeds, cloves, cinnamon stick, and cayenne. Pour this seasoned butter into the cooked dal, along with the garam masala and lemon juice. Give everything a good stir. Cover the dal and let it sit for 15 minutes to allow all the flavors to meld and all the vegetables to be fully cooked and tender. Serve in a big bowl with an extra pat of butter or a drizzle of cream and a sprinkle of fresh cilantro if you like. And don't forget the potato chips.

SAVORY BLACK-EYED PEA GRIDDLE CAKES

MAKES 12 TO 15 SMALL PANCAKES

Like many of my fellow Southerners, and many of my fellow Indians, I love black-eyed peas. My mom seemed to know dozens of ways to prepare them. The variation kept us satisfied, and looking back I now realize that it probably helped her stave off boredom in the kitchen as well. She served these griddle cakes for breakfast or as a quick afternoon snack. After the peas soak, the batter is simple to prepare and the cakes cook very quickly.

I used to think that soaking, grinding, and deep-frying or griddle-frying black-eyed peas was a uniquely Gujarati thing until I realized that the West African pea fritters called accara use much the same technique. Black-eyed peas migrated both east and west from their West African origins, to the Indian subcontinent and to the Americas. Their myriad preparations—distinct, but showing threads of kinship—offer ties that bind diverse cultures.

I like these cakes best as a weekend breakfast. I'll soak the peas when I first wake up. By the time I've had a leisurely morning around the house, the peas are ready to go. If you're not an early riser, you could also soak them overnight.

This batter lends itself to all kinds of variations. Try folding in some chopped leftover bacon or sausage. I like to serve the griddle cakes with Tomato-Coconut Chutney (page 99).

- 2 cups dried black-eyed peas, rinsed and picked over
- 1 teaspoon cumin seeds
- ½ small sweet onion, diced (about ½ cup)
- 1 or 2 garlic cloves, chopped
- 1-inch piece ginger, chopped
- 1 small serrano chile, stemmed and chopped
- 2 tablespoons chopped fresh cilantro leaves
- 1 tablespoon chopped fresh mint leaves
- ½ teaspoon salt
- ½ teaspoon freshly ground black pepper
- 2 to 3 tablespoons sorghum syrup, divided (you may substitute molasses, cane syrup, or honey)
- ¼ to ½ cup neutral oil, such as peanut or canola

Place the peas in a large bowl and add enough warm water to cover them by 2 inches. Set aside, uncovered, to soak for 3 hours or overnight. Drain the peas, reserving 1½ cups of the soaking liquid.

Toast the cumin seeds in a small, dry pan over medium heat, shaking the pan gently so that the seeds toast evenly and do not burn, about 1 minute. Remove from the heat. When cool enough to handle, grind in a spice grinder or coffee grinder, or with a mortar and pestle. Transfer the ground cumin to the bowl of a food processor.

Add the peas, onion, garlic, ginger, serrano, cilantro, and mint and pulse, adding the reserved soaking liquid as needed, until the mixture resembles the consistency of cornbread batter. Depending on the size of your food processor, you may need to work in two or three batches. If that's the case, scrape the first batch of processed pea batter into a bowl, then repeat with the remaining mixture. Once all of the mixture is processed, give it a stir to incorporate for a uniform consistency. (If you do not have a food processor, you can also process the ingredients in a blender. Since most blenders have a narrower bowl and a smaller blade than a food processor, you may need to stop the motor

RECIPE CONTINUES

and stir the ingredients a few times while blending to achieve that cornbread batter–like consistency. Be careful not to blend too fine or to add too much liquid to speed up the blending process.) Stir in the salt, pepper, and 1 tablespoon sorghum syrup.

Heat 2 tablespoons oil in a large nonstick skillet or griddle over medium heat. When the oil begins to shimmer, spoon in dollops of the batter to make silver dollar–size griddle cakes. (Alternatively, you can use a 1-ounce cookie scoop.) Do not crowd your skillet; leave a bit of room between each dollop of batter all around. Cook until crispy and golden brown on one side, 2 to 3 minutes. Flip and finish cooking on the other side, adding a few drops of oil as necessary. Transfer the finished griddle cakes to a paper towel–lined plate. If not serving them right away, you can transfer them to a sheet pan instead and keep them warm in a 200°F oven.

If needed, scrape any burned bits off the skillet or griddle before beginning the next batch. (You do not need to wipe it clean.) Repeat with the remaining batter, adding additional oil and letting it heat until it shimmers between each batch.

Drizzle the hot griddle cakes with the remaining sorghum syrup and serve.

STEWED GUJARATI-STYLE BLACK-EYED PEAS SERVES 6 TO 8

Growing up, we ate a thali almost every day for lunch. There were always one or two legume-based dishes in the mix, and this black-eyed pea stew was one of my mother's standbys. Like many Gujarati stews, it has a hint of sweetness from jaggery. I recognize a kindred flavor profile in American baked beans; in fact, this dish would be a welcome addition to a summer barbecue spread. Or I'll make a big pot as the centerpiece of a vegetarian meal and serve the beans alongside collard greens, marinated cucumbers and onions, and black pepper cornbread. The next day for lunch, I like to crumble my cornbread into a bowl of the steaming black-eyed pea stew and top it with a dash or two of hot sauce and some raw sweet onion.

This dish calls for tamarind concentrate, which you may also see labeled as tamarind paste. Made from the tropical tamarind fruit, the paste has a fruity-sour flavor. You can find it at many international markets, including Indian, Latino, or Caribbean grocery stores, or you can order it online.

2 cups dried black-eyed peas, rinsed and picked over

2 tablespoons neutral oil, such as peanut or canola

1 teaspoon cumin seeds

⅛ teaspoon asafoetida

1 sprig curry leaves

¼ cup chickpea flour

1½ cups diced ripe tomatoes

1 tablespoon minced ginger

1 teaspoon ground turmeric

1 teaspoon ground cayenne pepper

1 tablespoon tamarind concentrate

1 tablespoon jaggery or light brown sugar

1½ tablespoons minced fresh cilantro stems, plus 1½ tablespoons fresh cilantro leaves, for garnish

1 teaspoon salt, or to taste

Place the dried black-eyed peas in a bowl and add enough water to cover them by 1 to 2 inches. Leave the bowl on the counter and let the peas soak overnight. When ready to begin cooking, drain the peas, rinse them, and drain them again. Set aside.

Heat the oil in a large, heavy-bottomed pot over medium-high heat. When the oil begins to shimmer, add the cumin seeds and stir until they are toasted and fragrant, about 30 seconds. Add the asafoetida and curry leaves and give it all a good stir. Add the chickpea flour and stir until it is toasted and smells nutty, 2 to 3 minutes. Whisk in 1 cup water to make a smooth paste. Add the tomatoes and ginger. Lower the heat to medium, cover, and cook until the tomatoes have broken down and the mixture begins to thicken, 10 to 12 minutes. Stir in the turmeric, cayenne, tamarind concentrate, and jaggery.

Add the black-eyed peas to the pot and pour in enough water to cover the peas (about 7 cups). Cover and bring to a boil. Once the beans are boiling, uncover and adjust the heat to maintain a simmer. Simmer, uncovered, stirring occasionally, until the peas are tender but not falling apart, 30 to 40 minutes. Add the cilantro stems and salt and simmer for another 5 minutes. Taste and add more salt if necessary. Serve sprinkled with fresh cilantro leaves.

LADY PEAS WITH COUNTRY HAM AND THYME SERVES 6 TO 8

In September 2008, Teresa and I flew to Durham, North Carolina, to celebrate our wedding anniversary at Magnolia Grill. Husband and wife Ben and Karen Barker opened the restaurant in 1986, with Ben as chef and Karen as pastry chef. I considered the Barkers mentors and friends, and I admired Magnolia Grill's service as much as its elegant, understated interpretation of Southern food. For nearly three decades, it maintained a reputation as one of the best restaurants in the region—for me, one of the best in the country. Ben and Karen closed Magnolia Grill in 2012 to enjoy an early retirement. Sadly, Karen passed away from metastatic lung cancer in 2019 at age sixty-two.

I remember vividly a small bowl of lady peas cooked with smoked ham and served with a beautiful cornbread: fluffy and hot out of the oven and topped with a pat of sorghum butter. The peas were so simple, yet so profoundly good that, years later, I've used them as the inspiration for this dish. First, you make a stock from ham hocks and aromatic vegetables, then you cook the peas in this stock, adding the reserved meat at the end. For the stock, don't worry about the size of the chop on the vegetables, nor the exact measurements. You can even make the stock a day in advance. When I make this dish, whether with dried or fresh summer lady peas, I always think fondly of Magnolia Grill and the Barkers.

Camellia Beans out of New Orleans (best known for their red kidney beans, the foundation of the classic New Orleans red beans and rice) is a good mail-order source for dried lady peas, which they call lady cream peas. Remember to allow yourself time to soak the peas if you are using dried. If you have access to fresh lady peas at your local farmers' market, by all means, use those. They are small and light green to almost white in color, with a delicate flavor and creamy texture when cooked.

3 cups dried lady peas, rinsed and picked over, or 3 cups fresh lady peas

3 tablespoons olive oil

1 small yellow onion, minced (about 1 cup)

2 celery stalks, minced

4 medium carrots, diced

4 garlic cloves, thinly sliced

1½ teaspoons red pepper flakes

1 teaspoon dried thyme

2 bay leaves

7 cups Ham Stock (page 52), plus ham hock meat

2 teaspoons apple cider vinegar

Salt

½ cup thinly sliced scallion greens, for garnish

If using dried lady peas, place them in a bowl and add enough water to cover them by 1 to 2 inches. Leave the bowl on the counter and let the peas soak overnight. When ready to begin cooking, drain the peas, rinse them, and drain again.

To cook the lady peas, heat the oil in a Dutch oven or other wide, heavy-bottomed pot over medium heat. When the oil begins to shimmer, add the onion, celery, carrots, and garlic and cook until the onion is golden and the carrots are just soft, 7 to 8 minutes. Add the lady peas, red pepper flakes, dried thyme, bay leaves, and enough ham stock to cover the peas. Bring to a boil, then lower the heat and gently simmer until the peas are soft but not mushy, about 30 minutes, adding more ham stock as needed to keep the peas covered. (If you run out of stock and need additional liquid, use water, adding ½ cup at a time.) When the peas are done, turn off the heat and stir in the vinegar and reserved chopped ham hocks. Taste and add salt to your liking, if needed.

Garnish each serving with a sprinkle of sliced scallions.

HAM STOCK

MAKES ABOUT 7 CUPS

2 smoked ham hocks

1 small yellow onion, sliced or roughly chopped

2 celery stalks, roughly chopped

2 carrots, roughly chopped

2 bay leaves

10 sprigs thyme

2 teaspoons hot sauce

1 cup dry white wine, such as sauvignon blanc or Chablis

Place all the ingredients in a large stockpot. Add 14 cups water and bring to a boil over high heat. Reduce the heat and simmer for 3 to 4 hours, until the hocks are very tender. Remove from the heat. You should have about 7 cups stock.

If using immediately, strain the stock into a bowl with a lip for pouring. Reserve the ham hocks and discard the vegetables and herbs. If preparing the stock in advance, allow to cool completely before storing in a sealed glass or plastic container in the refrigerator. When the ham hocks are cool enough to handle, chop and reserve the meat, discarding the bones and skin. When the meat is completely cool, store it in a separate container in the refrigerator if cooking the peas the next day.

SAUTÉED LIMA BEANS WITH MUSTARD SEEDS AND GINGER SERVES 6 TO 8

Lima beans, more often called butter beans in the South, are a summer staple. They anchor succotash alongside fresh corn. When cooked by themselves, they're most often seasoned with bacon or another smoked pork product. Yet when I was growing up in Gujarat, lima beans were a late-winter vegetable. My mother usually prepared them in a fragrant broth, occasionally with eggplant. She always saved the tender green pods along with the beans, but here in Mississippi, butter beans are virtually always shelled before they arrive at the farmers' market.

A few times, nostalgia has gotten the better of me. I've driven to the Indian grocery store in Memphis (some 150 miles round-trip) to buy frozen lima beans in their pods, just so I can try to recreate this dish as my mother made it. What I've found, though, is that fresh beans yield a better dish—this is one of those simple recipes that highlights the natural flavors of the beans rather than masking them with spice. This same preparation also works well with fresh fava beans or green chickpeas.

- 2 tablespoons neutral oil, such as peanut or canola
- 2 teaspoons brown mustard seeds
- 1 cup sliced scallions, white parts only
- 2-inch piece ginger, minced
- 1 tablespoon minced garlic
- 1 serrano chile, stemmed and chopped
- 4 cups fresh lima beans (see Note below; substitute frozen if you must)
- 1 teaspoon salt
- ¾ teaspoon ground turmeric
- Juice of 1 lime
- 1 teaspoon light brown sugar

Heat the oil in a wide, heavy-bottomed pot over medium heat. When the oil begins to shimmer, add the mustard seeds and cook until they start popping, about 30 seconds. Add the scallions, ginger, garlic, and serrano and sauté until the scallions are soft and the ginger and garlic are fragrant, about 5 minutes. Reduce the heat to medium-low and add the beans, salt, turmeric, and 1 cup water. Stir the mixture to combine everything. Cover and cook until the beans are soft, 9 to 12 minutes. Stir in the lime juice and brown sugar and simmer for 2 to 3 more minutes to incorporate. Remove from the heat and serve warm.

NOTE: If you are fortunate enough to find whole lima bean pods, destring the beans and cut them into ½-inch pieces before beginning the recipe. Many of the beans will fall out of the pods, and that is fine. Just cook everything together.

SPROUTED RED PEA STIR-FRY SERVES 6 TO 8

Sprouted moong beans, red peas, or even black chickpeas were a standard breakfast dish when I was growing up. When dry pulses make up a large portion of your diet, you learn to vary their preparation. Sprouting peas for a few days before cooking them was one of the tricks in my mom's seemingly endless bag.

After I moved to the South, I was surprised to learn that, as common as peas and beans are here, few cooks sprout them. Due to health code restrictions, we don't serve these at the restaurant. But I love the fresh green flavor the beans acquire when they are sprouted, so at home I make these regularly. It's a three-day process, but most of that time is hands-off. I especially like to serve them for company; Southern friends who grew up on field peas find the preparation at once familiar and surprising.

For this recipe, I like Sea Island red peas the best. An heirloom variety grown in the Lowcountry and associated with the cuisine of the Gullah-Geechee communities, the peas are available online through a handful of purveyors, including Anson Mills and Marsh Hen Mill. Last year I revisited the bean-planting forays of my childhood, growing several in a raised bed behind my house. Once the pods matured, I let them dry on the vine and harvested more than a pound of peas at the end of the summer. For a more accessible alternative, head to your nearest Indian grocery store and look for the small red beans called chori.

2 cups dry Sea Island red peas or chori

3 tablespoons neutral oil, such as peanut or canola

2 teaspoons brown mustard seeds

1 teaspoon cumin seeds

2 teaspoons minced garlic

2 teaspoons minced ginger

1 small serrano chile, stemmed and cut in half lengthwise

1 teaspoon ground turmeric

½ teaspoon ground cayenne pepper

1 teaspoon salt, plus more to taste

Juice of 1 lime

½ teaspoon sugar

Freshly ground black pepper

FOR GARNISH:

¼ cup chopped fresh cilantro leaves

¼ cup minced red onion

¼ cup small-diced cucumber

¼ cup chopped roasted peanuts

Lime wedges

Put the peas in a large bowl, pour in 6 cups lukewarm water, and leave to soak on the counter overnight. The next day, drain the peas and place them in a colander. Cover the colander completely with a clean kitchen towel and set aside in a warm corner of the kitchen. The peas should take 2 days to sprout.

Heat the oil in a large, heavy-bottomed pot over medium-high heat. Once the oil is shimmering, add the mustard seeds and cook until they start popping, about 30 seconds. Add the cumin seeds and cook, stirring, until fragrant, 20 seconds. Add the garlic, ginger, and serrano and stir until the garlic and ginger are fragrant and starting to brown just a little bit, about 30 seconds. Reduce the heat to medium-low and stir in the turmeric, cayenne, and ½ cup water. Scrape up any bits that may have stuck to the bottom of the pot, then stir in the sprouted peas. (Be gentle so as not to break the little sprouts that you have been so patiently waiting for.) Add the salt and another ½ cup water, if the beans are looking dry. They should be stewy but not soupy. Cover and continue to cook for 10 to 12 minutes, until the peas are cooked through, tender but not mushy.

Remove the pot from the heat. Stir in the lime juice and sugar. Season with salt and pepper to taste. Serve the garnishes on the table in small bowls and let guests top their own peas.

SAUTÉED GREEN BEANS WITH GARLIC AND SESAME SEEDS SERVES 6 TO 8

This recipe brings back wonderful memories of my mom and dad sitting across from each other at the kitchen table, picking and cleaning a pile of green beans. Mom would remove the stems and stack the pretty green pods in bundles of fifteen or twenty beans, while Dad would meticulously chop them into ¼-inch pieces. The older beans that had mature seeds would get shucked and the peas would be set aside for a different use. Once all the beans were picked through, Dad would clean up the table, wash the cut beans, and set them in a colander to drain. The familiar ritual took them an hour or so, during which they worked in a companionable near-silence. It was a beautiful thing to watch. This was their regular routine while the beans were in season in the late winter, and it continued until Mom passed away in 2008.

Now, when my father comes to visit Oxford from Ahmedabad, which he does about once a year, he and I sit across my kitchen table from each other and do the same. More often, Teresa trims the beans as my mother used to do. I'll come home from work to find that she has arranged them in bundles, and I will know that my job is to chop.

While the chopping ritual is special to our family, it is not essential. The trimming, however, is. At the very least, wash the beans, pick through them for dried-out beans or debris (such as a stowaway bug from the farm), and remove the tough stem ends. The whole beans will need a few additional minutes to cook through.

For the most part, this is a faithful adaptation of my mother's recipe. She often used to garnish these with grated fresh coconut and chopped cilantro. I can't always find fresh coconut, so I don't use it all the time. It is definitely worth adding if you have it.

3 tablespoons neutral oil, such as peanut or canola

1 teaspoon brown mustard seeds

5 garlic cloves, thinly sliced lengthwise

1½ tablespoons white or brown sesame seeds

1½ pounds small green beans, cut into ½-inch pieces (about 6 cups)

1½ teaspoons salt

¾ teaspoon granulated sugar

½ teaspoon ground turmeric

½ teaspoon ground cayenne pepper

Grated zest and juice of 1 lemon

Chopped fresh cilantro leaves, for garnish (optional)

Grated fresh coconut, for garnish (optional)

Lemon wedges, for serving (optional)

Heat the oil in a deep sauté pan or heavy-bottomed pot over medium-high heat. When the oil begins to shimmer, add the mustard seeds and cook until they start popping, about 30 seconds. Add the garlic and cook, stirring, until it is very fragrant, another 20 seconds. Add the sesame seeds and stir until they smell toasted, another 30 seconds.

Add the green beans, salt, sugar, turmeric, cayenne, and 1 cup water to the pan and mix well. Reduce the heat to medium-low, cover, and cook for 15 to 20 minutes. You want the beans to maintain some texture. If they are still crunchy, they need a few more minutes, but do not let them get so soft that they become mushy. The water will not completely evaporate but will create a delicious potlikker. Remove the pot from the heat and stir in the lemon zest and juice before serving.

Garnish individual bowls with chopped cilantro and/or grated fresh coconut. I like to serve with lemon wedges for squeezing over the beans.

STEWED LIMA BEANS WITH WINTER SPICES

SERVES 6 TO 8

I love the green, slightly astringent taste of lima (butter) beans, which comes through whether they are fresh or dried. Unlike most of the recipes in this chapter, this one is decidedly wintry, so the recipe calls for dried beans. Remember that you'll need to allow yourself time to soak the beans overnight. Warm and comforting, with a creamy mouthfeel, this dish was a favorite of mine when I was a child. My mother didn't make it often, but when she did, there were never any leftovers. Like her, I cook this dish in the winter and let the aroma of warm spices fill the house. If you are familiar with soup beans, a staple dish of Appalachia usually made with pinto beans, think of this dish as a sort of cousin. And just like soup beans, this dish can be paired with cornbread (see Not Your Mama's Cornbread, page 137, or use your favorite recipe) for a humble, hearty vegetarian meal.

4 cups dried lima (butter) beans, rinsed and picked over

2 tablespoons black peppercorns

3 tablespoons ghee (store-bought or homemade, page 9) or neutral oil, such as peanut or canola

1 teaspoon cumin seeds

1 small red onion, finely diced (¾ to 1 cup)

2-inch piece ginger, minced

1 cinnamon stick

5 to 6 whole cloves

4 star anise pods

1 cup canned crushed tomatoes, such as San Marzano

2 bay leaves

2 teaspoons salt

1½ teaspoons jaggery or light brown sugar

2 tablespoons chopped fresh cilantro leaves, for garnish

Lemon wedges, for serving

Place the dried lima beans in a bowl and add enough water to cover them by 1 to 2 inches. Leave the bowl on the counter and let the beans soak overnight. When ready to begin cooking, drain the beans, rinse them, and drain them again. Set aside.

Toast the black peppercorns in a small, dry skillet over medium heat, shaking gently so that they toast evenly and do not burn, until fragrant, about 1 minute. Remove from the heat. When cool enough to handle, crack the peppercorns using the back of a spoon. Set aside.

Heat the ghee in a large heavy-bottomed pot over medium heat. When the ghee is hot and smells toasty, add the cumin seeds and cook, stirring, until fragrant, about 30 seconds. Add the onion and sauté until translucent, about 5 minutes. Add the ginger and cook for an additional minute. Add the cinnamon, cloves, and star anise and stir until fragrant, 30 seconds to 1 minute.

Add the lima beans and 10 cups water and bring to a boil. Reduce the heat to a simmer and add the tomatoes and bay leaves. Cover and simmer over low heat for 30 to 40 minutes, stirring frequently, until the beans are completely soft. If the beans seem to be absorbing the liquid too quickly, add water as needed, ½ cup at a time.

Once the beans are soft, stir in the salt and jaggery and simmer, uncovered, for an additional 10 minutes. Some of the beans will start to fall apart at this point. This is what gives the sauce that rich, creamy mouthfeel you want. Stir in the cracked black peppercorns. Serve each portion garnished with a sprinkle of chopped cilantro and a lemon wedge for your guests to squeeze over their beans if they like.

CHAPTER THREE

OKRA

For the longest time, I was under the impression that okra was native to India.

I once even tried to argue that with a friend from Senegal. (I lost.) I may be forgiven for being misinformed, given that okra is a staple across India. You'll find it fried, stewed, grilled, and stuffed. Even some Caribbean nations know the vegetable by its Hindi name, bhindi.

My friend and mentor, the culinary historian Dr. Jessica B. Harris, writes about the foodways of the African Diaspora. She gave me an invaluable education on okra's African origins. I hadn't realized that, like rice and black-eyed peas, okra came to the US South with the uprooted and enslaved peoples of West Africa. I realized then just how many mainstays of Southern cuisine owe a great debt to the women and men of African descent who were brought here violently and against their will. I've come to view okra as a vegetable inextricably linked with the South's tragic history. But I believe that even as we acknowledge that history, we can honor okra and its place on our region's table.

Okra traveled east, too. It arrived to the shores of India, Lebanon, Syria, and elsewhere via trade and became an important part of the culinary fabric of those places. The Lebanese Lamb, Okra, and Tomato Stew (Bamia) in this chapter (page 78) is but one example.

Okra made its way to the United States and to India by very different means. But it has made an impact on both places and appears in some of each country's iconic dishes. Okra remains my favorite vegetable. I hope that once you see how versatile it is, it will become one of your favorites as well.

A note on selecting and preparing okra: Okra is most often green, but you may find beautiful red or purple heirloom varieties at your farmers' market. Try them! In general, look for small pods. Larger pods tend to have an unpleasantly tough or woody texture. If you buy your okra at a farmers' market, you might not run into this problem—a good farmer knows to harvest her okra often so that the pods don't grow too big. I've found that the best way to clean fresh okra is to wipe each individual pod with a damp kitchen towel. This method gets rid of dirt, as well as some of the excess prickles on the skin. For most of the recipes in this chapter, you will also want to trim off the tough cap at the top of each pod.

WHOLE GRILLED OKRA SERVES 6

The grilled okra recipe in chef Floyd Cardoz's 2006 cookbook *One Spice, Two Spice* inspired this one. His was the first grilled okra I encountered.

If you haven't experienced the joy of grilled okra, and especially if the vegetable's reputation for slime has made you a doubter, you are in for a treat. And if you do not have an outdoor charcoal or gas grill, don't let that stop you. A cast-iron skillet or stovetop griddle will do the trick. Be sure to select tender okra pods, but for this particular recipe, since you're grilling, you want to look for medium pods rather than the very smallest ones. If you're still worried that they will fall through the grates on your grill, skewer them before grilling or use a grill basket.

This recipe makes an ideal appetizer or cocktail snack. The flavors are intense, and the cayenne packs a punch. (If you're sensitive to spice, you can dial it back a bit.) Be prepared to have your mind blown by how simple and delicious it is. Repeat until the summer okra is gone.

1 tablespoon coriander seeds

2 teaspoons black peppercorns

2 teaspoons cumin seeds

1 teaspoon fennel seeds

1 teaspoon ground cayenne pepper

1½ pounds tender okra pods, wiped clean and tough tops trimmed

3 tablespoons olive oil

1 teaspoon salt, divided

Grated zest and juice of 1 lemon

1 small red onion or 2 medium shallots, minced (¾ to 1 cup)

¼ cup chopped fresh cilantro leaves or scallion greens, for garnish

Heat the grill to medium. If you will be placing the okra on wooden skewers to grill, soak the skewers in water for 10 to 15 minutes so that they do not catch fire on the grill.

Meanwhile, toast the coriander seeds and peppercorns in a small, dry pan over medium heat, shaking the pan gently so that they toast evenly and do not burn. After about a minute, as you begin to smell the pepper, add the cumin seeds and fennel seeds. Continue to toast, shaking the pan gently, until the cumin and fennel seeds are fragrant, another 30 seconds to a minute. Remove from the heat and, when cool enough to handle, crush with a mortar and pestle. You are not trying to grind the spices to a powder, but nor do you want them so coarse that they fall off the okra. (If you're using a spice grinder or coffee grinder, keep it brief to achieve a texture that is more crushed than ground.)

Combine the toasted ground spices with the cayenne in a small bowl.

(If you do not have a grill and you will be cooking the okra in a cast-iron skillet on the stove, set the skillet over medium-high heat at this point. You want it to get very hot so that it will char the okra just like a grill would.)

In a large mixing bowl, combine the okra with the olive oil, ½ teaspoon salt, and half the spice mixture. Grill the okra (or cook in the skillet) until it is soft, blistered, and charred in spots, about 5 minutes. If you've skewered the okra for grilling or are using a grill basket, flip halfway through so that the okra chars on both sides. As soon as the okra comes off the grill or out of the skillet, slide it off the skewers (if you used them) and back into the bowl. Toss with the lemon zest and juice, onion, remaining spice mixture, remaining ½ teaspoon salt, and chopped cilantro or scallion greens. Serve immediately.

OKRA CHAAT SERVES 6 TO 8

This might be Snackbar's best-known dish—thin strips of flash-fried okra tossed in chaat masala. In mid- to late July, when my backyard okra begins producing pods, I know that Snackbar's farmer-suppliers will be knocking at the back door with okra soon. That's when we add this chaat—the catch-all term for savory snacks in India—to the Snackbar menu.

The idea for this dish came from chef Suvir Saran. Cooking a pop-up dinner at Snackbar in the fall of 2009, he served his version of fried okra, which had become a hit at his Michelin-starred restaurant Dévi in New York City. The recipe involved cutting the okra very thin lengthwise and frying it until crispy without using any breading. I had never seen this technique before that night. In fact, I was afraid that the okra wouldn't hold its texture through service. I was wrong. The dish turned out to be one of finest okra preparations I had ever tasted.

The following year, as soon as okra came in season, I decided to develop a new dish based on the technique I had learned from Chef Saran. The result was this okra chaat. It was a hit with the guests, including one local writer who mentioned it in a magazine. Word spread, and okra chaat has been a part of summer at Snackbar for a decade now. I think its appeal lies in its twist on a traditional Southern favorite, fried okra. Most of our diners are familiar with cornmeal-breaded fried okra. In this batterless preparation, the flavors take center stage. What was once a local novelty is now a local favorite. I hope one day you'll join us in Oxford and order it. Until then, here is the recipe. Serve it as an appetizer or cocktail snack.

3 cups neutral oil, such as peanut or canola

2 pounds okra pods, wiped clean and tough tops trimmed

1½ tablespoons chaat masala (store-bought or homemade, page 8), divided

Salt

2 jalapeño chiles, stemmed and minced

½ cup diced red onion

½ cup seeded and diced tomatoes

⅓ cup chopped dry-roasted peanuts

3 tablespoons chopped fresh cilantro leaves

1 teaspoon ground cayenne pepper

2 tablespoons cane syrup or sorghum syrup

Juice of 2 limes

Pour the oil into a Dutch oven or other large, heavy-bottomed pot and heat to 350°F over medium-high heat.

Slice the okra lengthwise into very thin strips (⅛ to ¼ inch). When the oil is hot, carefully add one-quarter to one-third of the okra to the hot oil. Fry the okra until it is dark and very crisp, about 1 minute. (You'll notice that the water bubbles begin to subside when the okra is done.) Use a slotted spoon to transfer the okra to a paper towel–lined plate. Immediately season it lightly with a couple of pinches of the chaat masala and a pinch of salt. Repeat with the remaining okra. Once all of the okra is fried and cool enough to handle, gently toss it in a medium bowl with the jalapeños, red onion, tomatoes, peanuts, cilantro, cayenne, cane syrup, lime juice, and remaining chaat masala. Serve immediately.

PICKLED OKRA, TWO WAYS

After all these years, I have yet to acquire a taste for most Southern-style pickles. In Gujarat, as in most of India, fruits and vegetables are pickled in a base of oil and spices rather than vinegar. I grew up eating green mango, chiles, and an olive cousin called gunda, all preserved in oil spiked with fenugreek and mustard. In fact, the one time I saw a bottle of vinegar in our house, my mother had bought it to use as a cleaning solution.

The major exception is okra. At City Grocery, we pickled okra to garnish Bloody Marys. Sometimes we would cut the okra in half lengthwise and stuff it with John Currence's excellent pimento cheese. I eventually took to slicing it thin and adding it to salads and slaw, or rolling it in cornmeal and frying it. These pickled okra tricks still find their way onto summer menus at Snackbar and my own dinner table at home. The City Grocery pickled okra manages to pack heat from hot sauce and red pepper flakes without masking the flavor of the vegetable itself.

Of course, I'm still loyal to the oil-based pickles of India. I would be remiss not to share at least one such recipe, so why not my beloved okra? I developed this version of pickled okra a few years back for a summer dinner I served with cookbook writers and brothers Matt Lee and Ted Lee in Atlanta. My course was fish cooked with tomatoes and coconut milk. It needed a bit of a sharp kick to round it out, so I decided to add a Gujarati-style spicy pickle as a garnish. Okra was a natural choice because of the season and the setting.

For the Gujarati-style pickle, you can find the split fenugreek, split mustard seeds, and mustard seed oil at Indian markets. The mustard seed oil is worth seeking out for its sharp, unique flavor. If you cannot find it, or if you prefer an oil that is a bit milder, substitute raw sesame oil or peanut oil. If you already have whole fenugreek seeds and mustard seeds at home, you can approximate the texture of split seeds by cracking them with a mortar and pestle or pulsing a couple of times in a coffee grinder or spice grinder.

Below you'll find the recipes for both the City Grocery pickled okra and my oil-based okra pickle. Neither one requires water-bath canning. Try them both—you might be surprised by which one you prefer.

CITY GROCERY PICKLED OKRA

MAKES 1½ QUARTS

1½ cups red wine vinegar

½ cup dry white wine, such as sauvignon blanc or Chablis

1 small shallot, sliced very thinly lengthwise

4 garlic cloves, thinly sliced lengthwise

1 tablespoon red pepper flakes

1 tablespoon brown mustard seeds

1 tablespoon coriander seeds

1 tablespoon salt

2 teaspoons dried dill (may be labeled dill weed)

1 teaspoon sugar

½ teaspoon ground turmeric

2 teaspoons hot sauce

1 pound okra pods, wiped clean and tough tops trimmed

Combine the vinegar, wine, shallot, garlic, red pepper flakes, mustard seeds, coriander seeds, salt, dill, sugar, turmeric, and hot sauce in a medium saucepan. Bring to a boil over medium-high heat. Add the okra, reduce the heat to medium-low, and simmer for 5 minutes. Remove from the heat and allow to cool completely before transferring the pickles and brine to glass or plastic containers for storage. The pickles will keep in the refrigerator for up to 10 days. If you don't think you will be able to finish them in that time, bring a jar to your neighbors.

GUJARATI-STYLE OKRA PICKLE

MAKES 2½ TO 3 CUPS

8 ounces okra pods, wiped clean, tough tops trimmed, and cut lengthwise into quarters

1 tablespoon fresh lemon juice

2½ teaspoons salt

2 teaspoons ground turmeric

1 teaspoon ground cayenne pepper

1 teaspoon Kashmiri chili powder or hot paprika

2 teaspoons toasted white or brown sesame seeds (You can buy toasted sesame seeds or toast them yourself in a dry pan until fragrant.)

2 tablespoons plus 2 teaspoons Gujarati Pickle Base

In a bowl, combine the okra, lemon juice, salt, and turmeric. Mix very well and set aside for 20 minutes. Drain in a colander (the okra will have leached some liquid) and transfer to a clean, dry bowl.

Add the cayenne, Kashmiri chili powder, sesame seeds, and pickle base and toss well. Allow the pickles to sit, covered, in the refrigerator for a day before using. They will keep in a covered plastic or glass container in the refrigerator for up to 10 days.

GUJARATI PICKLE BASE

6½ tablespoons split fenugreek seeds

3 teaspoons split mustard seeds

4 teaspoons fresh lemon juice

6 tablespoons mustard seed oil

Mix all the ingredients together. Store in an airtight container in the refrigerator for up to 1 month. You can use leftover pickle base for other vegetables and fruits. Try it with carrots, chiles, mangoes, or green apples.

GRILLED OKRA, CORN, AND TOMATO SALAD WITH JALAPEÑO DRESSING

SERVES 6 TO 8

Almost every time I think about making a salad, I'm haunted by a scene in *The Simpsons* where Bart and Homer taunt Lisa: "You don't win friends with salad! You don't win friends with salad!" Yet I know that a well-made salad can be a showstopper or a centerpiece, especially during the summer. I developed this dish for an August issue of *Food & Wine* magazine. I wanted to create a bold, colorful salad with some of the most beloved produce of the Southern summer. I'll admit that even I was surprised by how well it turned out. The next time okra, corn, and tomatoes are in season where you live, fire up your grill and try it for yourself. If you want a pop of cool sweetness, toss in some cubes of watermelon. I believe even Bart and Homer would approve.

If you do not have an outdoor grill, the recipe will work almost as well with a stovetop griddle or a cast-iron skillet. You just won't get the same char.

- 2 teaspoons coriander seeds
- 2 tablespoons cumin seeds
- 1 pound small, tender okra pods, wiped clean, tough tops trimmed, and cut in half lengthwise
- 3 tablespoons neutral oil, such as peanut or canola
- Salt
- Cracked black pepper
- 3 ears corn, husked
- 1 pound small mixed heirloom tomatoes, cut in half
- 1 small sweet onion, very thinly sliced from root to tip
- ½ English cucumber, thinly sliced
- 1 recipe Jalapeño Dressing (page 69)
- Chopped fresh cilantro leaves, for garnish
- Toasted sesame seeds, for garnish

Heat the grill to medium-high.

Toast the coriander seeds in a small, dry pan over medium heat for about 1 minute. Add the cumin seeds and toast, shaking the pan gently so that the seeds toast evenly and do not burn, until both spices are fragrant, about 1 more minute. Remove from the heat and, when cool enough to handle, grind in a spice grinder or coffee grinder, or with a mortar and pestle. Set aside.

Combine the sliced okra with the oil in a large bowl. Season with salt and black pepper and toss evenly to coat. Skewer the okra or put it in a grill basket so that the pieces do not fall through the grates. Grill until slightly blistered and just soft, about 5 minutes. Return the cooked okra to the bowl, add the toasted and ground seeds, and toss well to coat. Set aside.

Place the ears of corn on the grill and, as you begin to hear the kernels pop, turn the ears. Continue grilling and turning, using the popping sounds as your guide, until the corn is lightly charred on all sides. Remove from the grill and, when cool enough to handle, cut the kernels off the cobs. Add these to the bowl with the okra, then add the tomatoes, onion, and cucumbers.

Gently toss the okra-corn-tomato mixture with the jalapeño dressing. Garnish each serving with a little chopped cilantro and a sprinkle of toasted sesame seeds.

JALAPEÑO DRESSING

MAKES ABOUT ½ CUP

2 small jalapeño chiles

½ cup chopped fresh cilantro leaves

½ cup fresh basil leaves

Juice of 2 limes

1 teaspoon sugar

⅓ cup canola oil

½ to 1 teaspoon salt

Heat the grill to medium-high. Grill the jalapeños, turning until the skin is charred, about 8 minutes. (If you don't have a grill, you can approximate this step over the open flame of a gas stove, or even under your oven's broiler. If working over an open flame, char one pepper at a time. Use tongs and an oven mitt and be careful not to burn yourself.)

Once the peppers are charred all the way around, carefully transfer them to a small plastic bag or a small bowl covered with plastic wrap. Allow them to sit for about 10 minutes. The resulting steam and heat will finish cooking the peppers and make the skin easier to peel. Once the peppers are cool enough to handle, peel off the blistered skin. Slice the peppers in half lengthwise and remove the stems and seeds.

Put the peppers in the bowl of a food processor or blender and add the cilantro, basil, lime juice, sugar, and oil and blend until smooth. Transfer the dressing to a bowl. Add ½ teaspoon salt and stir. Taste the dressing and add another ¼ to ½ teaspoon if you like. When you are happy with the flavor of the dressing, set it aside.

If you like, you can make the dressing a few hours or a day in advance. If you make it in advance, cover and store it in the refrigerator until you are ready to proceed with the rest of the salad.

ROASTED OKRA SALAD WITH HARISSA SERVES 6

During summer, when local farmers supply Snackbar with okra by the bushel, I am always looking for new ways to use it. This particular recipe is inspired by a dish Teresa and I had on a trip to Paris. We had been in the city for four days, and we both needed a break from bistros. So we wandered through the Latin Quarter in search of a Moroccan restaurant. Someone pointed us in the direction of Le Méchoui du Prince on Rue Monsieur le Prince. The meal was a welcome departure from steak frites and coq au vin, with solid interpretations of lamb tagine, couscous, and chicken basteeya.

One plate stood out. It was a dish of baby zucchini, served at room temperature and tossed with spicy harissa and preserved lemons. Teresa knew right away that I was going to have to re-create that dish as soon as we got home. It had all of the flavors, textures, and colors I love in Moroccan cuisine—heat from the harissa, acid from lemon juice, salt from olives, and toasted pistachios for crunch. After much tinkering, I created this okra version.

I enjoy making my own harissa. My recipe is milder and a bit less oily than most Tunisian or Moroccan versions. But you can certainly make this salad with prepared harissa from the grocery store. If you don't want to make the Moroccan Seasoning (page 264), you may substitute baharat. This spice blend, a staple of Middle Eastern cooking, is available at Middle Eastern markets or online.

1 pound tender okra pods, wiped clean, tough tops trimmed, and cut in half lengthwise

¼ cup good-quality extra virgin olive oil, divided

Grated zest and juice of 2 lemons, divided

2 tablespoons Moroccan Seasoning (page 264) or baharat, divided

1½ teaspoons salt plus a pinch

1 cup halved cherry tomatoes and/or grape tomatoes

1 small red onion, sliced very thin from root to tip

¾ cup mixed green and black pitted olives

½ cup Vish's Harissa (page 72) or store-bought, divided

½ cup toasted pistachios, roughly chopped

¼ cup torn fresh mint leaves

NOTE: Use good-quality jarred olives or get a scoop from the olive bar near your grocery store's cheese counter. Do not use canned olives.

Preheat the oven to 400°F. Line a sheet pan with parchment.

In a medium bowl, toss the okra with half the oil, half the lemon zest and juice, half the Moroccan seasoning, and a pinch of salt. Spread out the seasoned okra in a single layer on the prepared sheet pan and roast for 15 minutes, or until cooked through and charred in spots.

Meanwhile, combine the tomatoes, onion, and olives in a medium bowl and add the remaining olive oil, lemon zest and juice, and salt. Mix well.

Once the okra is roasted, remove it from the oven and let cool on the pan for about 5 minutes. Add it to the tomato, onion, and olive mixture. Add 3 tablespoons harissa and give everything a gentle stir to combine.

Using the back of a spoon, spread the remaining harissa on the bottom of individual serving plates (or a platter, if serving family style). Spread the dressed okra salad over the harissa and sprinkle the toasted pistachios and mint leaves on top. Serve warm or at room temperature.

VISH'S HARISSA

MAKES ABOUT 3 CUPS

4 large red bell peppers

2 teaspoons coriander seeds

1 teaspoon caraway seeds

½ cinnamon stick

1 dried chipotle chile

2 teaspoons hot smoked paprika

2 garlic cloves, minced

1 tablespoon tomato paste

1½ tablespoons fresh lemon juice

¼ cup olive oil

Salt

To roast the bell peppers, turn the flame of a gas stovetop to medium-high. Using tongs and an oven mitt, hold one pepper directly over the flame, turning until it is charred on all sides, about 5 minutes. Repeat with the remaining peppers. (Alternatively, you can roast the peppers under the oven broiler. Watch them carefully and turn with tongs as each side chars.) Once the peppers are charred all the way around, carefully transfer them to a large plastic bag or a bowl covered with plastic wrap. Allow them to sit for about 10 minutes. The resulting steam and heat will finish cooking the peppers and make the skin easier to peel. Once the peppers are cool enough to handle, peel off the blistered skin. Cut the stem off each pepper, cut the peppers in half, and remove the seeds. Roughly chop the peppers.

Toast the coriander seeds in a small, dry skillet over medium heat, shaking gently so that they toast evenly and do not burn. After 1 minute, add the caraway seeds, cinnamon stick, and chipotle chile and toast, shaking gently, until everything is fragrant, about 1 more minute. Remove from the heat and, when cool enough to handle, coarsely grind the mixture in a spice grinder or coffee grinder, or with a mortar and pestle. Set aside.

Place the roasted peppers in the bowl of a food processor. Add the toasted and ground spice mixture, paprika, garlic, tomato paste, and lemon juice and blend. With the motor running, slowly add the olive oil through the feed tube, emulsifying to a smooth paste. Taste and season with salt to your liking. Use immediately or store for up to 2 weeks in a tightly sealed container in the refrigerator.

STUFFED OKRA SERVES 6

Next to my mother, my Uncle Paresh's wife, Aunt Janu, was the best cook in our family. The first time she visited our house, she showed my mother how to make an egg-free cake in a Dutch oven on the stovetop. The next day, extended family and friends descended on our house to celebrate Uncle Paresh's engagement and meet his new fiancée. Janu and my mother created a feast that my relatives still talk about. I remember a dessert called laapsi, which was reserved for special occasions, and I remember Janu's stuffed okra.

As I grew older, I considered her a teacher and a mentor. She knew I liked to eat and cook, so she would teach me how to prepare my favorite dishes as I took notes. After my mother passed away, she became our family's keeper of the flame, remembering every recipe and orchestrating family commitments and celebrations.

Unfortunately, Janu passed away quite suddenly in 2016, leaving a massive hole in all of our lives. I do have this recipe, which I make as a labor of love and a way to remember Aunt Janu. It is one of the more complex and time-consuming recipes in this book, but I promise you the result—nutty and a bit sweet, with a slight crunch from the sesame seeds—is worth it. Whether you serve this as an appetizer or side dish, keep the rest of the menu simple to let the okra shine.

2 tablespoons coriander seeds

1 tablespoon cumin seeds

1½ pounds medium okra pods, wiped clean

2 cups chickpea flour

2 tablespoons sesame seeds

2 teaspoons garam masala (store-bought or homemade, page 8)

1½ teaspoons sugar

1 teaspoon salt, or to taste

1 teaspoon ground cayenne pepper

½ teaspoon ground turmeric

½ teaspoon asafoetida

5 tablespoons neutral oil, such as peanut or canola, divided

3 tablespoons finely chopped fresh cilantro leaves

Toast the coriander seeds in a small, dry pan over medium heat for about 1 minute. Add the cumin seeds and toast, shaking the pan gently so that the seeds toast evenly and do not burn, until both spices are fragrant, about 1 more minute. Remove from the heat and, when cool enough to handle, grind in a spice grinder or coffee grinder, or with a mortar and pestle. Set aside.

Using a paring knife, cut a lengthwise slit in each okra pod, leaving about ⅛ inch on either end to make a pocket. Do not cut all the way through the bottom of the pod—you do not want the stuffing to fall out.

To make the stuffing, combine the chickpea flour, ground cumin-coriander mixture, sesame seeds, garam masala, sugar, salt, cayenne, turmeric, and asafoetida in a medium bowl with 2 tablespoons oil. Stir to combine all the ingredients and incorporate the oil. Set a large dry skillet over low heat, add the flour mixture and cook, stirring, until it smells nutty and the spices are fragrant, 10 to 12 minutes. This step gives the stuffing a deep, toasty-nutty flavor and keeps it from getting soggy in the okra.

Transfer the cooked stuffing mixture to a mixing bowl. Add the chopped cilantro and 2 to 3 tablespoons water. Stir to combine. Wipe out the skillet.

Using your fingers, gently open up each okra pod where it was split and spoon in as much stuffing as it can hold without breaking (roughly 1 heaping teaspoon

RECIPE CONTINUES

per pod), mounding it on top. I do this one pod at a time, working over the bowl of stuffing so that the excess falls back into the bowl and doesn't make a mess.

Once all the okra is stuffed, set the skillet over medium heat and add the remaining 3 tablespoons oil. Once the oil shimmers, gently add the stuffed okra. (Try to keep it in a single layer). Sprinkle any remaining stuffing over the okra. Sprinkle the pan with 2 to 3 tablespoons water to create steam. Cover and cook over low heat until the okra is softened, 12 to 15 minutes. Serve hot or warm. Leftovers will keep for a day or two in the refrigerator. To reheat, arrange the pods on a sheet pan and heat in a 350°F oven for about 15 minutes, until warmed through.

OKRA WITH POTATOES SERVES 4 TO 6

For many years of my childhood, Mom was cooking three meals a day for a crowd—not just my father, my sister, and me, but also several of my aunts and uncles. She learned how to be resourceful and to stretch more expensive ingredients by combining them with inexpensive ones, especially potatoes. As part of the lunchtime thali, she'd make eggplant with potatoes, squash with potatoes, tomatoes with potatoes . . . you get the idea. My favorite was always okra with potatoes. When she didn't have as many mouths to feed and the budget was not as tight, I still wanted her to make okra with potatoes. Today, I make the same dish at home. Instead of a thali, these days I serve it to Teresa alongside fried chicken (page 250) and cornbread. It's not just about nostalgia; I have realized that crisping the potatoes adds a flavor and texture dimension that you can't achieve with okra on its own. Here is the recipe exactly as my mother prepared it.

1½ tablespoons coriander seeds

2 teaspoons cumin seeds

¼ cup neutral oil, such as peanut or canola

1 teaspoon brown mustard seeds

½ teaspoon fenugreek seeds

8 ounces russet or gold potatoes, peeled and cut into ½- to 1-inch cubes

1 pound tender okra pods, wiped clean, tough tops trimmed, and cut into 1-inch pieces

½ teaspoon ground turmeric

½ teaspoon ground cayenne pepper

Salt

Toast the coriander seeds in a small, dry pan over medium heat for about 1 minute. Add the cumin seeds and toast, shaking the pan gently so that the seeds toast evenly and do not burn, until both spices are fragrant, about 1 more minute. Remove from the heat and, when cool enough to handle, grind in a spice grinder or coffee grinder, or with a mortar and pestle. Set aside.

Heat the oil in a wide-bottomed skillet over medium heat. Once the oil is shimmering, add the mustard seeds and cook until they start popping, about 30 seconds. Add the fenugreek seeds, then the potatoes. Reduce the heat to medium-low and cook the potatoes until they start to soften, about 10 minutes. Increase the heat to medium-high so the potatoes can start to crisp up on the outside. Continue to stir and shake the pan so the potatoes brown evenly and don't stick, about 5 minutes. Add the okra, turmeric, and cayenne and stir to combine. Turn the heat back down to medium, cover, and cook for 5 minutes. Remove the lid and season with salt to taste. Reduce the heat to low and continue to cook, uncovered, until the potatoes are tender all the way through.

When the potatoes are fully cooked, the okra should be done as well. Taste a piece to check for tenderness. If you prefer your okra crispy and browned on the outside, cook for an additional 3 to 4 minutes over low heat, being careful not to burn the potatoes. Remove from the heat and gently stir in the ground coriander and cumin. Serve immediately.

SLOW-COOKED OKRA WITH GARAM MASALA AND YOGURT SERVES 4

For a few years, while I was in high school, we lived in housing provided by my dad's work, the Physical Research Laboratory in Ahmedabad. Since the research lab was run by the federal government, many of my father's coworkers came from different parts of India. It was a wonderful community, at once diverse and tightly knit. Despite different customs, diets, and even languages, we dined often with our neighbors. In those years, I got to sample many regional Indian foods that were new to me: rajma, or Punjabi-style red beans; banana blossom curry from Maharashtra; and a flatbread called paratha stuffed with radish.

Our neighbors the Varmas were from Ambala, a city in the northern state of Haryana. Their son Hemant had been my friend since childhood. When we became neighbors, I took every opportunity to eat dinner with his family in order to enjoy his mother's exceptional cooking. One of my favorite dishes Mrs. Varma used to make was okra in a spiced yogurt sauce. I had never had okra like this at home, and I discovered that the funky tartness of the yogurt is a perfect foil for the mellow okra. Serve this dish with rice or flatbread.

- 1 shallot, roughly chopped
- 2-inch piece ginger, roughly chopped
- 1 green chile, such as serrano or jalapeño, stemmed and roughly chopped
- 10 sprigs cilantro, leaves and tender stems roughly chopped, plus additional chopped fresh cilantro leaves, for garnish
- 3 tablespoons neutral oil, such as peanut or canola
- 1 pound small, tender okra pods, wiped clean, tough tops trimmed, and cut into 1-inch pieces
- 1 teaspoon brown mustard seeds
- 1 teaspoon cumin seeds
- 1 tablespoon chickpea flour
- 2 teaspoons garam masala (store-bought or homemade, page 8)
- 1 teaspoon ground turmeric
- ½ teaspoon paprika
- 1½ cups plain, full-fat yogurt (preferably Greek-style)
- Salt
- 1 teaspoon chaat masala (store-bought or homemade, page 8), for garnish (optional)

Combine the shallot, ginger, green chile, and chopped cilantro sprigs in the bowl of a food processor and blend until smooth. Set aside.

Heat the oil in a wide skillet over medium heat. Once the oil starts to shimmer, add the okra and cook until it is lightly browned and crisp on the outside, about 2 minutes. Using a slotted spoon, transfer the okra to a bowl. Add the mustard seeds to the same skillet. Once they start popping, about 30 seconds, add the cumin seeds and chickpea flour. Cook, stirring, until the flour is toasted and nutty, about 5 minutes. Take care not to let the flour burn. Add the shallot mixture and sauté until it is cooked through and slightly darker in color, 6 to 7 minutes. Add the garam masala, turmeric, and paprika and cook until fragrant, about 3 minutes. Whisk in the yogurt, mixing until everything is well incorporated. Add the okra and stir. Reduce the heat to low, cover, and cook until the okra is cooked through and soft, 5 to 6 minutes. Taste and season with salt to your liking. Garnish with chopped cilantro leaves and a sprinkle of chaat masala, if using.

LEBANESE LAMB, OKRA, AND TOMATO STEW (Bamia) SERVES 6

My good friend Michael Koury descends from the Mississippi Delta's Lebanese community. This population is all but unknown outside of Mississippi, but it has been part of the fabric and food of the Delta for more than a century. If you see kibbe or labneh on a menu in Mississippi, you have the Delta Lebanese to thank. They, along with small but important populations of Italian Americans and Chinese Americans, make the Delta a place whose cultural and culinary diversity surprises many outsiders.

One night, Michael told our supper club that he would be serving his great aunt's stew. When it was time to eat, Michael brought a large Dutch oven to the table. It was brimming with chunks of lamb and okra pods. I smelled cinnamon, cumin, and coriander. *Huh?* I thought. *There's okra in Lebanon?* After dinner, Michael talked me through the stew ingredients, and I adapted it into this recipe. It reminds me a little of the stewed okra and tomatoes I grew up eating in India, but brought to Mississippi by way of Lebanon. What a small world. If you can't find lamb stew meat for this recipe, you can substitute beef, or even goat. Use the smallest okra pods you can find. This is the one recipe in this chapter where you can use whole frozen okra.

- 1 pound lamb stew meat
- 3 teaspoons salt, divided
- 1½ teaspoons freshly ground black pepper
- 2 teaspoons coriander seeds
- 2 teaspoons cumin seeds
- 3 tablespoons olive oil
- 1 medium onion, diced (about 1¼ cups)
- 4 garlic cloves, minced
- 2 cups diced fresh tomatoes
- 2 cups crushed canned plum tomatoes
- 1 pound okra pods, wiped clean and tough tops trimmed
- 1 cinnamon stick
- 2 teaspoons red pepper flakes
- 1 teaspoon paprika
- ½ teaspoon allspice
- ½ teaspoon ground cloves or 3 whole cloves
- 8 cups Chicken Bone Stock (page 247) or store-bought unsalted chicken stock (You may also use water, or a combination of stock and water.)

Season the lamb with 1½ teaspoons salt and the pepper; set aside.

Toast the coriander seeds in a small, dry pan over medium heat for about 1 minute. Add the cumin seeds and toast, shaking the pan gently so that the seeds toast evenly and do not burn, until both spices are fragrant, about 1 more minute. Remove from the heat and, when cool enough to handle, grind in a spice grinder or coffee grinder, or with a mortar and pestle. Set aside.

Heat the oil in a Dutch oven or other wide, heavy-bottomed pot over medium-high heat. Once the oil shimmers, add the lamb to the pot and sear, turning the meat as needed until the pieces are evenly browned on all sides, 4 to 5 minutes total. Transfer the seared lamb to a plate. Depending on the size of your pot, you may need to sear the lamb in two batches. Turn the heat down to medium and add the onion. Cook until the onion starts to release water and soften, about 5 minutes. Add the garlic and cook for another 2 to 3 minutes. Add the fresh and canned tomatoes and cook until they start to thicken, about 10 minutes.

Return the seared lamb to the pot and add the okra, coriander-cumin mixture, cinnamon stick, red pepper flakes, paprika, allspice, and cloves. Stir to mix well. Add the stock and remaining 1½ teaspoons salt and bring to a simmer. Reduce the heat to low, cover, and cook until the lamb is falling-apart tender, about 1 hour. Taste for seasonings before serving and add a bit more salt if needed.

Alternatively, once you've added all the ingredients to the pot, you can cover it and cook in a 300°F oven for 1½ hours. (The oven technique is nice if you need to make room on the stove for other dishes or you want to begin cleaning up before your guests arrive.)

CHAPTER FOUR

TOMATOES

In Gujarat, with its long growing season, tomatoes were always available. So my relationship with tomatoes was a sort of everyday affection, rather than the excitement I felt when a vegetable like okra appeared for its brief season.

I savored my mother's tomato soup, with its hints of clove, black pepper, and cinnamon. I loved it when she cooked the tomatoes down with onions and ginger and garam masala and added fresh homemade paneer to the resulting sauce.

I was well into my thirties and living in Mississippi before I truly understood the cult status tomatoes enjoy among Southerners. One summer afternoon, my neighbor, who kept a couple of scraggly tomato plants growing in pots on her back stoop, came over with three cracked and gnarly-looking specimens. They looked nothing like the perfectly uniform, perfectly tasteless orbs piled high at the supermarket. She offered me a slice, sprinkled with a pinch of salt. I was hooked.

That summer, I learned about tomato and mayonnaise sandwiches on white bread, BLTs, stewed okra and tomatoes, and even fried green tomatoes. I waited anxiously for the next summer so that I could grow some imperfect tomatoes of my own. Nowadays I leave most of the growing to the farmers who show up at our local markets with all sorts of tomato varieties—I especially love the Cherokee Purples, Green Zebras, Sungolds, and Big Boys. There is something magical about a hot, sticky summer day in Mississippi punctuated with cool slices of tomato.

By now, you've seen that tomatoes show up throughout these pages. When tomatoes are out of season where you live, I recommend using good-quality canned tomatoes rather than subpar "fresh" ones that have been trucked to your supermarket from far off. What's special about the recipes in this chapter is that they are the ones where fresh, in-season tomatoes really shine. There is one exception, the All-Weather Tomato Tart (page 89), which comes to the rescue when you are craving tomatoes at the wrong time of year.

UDIPI TOMATO "OMELET" MAKES 5 TO 6 OMELETS

The saying goes that you can't make an omelet without breaking some eggs. But in Mumbai's Udipi cafés, you'll find exactly that: a vegan dish called "omelet" made with chickpea flour rather than eggs.

Think of Mumbai as you would New York City: a metropolis that has long lured domestic and international migrants with the promise of jobs and a better life. In the 1920s, migrants from the town of Udipi (also spelled Udupi), some five hundred miles south of Mumbai along India's western coast, came to Mumbai to work in the city's booming textile mills. They brought with them their vegetarian cuisine. Soon, there were hundreds of Udipi cafés across the city. Before long, Udipis, as they are called for short, became the go-to establishments for people of all classes and professions to eat a cheap, quick breakfast or lunch. Essentially, the Udipi is to Mumbai what the diner is to New York. Today, there are even Udipi cafés in Indian neighborhoods of US cities such as Houston, Chicago, and Queens, New York.

The menu at an Udipi café follows a reliable formula. Beneath the South Indian standards, above the bread and toast section, you'll find the tomato omelet. This "omelet"—it's really more akin to a vegetable pancake—might sound unusual to you, but it is so easy and satisfying that it might become a new favorite. Serve it for breakfast with Tomato-Coconut Chutney (page 99). You can add spinach, shredded potatoes, cabbage, mushrooms, or any other vegetable you like. Have fun!

2 cups chickpea flour

1 teaspoon ajwain seeds

1 teaspoon salt

1 teaspoon freshly ground black pepper

½ teaspoon garam masala (store-bought or homemade, page 8)

½ teaspoon ground turmeric

Pinch asafoetida

3 large ripe tomatoes, diced (about 3½ cups)

2 bunches scallions (12 to 14 total), thinly sliced

2-inch piece ginger, minced (2 heaping tablespoons)

2 serrano chiles, stemmed and minced

⅓ cup chopped fresh cilantro leaves and tender stems

Neutral oil, such as peanut or canola, for cooking

To make the batter, combine 1½ cups water with the chickpea flour, ajwain seeds, salt, pepper, garam masala, turmeric, and asafoetida in a medium bowl and mix well to blend. Add the tomatoes, scallions, ginger, serrano chiles, and cilantro and mix gently using a whisk. Cover the bowl and set aside at room temperature to allow the flavors to meld.

Set a 10-inch nonstick pan or stovetop griddle over medium-high heat and add a teaspoon or two of oil. When the oil starts to shimmer, add ⅓ to ½ cup of batter to the center of the pan. Using a spatula, spread the batter as thin as possible to form a circle 5 to 6 inches in diameter. Once you see bubbles appear on the surface and the edges start to brown lightly, about 90 seconds, gently flip the omelet, drizzle a few drops of oil around the edges, and cook for an additional 90 seconds. If you're a nervous omelet flipper, you'll be glad to know that this batter actually lends itself to an easier flip than an egg omelet, with no folding required. The look and consistency of the finished omelet should be lacey and golden. It will be reminiscent of an egg omelet, but not exactly the same. Remove from the griddle and serve immediately.

Wipe out the pan, set it back over medium heat, add another teaspoon or so of oil, and repeat with the remaining batter until all the omelets are cooked.

PARSI-STYLE SCRAMBLED EGGS WITH TOMATOES (Akuri) SERVES 4

There are scrambled eggs, and then there is akuri, a dish made popular in India by the Parsi community. The Parsis, followers of the Zoroastrian faith, migrated to India from Persia around the eighth century AD, following the Islamic conquest of Persia. Parsis first settled on the coast of Gujarat. Descendants of a later wave of Persian migration to India are called Iranis. Eventually, many Parsis and Iranis made their way to Mumbai. There, they took up many professions—medicine, law, bureaucracy. A large number of Parsis and Iranis became restaurateurs. There was a time when there was a Parsi or Irani café at almost every street corner in Mumbai. Unlike the Udipis, the Irani cafés served both meat and eggs. They also offered bread and baked goods. The most famous Parsi and Irani cafés—Britannia, Kyani & Co., Yazdani Bakery, and Cafe Military—became household names. They were symbols of modernity in Mumbai and a testament to India's welcoming attitude toward immigrants.

Every time I visit Mumbai, I order akuri for breakfast at Kyani & Co., the oldest remaining Parsi café in the city. I often make it at home as well. There are a few elements that elevate akuri beyond everyday scrambled eggs. The flavors are bold, fresh, and spicy, with plenty of heat from fresh chiles and cayenne. The texture is light: a super-fluffy scramble with the eggs just set. But most of all, it's the tomatoes. You'll use both fresh and roasted confit tomatoes for extra sweetness and concentrated flavor. Once you've tried akuri yourself, you'll be ruined for plain scrambled eggs.

- 8 large eggs
- ⅓ cup heavy cream
- ½ teaspoon coriander seeds
- 2 tablespoons ghee (store-bought or homemade, page 9)
- 2 tablespoons neutral oil, such as peanut or canola
- 1 small red onion, minced (¾ to 1 cup)
- 2 serrano chiles, stemmed and minced
- 2 small tomatoes, diced (1 to 1¼ cups)
- 4 halves Roasted Tomato Confit (page 85), diced
- ½ teaspoon ground turmeric
- ½ teaspoon ground cayenne pepper
- ½ cup chopped fresh cilantro leaves and tender stems, divided
- 1 teaspoon salt
- Salted butter, for serving
- Toasted sourdough bread, for serving

Whisk the eggs and cream together in a large bowl until light and frothy. Set aside.

Toast the coriander seeds in a small, dry pan over medium heat until fragrant, shaking the pan gently so that the seeds toast evenly and do not burn, 1 to 2 minutes. Remove from the heat and, when cool enough to handle, grind in a spice grinder or coffee grinder, or with a mortar and pestle. Set aside.

Set a large, nonstick skillet over medium heat and add the ghee and oil. When it starts to shimmer, add the onion and cook, stirring occasionally, until it starts to brown, about 5 minutes. Add the chiles, fresh tomatoes, and confit tomatoes and cook until most of the water from the fresh tomatoes has evaporated. Add the ground coriander, turmeric, cayenne, and half the cilantro and stir until fragrant, 30 to 45 seconds.

Whisk the salt into the egg mixture and pour over the tomatoes in the skillet. Shake the pan while gently stirring with a silicone spatula or a wooden spoon. Cook until the eggs are just set, 5 to 6 minutes. You want a soft, fluffy scramble.

Garnish with the remaining cilantro and a pat of salted butter and serve with thick slices of toasted sourdough.

ROASTED TOMATO CONFIT

MAKES 8 CONFIT TOMATO HALVES

Roasting low and slow cooks some of the water out of the tomatoes and concentrates the sugar without burning. You can double this recipe and use the extra tomatoes in salads or pasta sauce.

4 ripe red tomatoes

8 garlic cloves, thinly sliced

8 teaspoons olive oil, divided

1 teaspoon chaat masala (store-bought or homemade, page 8)

Salt

Freshly ground black pepper

Preheat the oven to 250°F. Line a sheet pan or baking dish with parchment.

Cut the tomatoes in half crosswise and gently remove all the seeds and partitions with a scoop or spoon. Place the tomato halves, cut side up, on the prepared sheet pan. Fill each tomato cavity with the thinly sliced garlic. Drizzle each tomato half with 1 teaspoon olive oil, then season lightly with chaat masala, salt, and pepper. Roast for 2 hours, or until most of the water has evaporated from the tomatoes and they start to caramelize. Cool completely, then transfer to an airtight container and store in the refrigerator. The tomatoes will keep for up to 1 week.

JANU AUNTY'S ROASTED TOMATO GRILLED CHEESE

MAKES 4 SANDWICHES

Who doesn't love a good grilled cheese sandwich? Growing up, I didn't get to eat them very often. When I was a child, there was not much domestic cheese available in Gujarat. If my parents splurged on imported cheese, it was a small amount for a special occasion, such as entertaining guests from Europe or the United States. There was no chance Mom would make me a grilled cheese with that.

Things started to change in the early 1980s, when Amul Dairy introduced a processed cheese flavored with cumin seeds and sold in a can. I would spend my allowance on roadside grilled cheeses made with this new cheese because my mother refused to buy it. One afternoon, as a young teenager, I went to visit my Uncle Paresh and Aunt Janu. As always, she asked me what I would like to eat, and I requested a grilled cheese. She dispatched Uncle Paresh to buy a can of the new Amul cheese with cumin seeds that I so coveted. I now judge all grilled cheese sandwiches by that one.

Today I use sharp white cheddar instead of Amul, and the Southern favorite Duke's mayonnaise.

- 2 teaspoons cumin seeds
- 8 slices sourdough bread
- Salted butter, at room temperature
- Mayonnaise (preferably Duke's)
- 2 cups shredded sharp white cheddar cheese
- 1 serrano chile, stemmed and minced
- 2 shallots, minced (about ½ cup)
- 1 teaspoon chaat masala (store-bought or homemade, page 8)
- 8 halves Roasted Tomato Confit (page 85)

Toast the cumin seeds in a small, dry pan over medium heat, shaking the pan gently so that the seeds toast evenly and do not burn, about 1 minute. Remove from the heat and set aside to cool.

To assemble one sandwich, take 2 slices of bread. Generously spread butter on one side of each slice and mayonnaise on the other side. The mayonnaise sides will face in, and the buttered sides will face out. Top one slice on the mayonnaise side with ¼ cup shredded cheese. On top of that, add one-quarter of the serrano, one-quarter of the shallots, ½ teaspoon cumin seeds, and ¼ teaspoon chaat masala. Layer 2 tomato halves on top, followed by another ¼ cup shredded cheese. Top with the other slice of bread, buttered side out. Repeat with the remaining ingredients until you have assembled all four sandwiches.

Set a nonstick skillet or stovetop griddle over medium-high heat. (If you have a panini press, you can use that instead.) Let it heat up for a couple of minutes and then add a sandwich. (If your skillet is large, you can cook two sandwiches at once. A griddle may be able to accommodate all four sandwiches.) Toast until crispy and golden brown on the bottom, about 90 seconds. Carefully flip the sandwich and cook until the cheese is melted and the second side is also nicely toasted. Repeat with the remaining sandwiches. Cut each sandwich in half and serve immediately.

SPICEWALLA

ALL-WEATHER TOMATO TART SERVES 4 TO 6

I am a sucker for tomato pie. Who isn't? However, making a perfect tomato pie could seem a bit daunting, what with the making of a proper pie dough, selecting the right cheese, and of course picking the perfectly ripe—but not too ripe—tomatoes. This is all well and good during peak tomato season, but what happens when you get a hankering for one in November or March, when the tomatoes at your grocery store may look shiny and red but the flavor is just not there? I have found the solution. This recipe uses a store-bought puff pastry crust, a bit of smoky bacon, a smear of crème fraîche, a grating of pecorino, and a sprinkle of coriander seeds and cracked black pepper. Once you have a batch of Roasted Tomato Confit (page 85) made, the tart comes together quickly and easily. It uses two kinds of tomatoes, fresh and roasted, for a pleasing contrast of colors, flavors, and textures.

All-purpose flour, for dusting

1 sheet puff pastry

1 teaspoon ajwain seeds

¾ cup crème fraîche (store-bought or homemade, page 90)

1 cup roughly chopped Roasted Tomato Confit (page 85; this will be about 5 confit tomato halves, depending on their size)

½ cup cherry and/or grape tomatoes, cut in half

⅓ cup thinly sliced sweet onion

⅓ cup diced smoky bacon, cooked

2 teaspoons cracked coriander seeds

2 teaspoons cracked black pepper

½ cup pecorino cheese, shaved

Preheat the oven to 400°F.

While the oven is heating up, sprinkle a little flour on a clean work surface and lay out the puff pastry sheet. Sprinkle with the ajwain seeds. Gently roll the puff pastry out until it is about twice its original size. Do not worry if you are not able to maintain a perfectly rectangular shape. Dock the surface five or six times with a fork. Slide a baking sheet under the dough. (If you do not have a flat cookie sheet, carefully transfer the puff pastry to a sheet pan. Either way, there is no need to grease the pan because the pastry contains so much butter.) Spread the pastry with an even layer of crème fraîche. Top with the chopped roasted tomatoes, cherry tomatoes, onion, and bacon. Sprinkle the coriander seeds and black pepper on top.

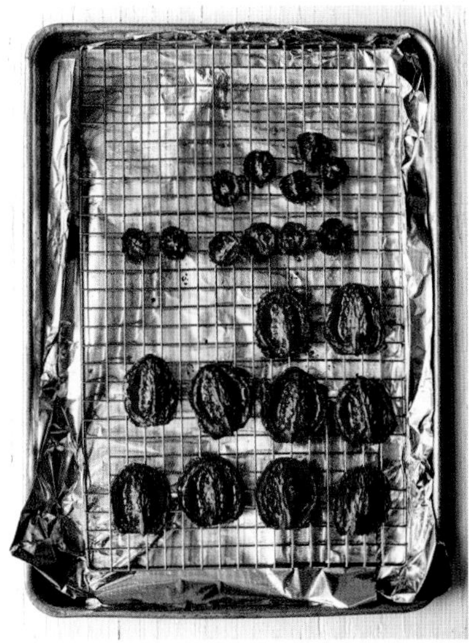

RECIPE CONTINUES

Bake for 20 to 25 minutes, until the pastry is puffed and golden brown. Cut into four to six squares. Garnish each square with a sprinkle of shaved pecorino before serving.

NOTES: Puff pastry is usually sold in 17.3-ounce packages. Depending on the brand, it may be refrigerated or frozen. If frozen, thaw before proceeding with the recipe. Rolling out and docking (poking holes in) the puff pastry will make for a crispier crust and keep it from puffing too much as it cooks. You can use any small tomatoes, such as cherry or grape. If you can find various colors, they will make for an especially lovely presentation.

CRÈME FRAÎCHE

MAKES ABOUT 2 CUPS

You'll need to find cultured buttermilk for this recipe because the live, active cultures are essential to the fermentation process that turns these ingredients into crème fraîche and gives it its flavor and texture. Warming the cream and buttermilk "wakes up" the cultures, making them happy and ready to go to work.

2 cups heavy cream

2 tablespoons cultured buttermilk

¼ teaspoon fresh lemon juice

Salt

Combine the cream and buttermilk in a small pot. Warm the mixture over low heat until it is lukewarm to the touch, about 85°F.

Remove from the heat and stir in the lemon juice and a pinch of salt. Pour the mixture into a quart-size glass jar and cover with cheesecloth or a thin kitchen towel. Tie a string or a rubber band around the mouth of the jar to keep the cloth from sliding off. Place the jar in a warm spot in your kitchen overnight. (I find that 10 hours is ideal. If your kitchen is cold, the process might take longer.) The following day, remove the cheesecloth, cover the jar with a proper lid, and refrigerate for 8 hours. The mixture will continue to thicken. By the end of this time you will have a thick, slightly tangy yogurt-like product that is ready to use.

Crème fraîche will last for up to 1 week in the refrigerator. Give it a stir before using. Spread it on toast or crackers, or dollop it anywhere you would sour cream. You can substitute crème fraîche in savory recipes that call for heavy cream for a richer, tangier flavor.

MOM'S TOMATO SOUP SERVES 6 TO 8

Close your eyes and imagine that you are sitting in front of a steaming bowl of tomato soup accompanied by a crispy-on-the-outside, melty-gooey-in-the-middle grilled cheese. It is a great picture, isn't it? Can you think of anything more all-American than that?

Believe it or not, I grew up with tomato soup and grilled cheese sandwiches, too. I've had many tomato soups in my lifetime, but none comes close to the one my mother used to make. She used ripe, juicy tomatoes, fresh ginger, cloves, and cinnamon. Freshly cracked black pepper lent a touch of heat, and a pinch of sugar balanced the tomatoes' acidity. Next time you bring home a bushel of summer tomatoes from your farmers' market, give this recipe a try. My mother never peeled her tomatoes, but you can do so if you prefer a smoother texture.

This soup served with a Bombay Toastie (page 148) will become your new favorite soup-and-sandwich combination.

8 to 10 medium ripe tomatoes, cored and diced (8 to 9 cups)

2 carrots, peeled, cut in half lengthwise, and sliced into half-moons (¾ to 1 cup)

3 garlic cloves, sliced

3-inch piece ginger, minced (3 heaping tablespoons)

1 cinnamon stick

6 whole cloves

2 bay leaves

3 tablespoons minced fresh cilantro stems

Pinch ground turmeric

Pinch garam masala (store-bought or homemade, page 8)

3 tablespoons ghee (store-bought or homemade, page 9) or neutral oil, such as peanut or canola

1 teaspoon cumin seeds

2 tablespoons cracked black pepper

1 teaspoon salt

1 teaspoon granulated sugar

2 to 3 tablespoons fresh cilantro leaves, for garnish

Combine the tomatoes, carrots, garlic, ginger, cinnamon, cloves, bay leaves, cilantro stems, turmeric, garam masala, and 8 cups water in a large pot and bring to a boil over high heat. Reduce the heat to low and simmer for 20 minutes.

Heat the ghee in a small pan or pot over medium heat. When the ghee is shimmering, add the cumin seeds and black pepper and cook until very fragrant, about 30 seconds. Add the ghee mixture to the large pot and simmer for an additional 5 minutes. Remove from the heat and discard the cinnamon stick and bay leaves. Using an immersion blender, purée the soup. (If you do not have an immersion blender, you can purée the soup in a regular blender, working in batches.) If you prefer a smooth, fine purée, carefully strain through a chinois or fine-mesh strainer. Stir in the salt and sugar. Taste and adjust for seasonings as desired. Ladle into bowls and garnish each serving with a sprinkle of cilantro leaves.

TURKISH TOMATO SALAD (Ezme) SERVES 8 TO 10

Some of the best dishes are also the simplest. This salad—it is actually closer to a salsa—is a great example of that.

Dr. Gokhan Karahan, a former professor of economics at the University of Mississippi, has been a friend of mine for more than two decades. Every time he cooks for Teresa and me, he serves lamb kofta with tzatziki and bean soup with lemon and garlic. One summer, he invited us over to meet his sister, who was visiting from Turkey. As an afterthought, I packed a bag of produce from our garden—a few overripe tomatoes, some peppers, and a bunch of mint.

I handed the sack to our host, who handed it to his sister. She looked inside, smiled with delight, and disappeared into the kitchen. When she reappeared, she was carrying a bowl of what looked like salsa. Gokhan's eyes lit up. They explained that it was a Turkish salad called ezme, which we ate with the kofta.

As is her custom when she falls in love with a new dish, Teresa asked Gokhan's sister for the recipe. It looked so simple that I was convinced she had left out some secret ingredient. But when we made it, it was just as fresh, bright, and perfect as we remembered.

This recipe requires a great deal of mincing, but I promise that the result is worth it. (Please resist the temptation to use a food processor as a shortcut!) Make it when tomatoes are at their peak. You'll see that the recipe below serves a crowd. Feel free to cut the quantities in half for a smaller batch. But it is incredibly versatile, and I think you'll find that any leftovers will disappear quickly. You can serve the ezme as a salad or side dish, as part of a Mediterranean-style mezze platter with Ground Lamb (Kofta) Kebabs (page 288), as a dip with pita chips, or over eggs at breakfast.

2 teaspoons cumin seeds

8 large ripe tomatoes, peeled and minced (about 6 cups)

2 small yellow onions, minced (about 1½ cups)

1 red bell pepper, seeded and minced (about ¾ cup)

1 green bell pepper, seeded and minced (about ¾ cup)

4 to 6 Fresno or jalapeño chiles, stemmed and minced (⅓ to ½ cup)

3 garlic cloves, minced

1 bunch flat-leaf parsley, leaves chopped (Reserve a tablespoon or two for garnish.)

⅓ cup chopped fresh mint leaves

2 teaspoons ground sumac, plus a pinch for garnish

2 teaspoons red pepper flakes

⅓ cup extra virgin olive oil, plus a drizzle for garnish

¼ cup red wine vinegar or fresh lemon juice

3 tablespoons pomegranate molasses

1 teaspoon salt, or to taste

1 teaspoon freshly ground black pepper, or to taste

Toast the cumin seeds in a small, dry pan over medium heat, shaking the pan gently so that the seeds toast evenly and do not burn, about 1 minute. Remove from the heat. When cool enough to handle, grind in a spice or coffee grinder, or with a mortar and pestle.

Combine the tomatoes, onions, bell peppers, chiles, garlic, parsley, mint, ground cumin, sumac, red pepper flakes, olive oil, vinegar, pomegranate molasses, salt, and black pepper in a large bowl and mix gently to blend. Allow to sit for 30 minutes before serving to allow the flavors to meld. Before serving, taste and add additional salt and black pepper if desired. Garnish with an extra drizzle of olive oil, a pinch more sumac, and a little more chopped parsley before serving.

Store leftovers in a covered container in the refrigerator for up to 3 days. As the salad sits, the tomatoes will release more water. You may want to pour off this extra liquid before serving the leftovers.

PEELED TOMATOES

To peel the tomatoes, cut an X into the bottom of the tomatoes, lower them into boiling water for 25 seconds, then remove them with a slotted spoon and immediately plunge them into ice-cold water. The skin will peel right off.

NOTES: Traditionally, you want the heat from the chiles. If you think they are too hot for you, use 4 chiles rather than 6 and remove some or all of the seeds according to your taste. Pomegranate molasses adds a pleasantly tart flavor and just a hint of sweetness to the ezme. If your supermarket does not carry it, you can find it at Middle Eastern or international grocery stores or order it online. I love using it in salad dressings.

TOMATO STEW WITH CHICKPEA FLOUR NOODLES SERVES 4 TO 6

If you are a fan of tomato soup with dumplings or a spicy Mexican sopa de fideo, you are going to love this. This recipe is my recreation of a soup my grandmother made when we visited her in the city of Bhavnagar for Holi, the colorful Hindu festival of early spring. I have vivid memories of the vegetable vendor coming by the house in the morning, cart piled high with bright red plum tomatoes. Grandmother would always ask if it was okay to have tomato stew for dinner. I would enthusiastically say yes. Tomatoes would be bought. Dough for chickpea noodles/dumplings would be kneaded, and the kids would be banished from the kitchen until suppertime. The loud hiss of the pressure cooker was a sure sign that the tomatoes were very close to being ready. We would all run in, wash up, and help get ready for dinner. The shallow porcelain soup bowls that were stashed away in her cupboard for meals like this would be fished out, and the soup spoons from the ancient cutlery set that had been part of her dowry would make a rare appearance. We would all sit on the low wooden seats in a semicircle around her. She would ladle piping hot stew into our bowls—deep red, with flecks of green cilantro, little brown mustard seeds, and the yellow noodles bobbing up and down. We would all quietly tuck in as she turned her attention to rolling out light and fluffy chapatis to accompany the meal.

If you have a spaetzle maker or handheld pasta extruder, this is your chance to use it. Or, you can do as my mother did when she made this stew and scrape the dough through a colander to achieve the same effect. The technique takes a little practice and coordination. Have fun with it—the noodles do not have to be uniform. If you don't get it quite right the first time, the stew will still be delicious. And you'll just have an excuse to make it again.

FOR THE CHICKPEA FLOUR NOODLES:

¾ cup chickpea flour

½ teaspoon ajwain seeds

½ teaspoon salt

½ teaspoon cracked black pepper

½ teaspoon ground cayenne pepper

Pinch ground turmeric

Pinch asafoetida

1½ teaspoons neutral oil, such as peanut or canola

FOR THE STEW:

1½ teaspoons coriander seeds

½ teaspoon cumin seeds

6 garlic cloves, peeled

1 serrano chile, stemmed and roughly chopped

½ teaspoon ground cayenne pepper

2 tablespoons neutral oil, such as peanut or canola

1 teaspoon brown mustard seeds

1 sprig curry leaves

½ teaspoon asafoetida

4 cups diced ripe plum or Roma tomatoes (8 to 10 tomatoes)

2 teaspoons jaggery or light brown sugar

½ teaspoon garam masala (store-bought or homemade, page 8)

½ teaspoon ground turmeric

1½ teaspoons salt, or to taste

FOR SERVING:

¼ cup chopped fresh cilantro

Flatbread (optional)

To make the chickpea flour noodles, combine the chickpea flour, ajwain seeds, salt, black pepper, cayenne, turmeric, and asafoetida in a large bowl. Add the oil and mix well. Gradually add water, a tablespoon at a time, and knead until the dough starts coming together. Continue to add more water as needed and knead in the bowl until you have a firm but not dry dough. You will use about 6 tablespoons water in all. If you are used to working with wheat flour dough, this will feel very different. There is no gluten in chickpea flour, so the dough will go from sticky to firm without much give. The surface will remain tacky. Set the dough aside at room temperature while you make the stew.

Toast the coriander seeds in a small, dry pan over medium heat for about 1 minute. Add the cumin seeds and toast, shaking the pan gently so that the seeds toast evenly and do not burn, until both spices are fragrant, about 1 more minute. Remove from the heat and, when cool enough to handle, grind in a spice grinder or coffee grinder, or with a mortar and pestle. Set aside.

Put the garlic, serrano, and cayenne in the bowl of a food processor and process to a smooth paste.

Heat the oil in a Dutch oven or other wide, heavy-bottomed pot over medium heat. Once the oil is shimmering, add the mustard seeds and cook until they start popping, about 30 seconds. Add the curry leaves, asafoetida, and garlic paste and cook, stirring, until fragrant, about 20 seconds. Add the tomatoes, ground coriander-cumin mixture, jaggery, and garam masala. Stir and simmer until the tomatoes start releasing their water and soften, about 4 minutes. Add the turmeric and 4 cups water. Turn up the heat and bring the stew to a boil. If the stew seems too thick, add another ½ to 1 cup water.

Divide the noodle dough into five or six pieces. Working with one piece at a time, carefully press the dough into the boiling soup using a colander, spaetzle maker, or handheld pasta extruder. If using the colander technique, press a piece of dough into the bottom of the colander. Then, drag a bench or bowl scraper across the dough, applying pressure as you scrape. Small pieces of dough will fall through the holes and into the soup.

Make sure the stew is boiling as you add the noodles. If it stops boiling, wait for it to return to a boil before adding more noodles. Give the soup an occasional stir to distribute the noodles evenly. Once they start floating to the top, they are done. Reduce the heat, add the salt, and simmer for an additional 3 to 4 minutes. Taste and adjust seasonings if desired. Ladle into bowls and garnish each serving with chopped cilantro. If you like, serve with flatbread for dipping.

The soup is best served immediately, as the noodles will eventually break down in the liquid.

GRILLED STUFFED TOMATOES SERVES 8

If I were to invite my Turkish and Greek friends over for dinner, they would recognize this dish as dolma, the collective name for a leaf or vegetable stuffed with meat and rice. They would then proceed to argue with each other about who invented the dish. Our Lebanese neighbors would join in the argument. Imagine we had invited guests from the Levant and the Balkans; they, too, would stake a claim to dolmas. Very soon the dinner party would turn into a ruckus—that is, until the stuffed tomatoes were served. Then the talk would turn to memories. Memories of childhood and family gatherings. Memories of festivals and, inevitably, recollections of how wonderful tomatoes used to be back then. The bickering would subside, and the guests would begin to laugh in recognition of how much they had in common.

I have no idea who invented stuffed tomatoes. I just know that it is a wonderful dish to serve to a crowd and make your own memories.

I like this dish best with ground chicken or lamb, but use the meat that you prefer. For a vegetarian version, substitute crumbled tofu. Serve the tomatoes as a first course or alongside Ground Lamb (Kofta) Kebabs (page 288). For a lunch or lighter supper, a green salad on the side is all you need. And of course, you can halve this recipe for a small gathering.

8 large, firm, ripe tomatoes

Salt

5 tablespoons olive oil, divided

Freshly ground black pepper

1 large yellow or white onion, minced (about 1½ cups)

3 tablespoons minced garlic

2 teaspoons tomato paste

1½ pounds ground chicken or ground lamb

2 cups cooked long-grain white rice, such as basmati or jasmine

½ cup pine nuts or chopped pistachios

¼ cup chopped fresh flat-leaf parsley

1 teaspoon dried dill (may be labeled dill weed)

1 teaspoon red pepper flakes

1 cup crumbled feta cheese

Grated zest and juice of 1 lemon

NOTE: Depending on the size of your tomatoes, you may end up with extra stuffing. The stuffing is delicious on its own or with pita bread. It also makes a knockout omelet filling for breakfast the next morning.

Heat the grill to medium. If it is a charcoal grill, push the coals to one side to grill the tomatoes with indirect heat. If baking instead of grilling, preheat the oven to 350°F.

Slice each tomato horizontally ¼ to ½ inch from the top. Discard the tops and gently scoop out the inside of each tomato with a spoon, reserving a total of 1 cup pulp and seeds. Generously salt the inside of each tomato and turn them upside down on a wire rack over a sheet pan or over the sink. Allow the tomatoes to drain while you prep the rest of the ingredients.

Once the hollowed-out tomatoes have drained sufficiently, turn them cut-side up in a large baking dish or on a sheet pan. Drizzle them with 3 tablespoons olive oil and season lightly with pepper; set aside.

Heat the remaining 2 tablespoons olive oil in a large sauté pan over medium heat. When the oil begins to shimmer, add the onion and garlic. Cook, stirring occasionally, until the onion is golden brown and very soft, 8 to 10 minutes. Stir in the tomato paste, then add the ground meat and reserved tomato pulp. Cook, breaking up the meat with a wooden spoon or spatula, until the meat is browned and completely cooked through, 10 to 12 minutes. Remove the pan from the heat and mix in the rice, nuts, parsley, dill, red pepper flakes, feta, and lemon zest and juice. Taste and add salt, if needed.

When the mixture is cool enough to handle, spoon it into the prepared tomatoes, filling them to the top.

RECIPE CONTINUES

Using tongs, gently place the tomatoes directly on the grill. Use the cooler side of the grill, if possible, to reduce the chance of the tomatoes splitting and spilling. Close the lid and cook for 10 minutes.

Carefully remove the tomatoes from the grill using a spatula and tongs. If baking instead of grilling, leave the tomatoes on the rack in the baking dish or on the sheet pan and bake for 15 to 20 minutes. Serve hot.

TOMATO-COCONUT CHUTNEY MAKES ABOUT 4 CUPS

Chutneys were an integral part of every meal I ate growing up. Composed of nearly every combination of fruits and vegetables you can imagine, they can take various forms and textures. Some are more like pesto (see Peanut Pesto, page 170), some have yogurt as a base, and others resemble salsa. There are as many different variations on chutneys as there are households.

This tomato-coconut chutney is inspired by a trip Teresa and I took to a beach resort in the state of Kerala, at the southwestern tip of India. On the first morning of our stay, Teresa endeared herself to the dining staff by putting away a Keralan-style breakfast. For the next three days, the servers would bring out things for her to taste every time we sat down to eat in the restaurant or ordered a drink at the bar. One afternoon, the bartender offered us some crispy fried lentil fritters accompanied by a fiery tomato chutney. Teresa fell in love with that chutney and asked for the recipe. In typical Indian fashion, with much head nodding involved, we left with assurances that the chef would write down the recipe for us. He didn't.

Back home in Mississippi, I tried to recreate the Keralan tomato chutney. After much trial and error, I added coconut milk to tone down the heat from the fresh chiles. Try it with Ground Lamb (Kofta) Kebabs (page 288), Grilled Chicken Thighs with Peaches, Chiles, and Spiced Honey (page 258), or the Udipi Tomato "Omelet" (page 82).

3 tablespoons neutral oil, such as peanut or canola

1 sprig curry leaves

6 dried chiles de árbol, stemmed and broken in half

1 teaspoon brown mustard seeds

1 teaspoon cumin seeds

½ teaspoon ground turmeric

1 medium red onion, minced (about 1¼ cups)

2 pounds ripe tomatoes, diced (about 3 to 3½ cups)

1 cup tomato paste

1 tablespoon molasses

1 teaspoon Madras curry powder

1 teaspoon freshly ground black pepper

½ teaspoon ground cayenne pepper

¾ cup canned full-fat coconut milk

1 teaspoon salt

NOTE: This recipe calls for Madras curry powder, which has a bit more heat than regular curry powder as well as more fenugreek, which lends a pleasantly bitter note. If you cannot find it, substitute regular curry powder.

Heat the oil in a medium saucepan over medium heat. When the oil starts to shimmer, add the curry leaves, chiles, mustard seeds, and cumin seeds. Cook until the mustard seeds begin to pop, about 30 seconds. Add the turmeric and stir. Cook until the chiles darken to a deep brown, 1 to 2 minutes. Add the onion and cook until it is completely soft and golden, 6 to 7 minutes. Stir in the tomatoes, tomato paste, molasses, curry powder, black pepper, and cayenne. Simmer until the tomatoes break down and thicken, 6 to 7 minutes. Add the coconut milk and salt and simmer for an additional 4 to 5 minutes to let the liquid reduce and the chutney thicken. The finished chutney should be a consistency that you spoon rather than drizzle.

Serve warm or at room temperature. The chutney will keep for up to 1 week in the refrigerator. In my house, it's always gone in a matter of days!

MR. BUNZENDAHL'S GREEN TOMATO PIE

MAKES ONE 9-INCH PIE (SERVES 6 TO 8)

If you've spent any time in the South, you have come across green tomatoes—simply tart, unripe tomatoes that have not turned red yet. They are most often fried, pickled, or turned into a chutney or relish like piccalilli or chow-chow. I am willing to bet that you haven't had a green tomato pie for dessert. I learned of this wonderful creation from one of my oldest and dearest friends, EJ Bunzendahl.

One summer, EJ came to visit. As we sat on my porch, I lamented that our backyard tomatoes were late to ripen that season. I had several green tomatoes, but none that were ripe. To my surprise, EJ suggested that we make a green tomato pie, a recipe she'd learned from her father. Essentially, it takes the spices you would use in an apple pie and applies them to a filling of tart-sweet green tomatoes, baked into a double-crust pie. The experience reminded me that there's always more to learn about even the most familiar of ingredients.

5 cups diced green tomatoes (these are unripe tomatoes, not the Green Zebra heirloom variety)

1⅓ cups plus 1 tablespoon granulated sugar

½ teaspoon salt

2 Vish's Pie Crusts (page 101)

¼ cup plus 2 tablespoons tapioca flour or cornstarch

½ teaspoon ground cinnamon

¼ teaspoon ground cloves

1 tablespoon grated lemon zest

2 tablespoons fresh lemon juice

3 tablespoons unsalted butter, cut into 6 to 8 pieces

Vanilla ice cream, for serving (optional)

Toss the green tomatoes with 1 tablespoon sugar and the salt in a large bowl. Transfer to a colander and set aside over a large bowl or the sink for 30 minutes to drain.

Preheat the oven to 375°F.

Roll one pie crust between two sheets of parchment or waxed paper to a 10-inch circle about ⅛ inch thick. Fit the circle into a 9-inch pie pan. Fold and crimp the edge with the tines of a fork. Line the crust with a piece of aluminum foil and fill with pie weights or dried beans (this will help prevent shrinkage and puffing while the crust bakes). Bake for 5 minutes. Remove the foil and pie weights. Set aside.

Combine the remaining 1⅓ cups sugar, tapioca flour, cinnamon, cloves, and lemon zest and juice in a large bowl and mix well. The mixture will look like wet sand.

Shake the colander over the sink to drain the excess moisture from the tomatoes, then add them to the sugar-spice mixture, tossing gently to combine.

Spoon the tomato filling into the parbaked bottom crust, mounding it in the center. Dot the top with the butter. Roll the second pie crust between two sheets of parchment or waxed paper into a 9- to 10-inch circle. (The top crust can be slightly smaller in diameter and slightly thicker than the bottom crust since it does not have to cover as much surface area.) Drape the crust over the pie and seal the edges by pressing together with a fork all the way around or crimping with your fingers. Cut four or five vents in the top crust with the tip of a sharp knife. Bake for 45 to 60 minutes, until the top crust is a deep golden brown and you can see the filling bubbling through the vents.

Let the pie cool on a rack completely before cutting. The rest time allows the filling to set, but it will not become completely firm. I promise, the juice is so good, you will not complain! Slice the pie and serve warm, ideally with a scoop of vanilla ice cream.

VISH'S PIE CRUST

MAKES TWO 9-INCH PIE CRUSTS

1½ cups all-purpose flour, plus more for rolling

1½ cups cake flour

½ teaspoon salt

8 tablespoons (1 stick) unsalted butter, cold, diced

½ cup vegetable shortening or lard, very cold

½ cup cold whole milk

1 tablespoon white vinegar

Combine the all-purpose flour, cake flour, and salt in the bowl of a food processor fitted with a steel blade and pulse to mix. (For pie dough, a food processor is more effective than a stand mixer. The blade of the food processor does a better job of mixing the ingredients, and it is helpful to be able to see into the side of the food processor's clear bowl.) Add the butter and shortening. Pulse until the mixtures resembles coarsely ground cornmeal and no large pieces of butter or shortening remain visible.

Combine the milk and vinegar in a small bowl. Remove the lid of the food processor and sprinkle the milk mixture evenly over the top of the flour. Replace the lid and pulse just until the dough begins to form a ball. Add more cold milk if needed.

Sprinkle flour over a work surface and scrape the dough out onto it. Divide the dough in half. Place each dough half between two pieces of plastic wrap and press it into a 6-inch disk. Refrigerate the dough until firm, at least 1 hour. Proceed with your favorite pie recipe. (Alternatively, you can make the dough ahead of time and freeze it for several weeks. Wrap the dough tightly in two layers of plastic wrap to avoid freezer burn. When ready to use, defrost the frozen pie dough overnight in the refrigerator or at room temperature for about an hour and a half. The dough should be cold but not frozen when you begin working with it.)

NOTE: This pie crust recipe makes enough for two crusts. You will need both of them for this pie. Make sure the dough is cold before you roll it out. In a pinch, you can use store-bought pie crusts. The refrigerated, rolled-up ones (as opposed to pie shells) work well here. They are usually sold two to a box and shelved with the biscuits and cookie dough.

CHAPTER FIVE

EGGPLANT

When it comes to eggplant, I grew up in a house divided. My father hates the vegetable with a passion. My mother loved it with equal fervor.

When our family moved from India, first to France and then to the States, eggplant was one vegetable my mother could find and cook to taste just like it did back home. It was also the vegetable that allowed her to delve into cuisines from around the globe. She used the eggplant as her springboard to French ratatouille, Turkish imam bayildi, and her vegetarian version of Greek moussaka. Eggplant gave her—and by extension, me—a window into other cultures and cuisines. The Chinese and the Indians, the Greeks and Turks, the Jews and Arabs, the French and the Italians, the Creoles and the Cajuns, all have recipes for eggplant. And each of those dishes tells a story. To me, that speaks volumes about a simple vegetable's power to bring us together at the dinner table.

I am on my mother's side of this debate—next to okra, eggplant is my favorite vegetable. I'm drawn to its rich purple color, its texture, and its versatility. It can be smooth and creamy, meaty, or fried to a pleasant crisp. I look forward to eggplant season every summer. As soon as the first eggplants appear at the farmers' market, shining next to the red tomatoes, yellow squash, and green peppers, I add them to my menu. Eggplant Creole, ratatouille, and caponata are Snackbar staples during the summer months. And of course, I make eggplant dishes at home.

GUJARATI-STYLE CHARRED EGGPLANT (Olo) SERVES 6 TO 8

This is my mother's family recipe. Every fall we used to visit my maternal grandmother and spend a week at her home in the countryside. Grandma cooked this mashed eggplant, which is called olo in Gujarati, with much fanfare every time we visited. My uncles would visit nearby farms to pick just the right eggplants, dig up green garlic, and pluck chile peppers. Often, I went with them—with the house full of guests, it gave Grandma a little break. When we returned home, Mom and Grandma would supervise as the uncles built a fire with acacia wood and hay. Once the fire had burnt down to embers, the women would roast the eggplant until it was charred and soft. While the eggplant cooked, they would pulverize green garlic and ginger with a mortar and pestle and chop green chiles. They cleaned and mashed the smoked eggplant and folded it together with sautéed garlic, ginger, chiles, mustard seeds, and garam masala.

We would all sit out on the veranda and eat the olo with millet flatbread, cooked on a concave clay griddle over the fire. Also on the table were raw green onions with a squeeze of lime, mango or olive pickles, yogurt, and freshly churned butter. We'd wash it all down with glasses of fresh buttermilk.

When I make olo at home in Oxford, I no longer light a fire but use the grill instead. I serve the eggplant as a side dish, usually with something else that has been cooked on the grill, such as Grilled Chicken Thighs with Peaches, Chiles, and Spiced Honey (page 258). These flavors also work well with Confit Pork Ribs with Mexican Adobo Paste (page 274) or Punjabi-Style Fried Catfish (page 231). If young, green garlic is available at your farmer's market, use that in place of regular garlic. Thousands of miles from my grandmother's home, it still reminds me of her.

- 3 medium eggplants
- 3 tablespoons neutral oil, such as peanut or canola, divided
- 2 tablespoons coriander seeds
- 2 teaspoons cumin seeds
- 1 teaspoon brown mustard seeds
- ½ teaspoon asafoetida
- 1 small red onion, minced (¾ to 1 cup)
- 2-inch piece ginger, minced (2 heaping tablespoons)
- 2 to 3 medium ripe tomatoes, chopped (about 2½ cups)
- 1 bunch scallions, finely chopped, greens separated from whites
- 5 or 6 garlic cloves (preferably green garlic), minced
- 2 or 3 serrano chiles, chopped (scant ¼ cup)
- 1 teaspoon garam masala (store-bought or homemade, page 8)
- ½ teaspoon ground turmeric
- 1 teaspoon salt, or to taste
- Sliced chives or greens from top of a green garlic bulb, for garnish
- Lime wedges, for squeezing

Heat the grill to medium.

Brush the eggplants with 1 tablespoon oil and grill, turning often, until very soft and charred, 12 to 15 minutes. (Ideally you want to do this over a wood fire, but charcoal or gas works as well.)

Place the charred eggplants in a large bowl and cover with plastic wrap. Allow them to sit for about 10 minutes. The resulting steam and heat will finish cooking the eggplants and make the skin easier to peel. Once the eggplants are cool enough to handle, remove the stem and peel off and discard as much of the charred skin as possible. Mash the eggplant with a fork or chop it into small pieces.

Toast the coriander seeds in a small, dry pan over medium heat for about 1 minute. Add the cumin seeds and toast, shaking the pan gently so that the seeds toast evenly and do not burn, until both spices are fragrant, about 1 more minute. Remove from the heat and, when cool enough to handle, grind in a spice grinder or coffee grinder, or with a mortar and pestle. Set aside.

Heat the remaining 2 tablespoons oil in a large skillet over medium heat. Once the oil is shimmering, add

RECIPE CONTINUES

the mustard seeds and cook until they start popping, about 30 seconds. Add the asafoetida, onion, and ginger. Cook, stirring often, until the onion is soft and translucent, about 6 minutes. Add the tomatoes, scallion whites, garlic, and chiles and cook, stirring frequently, until all the water has cooked out of the tomatoes, 10 to 12 minutes. Add the coriander, cumin, garam masala, and turmeric. Mix well and cook for 3 to 4 minutes. Stir in the mashed eggplant and salt and cook for 5 to 6 more minutes. Taste and add additional salt if desired. Garnish with chives, scallion greens, or garlic greens. Serve with lime wedges to be squeezed on top as desired.

NOTE: If you don't have an outdoor grill, you can approximate the charred flavor by baking the eggplant, then broiling it. Cut the eggplant in half and place the halves, skin side up, in a baking dish. Add water to the baking dish to a depth of about ¼ inch. Bake at 375°F for 20 minutes, or until the eggplant is soft. Turn the oven to broil and broil until the skin begins to char, 3 to 4 minutes.

ITALIAN SAUSAGE AND EGGPLANT DRESSING SERVES 6 TO 8

Eggplant dressing is a common dish in homes and restaurants in Louisiana's Cajun country, which lies west of New Orleans in the southern third of the state. "Dressing" in this context means a substantial baked side dish, often involving meat, like a casserole. It's common at Thanksgiving. I have seen versions of the dressing on New Orleans restaurant menus as well. Some include shrimp, others ground beef or pork, and some combine two or more meats along with the vegetables. While I always enjoy the dish, I tend to find myself craving a bit more spice. Cajuns, of course, are descended from the French Canadians who were expelled by the British in the eighteenth century and eventually migrated to Louisiana. Germans immigrated to Acadiana, too, and their foodways have also become a part of Cajun home cooking. For years, I wondered why, given New Orleans's sizable Italian population, no one had created an eggplant dressing that used spicy Italian sausage. To me, it would be the perfect rural-urban crossover. So I developed my own. I think a rich dressing like this is best served alongside a simple roast meat like chicken or turkey. Or, make this the next time you're asked to bring a dish to a holiday dinner.

2 large eggplants, peeled and cut into 2-inch cubes

4 tablespoons (½ stick) unsalted butter, divided

1 pound spicy Italian sausage (remove casings if using links)

1 cup diced yellow onion

1 small red bell pepper, seeded and diced (about ¾ cup)

2 teaspoons minced garlic

1 tablespoon tomato paste

1 tablespoon fresh thyme leaves

1 tablespoon chopped fresh flat-leaf parsley

1 tablespoon chopped scallions, green parts only

1 teaspoon hot sauce

1 teaspoon Creole seasoning (store-bought or homemade, page 8)

1 teaspoon salt

1 large egg, lightly beaten

1 cup Italian-style bread crumbs, divided

¼ cup grated Parmesan cheese

Preheat the oven to 375°F. Lightly grease an 8-inch square baking pan.

Bring a large pot of salted water to a boil over high heat. Add the eggplant and cook until just soft, about 20 minutes. Drain and set aside.

Heat 2 tablespoons butter in a Dutch oven or other wide, heavy-bottomed pot over medium heat. Add the sausage and cook, breaking up the meat with a wooden spoon or spatula, until it is lightly browned, 5 to 6 minutes. Add the onion, bell pepper, and garlic and sauté until the onion is soft, 6 to 7 minutes. Add the tomato paste and cook for 2 to 3 minutes. Fold in the eggplant, herbs, hot sauce, Creole seasoning, and salt and mix well. Remove from the heat and fold in the beaten egg and ½ cup bread crumbs.

Transfer the mixture to the prepared pan and flatten lightly with the back of a spoon or spatula. Melt the remaining 2 tablespoons butter in a small skillet or saucepan, then stir in the remaining ½ cup bread crumbs and the Parmesan cheese. Sprinkle the mixture evenly over the eggplant.

Bake until the top is golden brown, 8 to 10 minutes. Allow the dressing to rest for 8 to 10 minutes before serving.

EGGPLANT AND RICE CROQUETTES

MAKES 16 TO 18 CROQUETTES

These croquettes draw inspiration from two Louisiana dishes: the fried balls of rice-filled boudin sausage that are a staple of the Snackbar menu, and Creole calas, or rice fritters. The feta cheese adds a nice salty kick without completely melting. Serve these as an appetizer or cocktail snack, figuring on about 3 croquettes per person. Try them with any number of sauces or chutneys for dipping, such as French Remoulade (page 203), Peanut Pesto (page 170), or Tomato-Coconut Chutney (page 99).

4 medium eggplants (about 2½ pounds)

Neutral oil, such as peanut or canola

2 cups cooked long-grain white rice (see page 18), at room temperature

1 large egg, beaten

½ teaspoon salt

½ teaspoon Creole seasoning (store-bought or homemade, page 8)

¼ cup chopped fresh flat-leaf parsley

5 ounces crumbled feta cheese

¼ cup grated Parmesan cheese

1½ cups plain bread crumbs, divided

NOTE: If you don't have an outdoor grill, you can approximate the charred flavor by baking the eggplant, then broiling it. Cut the eggplant in half and place the halves, skin side up, in a baking dish. Add water to the baking dish to a depth of about 1/4 inch. Bake at 375°F for 20 minutes, or until the eggplant is soft. Turn the oven to broil and broil until the skin begins to char, 3 to 4 minutes.

Heat the grill to medium.

Brush the eggplants with 1 tablespoon oil and grill, turning often, until very soft and charred, 12 to 15 minutes. (Ideally you want to do this over a wood fire, but charcoal or gas works as well.)

Place the charred eggplants in a large bowl and cover with plastic wrap. Allow them to sit for about 10 minutes. The resulting steam and heat will finish cooking the eggplants and make the skin easier to peel. Once the eggplants are cool enough to handle, remove the stem and peel off and discard as much of the charred skin as possible. Place the peeled eggplants in a colander over a bowl or sink and let them drain for 40 minutes. You can speed up this process by gently squeezing some of the water out.

Line a sheet pan with parchment. Put the drained eggplant in a large bowl and mash it with a fork. (It will already be soft, but you are trying to smooth out the texture and remove any large lumps. It does not have to be perfectly smooth.) Add the rice, egg, salt, Creole seasoning, parsley, feta, and Parmesan. Mix everything together gently with a fork. Add ¾ cup bread crumbs and combine until the mixture is just solid enough to hold its shape. Put the remaining ¾ cup bread crumbs in a shallow dish. Lightly grease your hands with a bit of oil and form the mixture into portions about the size of golf balls. Roll the formed portions in the bread crumbs and place in one layer on the prepared sheet pan. Chill for 30 minutes or up to several hours.

When ready to cook the croquettes, remove them from the refrigerator. You may deep-fry or pan-fry them—both methods yield delicious results.

First, line a large plate with paper towels and set it near the stove.

RECIPE CONTINUES

To deep fry, heat 2 to 3 cups oil to 350°F in a Dutch oven, cast-iron skillet, or electric fryer. If you don't have a deep-fry thermometer, break off a small piece of one croquette and drop it in the oil to test the temperature. If it sizzles and floats to the top, your oil is ready. If it sinks to the bottom of the pot, the oil still needs to heat up more. If the oil is too hot, the croquettes will burn on the outside while the center will be raw. In that case, lower the heat and wait a couple of minutes before you start to fry a batch.

When the oil has reached 350°F, gently drop the croquettes into the oil, about 6 at a time, depending on the size of your frying vessel. Fry for 2 to 3 minutes, turning with a slotted spoon so that they cook evenly. On the first batch, you might want to break open one of the croquettes to make sure it is cooked all the way through before taking the rest out of the oil. Transfer the cooked croquettes to the paper towel–lined plate. When all of the croquettes from the first batch are finished, let the oil temperature return to 350°F before adding more. Repeat until you have fried all of the croquettes.

To pan-fry, use your hands or a spatula to flatten the balls into patties ½ to 1 inch thick. Heat about ½ cup oil in a skillet over medium heat. When the oil is shimmering, add the patties, four to six at a time depending on the size of your skillet. Cook until crisp and golden brown on the outside and warmed all the way through, 2 to 3 minutes on each side, then transfer to the paper towel–lined plate. Repeat until you have fried all of the patties.

Transfer to a platter and serve immediately.

EGGPLANT WITH GREEN PIGEON PEAS

SERVES 6 TO 8

This was my mom's favorite dish to make for herself. She cooked it only a handful of times each year, in January and February, because it required pigeon peas and eggplant to both be in season. What works so well is the textural contrast between the velvety-soft eggplant and the pop of the pigeon peas. Beyond India, pigeon peas are a staple of Caribbean cooking. In Puerto Rico they are called gandules, and you're likely to find them labeled as such at a Latino or Caribbean market. I have also substituted baby limas, lady peas, and pink-eye peas, all with very good results.

Mom would serve eggplant with pigeon peas as part of a thali, along with rice, of course. She used Japanese eggplants, which tend to have fewer seeds and thinner skin than globe eggplants. They are ideal for a recipe like this one where you do not peel the eggplant. That said, globe eggplants make a fine substitute.

I think this dish pairs nicely with grilled chicken (such as Ahmedabad Street-Style Grilled Chicken, page 262) or pork tenderloin (such as Grilled Pork Tenderloin with Tandoori Spices, page 273). Or, it could be a vegetarian main dish served with steamed rice and/or flatbread.

3 tablespoons neutral oil, such as peanut or canola

1 teaspoon brown mustard seeds

1 teaspoon ajwain seeds

1 small red onion, diced (¾ to 1 cup)

4 garlic cloves, thinly sliced

3 medium tomatoes, diced (about 3½ cups)

Salt

6 medium Japanese eggplants or 3 large purple eggplants, cut into ½-inch cubes (about 7 cups)

2 cups fresh or frozen pigeon peas

1 teaspoon garam masala (store-bought or homemade, page 8)

¾ teaspoon ground turmeric

½ teaspoon ground cayenne pepper

½ teaspoon sugar

Heat the oil in a large skillet over medium heat. Once the oil is shimmering, add the mustard seeds and cook until they start popping, 30 to 40 seconds. Add the ajwain seeds, stir, and add the onion. Sauté until the onion is soft and taking on a bit of color, about 5 minutes. Add the garlic and stir. Add the tomatoes and a pinch of salt and cover. Cook, stirring occasionally, until the tomatoes have completely broken down and turned into a thick sauce, about 12 minutes. Stir in the eggplant and peas, followed by the garam masala, turmeric, and cayenne. Add 2 cups water and stir to mix well. Lower the heat to medium-low, cover, and simmer until the eggplant is very soft and the peas are completely cooked through, about 20 minutes.

Stir in the sugar and 1½ teaspoons salt. Simmer on low for an additional 5 minutes. Taste and season with additional salt, if necessary, before serving.

PEANUT MASALA–STUFFED BABY EGGPLANT

SERVES 6 AS A MAIN DISH OR 12 AS A SIDE DISH

John Currence and I were invited by Sarah Simmons to cook at the (now-defunct) City Grit supper club in New York City a few summers ago. This was a rare chance for me to cook for diners in the big city and show off a little. I wanted to make sure that I represented us well, while cooking something that would reflect my background.

I chose to serve baby eggplants stuffed with a richly seasoned paste of peanuts, shallots, ginger, chiles, and spices. This is a combination I knew from growing up. Since it was summer, I was confident we could source good eggplant in New York, and I knew that roasted peanuts would not be a problem. Neither would the spices I needed to execute the dish. I sent my recipe in, with instructions that I would like to use baby Indian eggplant. The baby eggplants were procured—with some difficulty, it turns out—by my friend Mary-Frances Heck, who was then the culinary director for City Grit. If I'd had the forethought to tell her that she could easily find them at any Indian or Caribbean grocery store in Queens, I could have saved her some stress, a lot of running around, and a couple of swipes on her MetroCard. If where you live is anything like our little Mississippi town, you won't even have to do that—just be on the lookout for them at your local farmers' market when eggplant is in season.

If you can't find the small eggplants, not to worry. You can still make a delicious dish with any available variety. If you are using larger eggplants, you could place them in a lidded baking dish, layer the stuffing on top, and bake, covered, at 375°F for about 45 minutes, until soft all the way through.

Since you will be processing the stuffing ingredients into a paste, it is okay to roughly chop the ginger, chiles, and shallots.

Whatever else you are cooking, let this dish be the star. I recommend it as the centerpiece of a vegetable-centric, summertime farmers' market supper.

- 12 baby eggplants, stem on (3½ to 4 inches long)
- 2 teaspoons coriander seeds
- 1½ teaspoons cumin seeds
- ¾ cup roasted unsalted peanuts
- ⅓ cup sesame seeds
- ½ cup chopped fresh cilantro
- 8 garlic cloves, peeled
- 2-inch piece ginger, roughly chopped
- 2 serrano chiles, stemmed and chopped (about ⅓ cup)
- 4 medium shallots or 1 large onion, chopped (about 1¼ cups)
- 1½ teaspoons salt
- 1 teaspoon sugar
- 1 teaspoon ground turmeric
- 1 teaspoon garam masala (store-bought or homemade, page 8)
- 2 teaspoons tomato paste
- 1 teaspoon peanut butter (preferably all-natural peanut butter with no added salt or sugar)
- 5 tablespoons neutral oil, such as peanut or canola, divided
- 1 sprig curry leaves (optional)

Slice each eggplant from the bottom toward the stem into quarters, making sure the stem is still attached, so that they open up like a flower. Put them in a large bowl, cover with cold water, and set them aside.

Toast the coriander seeds in a small, dry pan over medium heat for about 1 minute. Add the cumin seeds and toast, shaking the pan gently so that the seeds toast evenly and do not burn, until both spices are fragrant, about 1 more minute. Remove from heat and, when cool enough to handle, grind in a spice grinder or coffee grinder, or with a mortar and pestle. Set aside.

Heat a large Dutch oven or skillet with a lid over medium heat. (You want a vessel large enough to hold all 12 eggplants in one layer.) Lightly toast the peanuts and sesame seeds until fragrant and beginning to take on color, 1 to 1½ minutes. Transfer to a bowl to cool.

When the peanuts and sesame seeds are cool enough to handle, place them in the bowl of a food processor and add the cilantro, garlic, ginger, serranos, shallots, cumin-coriander mixture, salt, sugar, turmeric, garam masala, tomato paste, peanut butter, and ⅓ cup water. Pulse to a coarse paste. The mixture will be somewhat crumbly, but if it is so dry that it does not hold together at all, add a bit more water, a tablespoon at a time, and pulse again.

Heat 2 tablespoons oil over medium heat in the same pot you used to toast the peanuts. Once the oil is shimmering, add the curry leaves, if using. When the leaves stop crackling, add the peanut paste. Lower the heat to medium and cook, stirring frequently, until the stuffing mixture is softened and cooked through, about 10 minutes.

Transfer the cooked stuffing mixture to a bowl, turn off the heat, and wipe the pan clean. Allow the mixture to cool.

Once the mixture has cooled, drain the water from the eggplants. Using your fingers, gently open up the eggplants and stuff each one with 1 to 2 tablespoons of the mixture. Save any of the stuffing that won't fit or that falls out.

Heat the same pot and add the remaining 3 tablespoons oil. When it is hot and shimmering, gently add the stuffed eggplants, stem side up, one at a time. Add any leftover stuffing on top. Turn the heat to low, cover the pan, and allow the eggplants to cook slowly. After 8 to 10 minutes, gently rotate the pot 180 degrees on the stove so that the eggplants cook evenly. Sprinkle them with a bit of water, cover, and finish cooking them until they are cooked through, 10 to 12 minutes. The eggplants should be very soft, offering no resistance when pricked with the tip of a paring knife. Serve immediately.

EGGPLANT AND OKRA CAPONATA SERVES 6 TO 8

I first had caponata at Bayona, chef Susan Spicer's French Quarter institution in New Orleans. Chef Spicer's version of caponata—with its silky eggplant, tart-sweet confit tomatoes, salty pop of capers, and nutty bite of toasted pecans—bowled me over. How had I, a self-proclaimed lover of all things eggplant, never tasted this dish before?

In retrospect, it makes perfect sense that my first run-in with this Sicilian classic was in New Orleans, a city where Sicilian immigrants have made numerous contributions to the local cuisine. (If you've ever had a muffuletta sandwich, you've tasted that influence.) All these years later, I still serve caponata at Snackbar. Recently, I decided to try a nontraditional version that includes my other favorite vegetable: okra. I am happy to report that the combination works beautifully. You can serve caponata as a side dish or as the centerpiece of a vegetarian meal.

1 cup chopped pecans

½ cup olive oil

3 cups diced yellow onion (1 large or 2 small onions)

¼ cup sliced garlic (8 to 10 cloves)

4 cups diced eggplant (about 2 medium eggplants)

1 teaspoon salt, or to taste

4 cups diced fresh tomatoes (about 4 tomatoes)

4 cups small okra pods, wiped clean and tough tops trimmed

2 tablespoons fresh lemon juice

2 teaspoons red wine vinegar

¾ cup pitted green olives, such as Castelvetrano

3 tablespoons capers, rinsed

¼ cup finely sliced fresh basil

¼ cup chopped fresh flat-leaf parsley

2 teaspoons hot sauce

Toast the pecans in a small, dry skillet over medium heat until fragrant, about 2 minutes. Remove from the heat and set aside.

Heat the oil over medium heat in a Dutch oven or other wide, heavy-bottomed pot. Add the onion and garlic and cook until golden, about 6 minutes. Add the eggplant and salt and stir well. Cover, reduce the heat to medium-low, and cook until the eggplant is soft, 6 to 7 minutes. Add the tomatoes, okra, lemon juice, and vinegar and stir well. Cover and cook for 5 to 6 minutes more, until the okra is just soft. Stir in the olives and capers.

Remove the pot from the heat. Stir in the basil, parsley, pecans, and hot sauce. Taste and add salt, if desired. Serve.

Leftovers will keep for up to 3 days in the refrigerator. Enjoy the leftovers for lunch with toasted pita or baguette, or even folded into an omelet.

MOUSSAKA SERVES 6 TO 8

Moussaka is a classic Greek dish, a casserole of sorts layered with eggplant, potatoes, ground lamb or beef cooked in a tomato sauce, and rich, creamy béchamel. We didn't eat moussaka very often when I was growing up. In our flat in Ahmedabad, we did not have an oven—very few people have ovens in Gujarat. We did not have good cheese, either, so the success of the recipe depended on the quality of the eggplants and tomatoes. When we moved to France and had access to good cheese, good produce, and an oven, the quality of Mom's moussaka dramatically improved. She even bought a small cocotte to make it for just the two of us.

My dear friend Tim Hontzas, who used to cook at City Grocery and now owns Johnny's in Homewood, Alabama, makes a moussaka that is entirely different from my mother's, but is tied with hers for my favorite interpretation. In the summer, he uses eggplant and tomatoes from the Market at Pepper Place in Birmingham, ground lamb, fresh herbs, and just a touch of feta cheese that makes everything come together brilliantly.

Tim has some secrets he won't divulge, and I'll always believe that my own sauce falls just short of my mother's. But I've engineered a hybrid moussaka that combines the best elements of those two. It bridges disparate diets, origins, and families. It's a full meal all by itself, although you might want to serve it with some crusty bread and a simple green salad.

FOR THE VEGETABLES:

3 to 4 tablespoons olive oil

½ cup plain breadcrumbs

2 large Yukon Gold (or similar) potatoes, peeled and thinly sliced

1 medium red onion, thinly sliced

Salt

Freshly ground black pepper

6 to 8 tablespoons fresh thyme leaves, divided

2 large eggplants, thinly sliced

2 medium zucchini, thinly sliced

FOR THE MEAT:

2 tablespoons olive oil

1 small yellow onion, minced (about 1 cup)

2 or 3 garlic cloves, minced

1 pound ground lamb or beef

½ teaspoon ground cinnamon

½ teaspoon ground cloves

½ teaspoon ajwain seeds (optional)

2 tablespoons tomato paste

2 cups crushed good-quality canned plum tomatoes

2 tablespoons chopped fresh mint

Salt

Freshly ground black pepper

FOR THE BÉCHAMEL:

8 tablespoons (1 stick) unsalted butter

½ cup all-purpose flour

3½ cups whole milk, at room temperature

½ cup grated Parmesan cheese

⅓ cup crumbled feta cheese

½ teaspoon freshly grated nutmeg

Freshly ground black pepper

Grated zest of 1 lemon

3 large egg yolks

FOR ASSEMBLING THE MOUSSAKA:

½ cup grated Parmesan cheese

⅓ cup crumbled feta cheese

TO MAKE THE VEGETABLES: Preheat the oven to 375°F. Brush the bottom and sides of a 9 x 13-inch baking pan with a bit of olive oil. You will assemble and bake the entire moussaka in this pan, so choose one that is several inches deep. Sprinkle the bread crumbs in the bottom of the baking dish—these will help soak up the liquid that the vegetables release as they cook.

Toss the sliced potatoes and onion in a bowl with a generous tablespoon of olive oil. Season with salt, pepper, and one-third of the fresh thyme and arrange them in an even layer in the baking pan. Bake for 20 minutes, or until the potatoes and onion are just soft.

Meanwhile, toss the sliced eggplant with another tablespoon of olive oil in the same mixing bowl and season with salt, pepper, and half of the remaining thyme. Remove the baking dish from the oven, layer the eggplant on top of the potatoes and onion, and return it to the oven. Bake for another 20 minutes.

Meanwhile, toss the sliced zucchini with another tablespoon of olive oil in the same mixing bowl and season with salt, pepper, and the remaining fresh thyme. Remove the baking dish from the oven, layer the zucchini on top of the eggplant, and return it to the oven. Bake for another 20 minutes. (You will not take anything out of the pan, so the potatoes and onions cook for about 1 hour total, the eggplant for 40 minutes, and the zucchini for 20 minutes.)

Remove the pan from the oven and set aside. Leave the oven on.

TO MAKE THE MEAT: Heat the olive oil in a Dutch oven or heavy-bottomed skillet over medium heat. When the oil is shimmering, add the onion and cook until caramelized, 20 to 30 minutes. Be patient and do not rush this step, as you want the richness of the caramelized onions to bring a depth of flavor to the meat mixture. If you start caramelizing the onions while the vegetables are baking, don't let your attention stray from the onions for too long. Stir the onions frequently as they cook. If they are sticking, you can add a tiny bit of water and stir to scrape up any brown bits from the bottom of the pot. If the sticking is persistent, turn the heat down slightly. The onions will turn completely brown and begin to break down. If you taste a bite, it will have some sweetness. At this point, add the garlic, ground lamb, cinnamon, cloves, and ajwain (if using) and cook until the meat is browned and starts releasing its fat, about 15 minutes. Stir in the tomato paste. Add the crushed tomatoes and mint, lower the heat to medium-low, and cook, stirring frequently, until all the water has evaporated from the tomatoes and the lamb is fully cooked, about 12 minutes. Season with salt and pepper; set aside.

TO MAKE THE BÉCHAMEL: Melt the butter in a heavy-bottomed saucepan over medium heat. Whisk in the flour. Add the milk about 1 cup at a time, whisking constantly to incorporate. (If you add the milk too quickly, you will end up with lumps in your sauce.) Continue to whisk over medium heat. Once the sauce is smooth and begins to bubble, take it off the heat. Whisk in the two cheeses, nutmeg, pepper (I use six turns of the grinder), lemon zest, and egg yolks.

TO ASSEMBLE THE MOUSSAKA: Transfer the meat mixture to a large bowl and fold in one-third of the béchamel. Spread the béchamel-meat mixture in an even layer over the baked vegetables. Pour the remaining béchamel over the top and smooth it out.

Sprinkle the Parmesan and feta on top and bake for 25 to 35 minutes, until the top is golden brown and bubbly.

Remove from the oven and allow the moussaka to rest for at least 30 minutes before serving. This will allow it to set up and reabsorb some of the liquid that the vegetables released while cooking. Serve hot.

Any leftover moussaka can be refrigerated for up to 2 days and reheated in a 350°F to 375°F oven. Make sure the baking dish is completely cool and cover it with plastic wrap or aluminum foil before storing in the refrigerator.

NOTE: Moussaka has three components: vegetables, meat, and béchamel. You'll prepare each component separately, then assemble and bake in one large baking dish. When preparing the vegetables, slice them to a thickness of ¼ to ½ inch—you don't want them paper-thin. A mandoline makes quick, uniform work of the slicing.

CHAPTER SIX

CORN

Corn is a quintessential American crop, so we didn't eat much of it when I was growing up. Corn on the cob was a special treat that we waited for anxiously.

It showed up every year just at the beginning of monsoon season, usually in July. Vendors with their small charcoal braziers would set up on the sidewalks all around Ahmedabad and offer freshly grilled corn rubbed with lime, chiles, and spices. When fresh corn made its short-lived appearance in the market, Mom would make her famous "American corn." It was the way my parents had eaten corn while living in Tennessee: boiled, slathered in butter, and seasoned simply with salt and pepper.

When we moved to Texas, corn was everywhere, a staple of both Tex-Mex and Southern cuisine. I ate tortillas, chips, and corn salsa for the first time. Grits and cornbread, too.

Three decades of living in the South have exposed me to many incarnations of corn. From simple summer grilled corn to cornbread to Cajun maque choux and more, I have come to appreciate its many uses.

I also understand how commercial agriculture has led to the proliferation of hybrid corn, to the detriment (and sometimes loss) of heirloom and landrace varieties, meaning those strains that have evolved in their local environment.

Thanks to folks like Glenn Roberts of Anson Mills and Professor David Shields of the University of South Carolina, I've learned about heirloom corn varieties that have been recovered from the brink of extinction. I didn't know that native corn was almost wiped out and forgotten by the end of the twentieth century. Now, a revival of these varieties is being led by a coalition of farmers, scholars, chefs, and even distillers. In South Carolina alone, the Anson Mills team has revived varietals like Jimmy Red, Pencil Cob, and Henry Moore Yellow. It shows that chefs are as much stewards of tradition as anyone else. That makes cooking a noble profession.

The recipes in this chapter that begin with corn kernels taste best when made with fresh kernels cut off the cob. One ear of fresh corn yields ⅔ to ¾ cup of kernels. If you are substituting frozen corn kernels, allow them to thaw before proceeding with the recipe.

MONSOON GRILLED CORN SERVES 8

Monsoon season is a big deal in India. A good monsoon means a good harvest and refilled water reservoirs. It means the rest of the year will be worry-free for the farmers and nonfarmers alike. Rains bring life. No wonder there are songs, poems, dances, and prayers dedicated to monsoons.

During monsoon season, there was one thing in particular that I looked forward to: The rains brought corn. Vendors with their charcoal braziers would show up on street corners and next to tea stalls. They would grill fresh corn on the cob right in front of you, rub it with lime, season it, and pass it to you. As a kid, I would bite into it with joy, juices running down my chin, corn skin getting stuck between my teeth. That flavor combination—corn, tangy lime, salt, chile, and a hint of toasted cumin—continues to inspire me. At least once a week while corn is in season, I light the grill, char the corn, and rub it with lime and spices. My mind returns to the monsoons of my childhood, jumping in puddles and catching tadpoles with my friends. If I am very lucky, a late-summer Mississippi thunderstorm makes it all the more special.

Grilled corn makes the perfect side for a summer cookout. Serve them with anything from hamburgers and hot dogs to Confit Pork Ribs with Mexican Adobo Paste (page 274).

8 large ears corn in their husks

1 tablespoon cumin seeds

1½ tablespoons salt

1 teaspoon cracked black pepper

1 teaspoon ground cayenne pepper

½ teaspoon chaat masala (store-bought or homemade, page 8)

2 tablespoons ghee (store-bought or homemade, page 9) or unsalted butter, melted

2 limes, cut in half

NOTE: These corn taste best when grilled over charcoal, but charring them over a gas flame works well, too. You can scale the recipe up or down depending on how many people you are serving. Figure one ear of corn per person.

Heat the grill to medium.

Fold back the husks on the corn (but leave them attached) and remove the silk. Twist the husks so that each ear of corn has a "handle."

Toast the cumin seeds in a small, dry pan over medium heat, shaking the pan gently so that the seeds toast evenly and do not burn, about 1 minute. Remove from the heat and, when cool enough to handle, grind in a spice grinder or coffee grinder, or with a mortar and pestle. Combine the ground cumin with the salt, black pepper, cayenne, and chaat masala in a small bowl and set aside.

Grill the corn. Using the husks as handles, turn the ears as they cook to char the cobs evenly all the way around. As you hear the kernels begin to pop, that's your cue to turn the ears a quarter turn. This should take no more than 4 minutes. If charring the corn on a stovetop, cook directly over the gas flame, one ear at a time, turning to char the cobs all the way around. Transfer the grilled cobs to a platter and brush them lightly with ghee.

Rub 2 lime halves on the buttered cobs, squeezing to release the juices as you rub. Dip the cut side of the other 2 lime halves in the spice mixture and rub the spices evenly on each cob, dipping the lime halves back in the spice mixture to reload the spices as needed. Serve immediately.

If you have leftovers, cut the kernels off the cob and save them to use in a salad.

CORN AND ROASTED POBLANO SOUP

SERVES 6 TO 8 AS A FIRST COURSE, 4 TO 6 AS THE MAIN COURSE

Whether in the American Southwest or Gujarat, corn and chiles are a match made in heaven. This soup is easy and delicious proof. It uses the whole cob for a deep corn flavor. Serve it in the late summer or early fall, when corn and chiles are at their peak. Look for fresh corn with plump, juicy kernels and bright, shiny chiles without wrinkles. Serve as a main course or with Janu Aunty's Roasted Tomato Grilled Cheese (page 86) for lunch, or as a first course for dinner, followed by Shrimp Recheado (page 221). If you want the soup to be vegetarian-friendly, simply omit the bacon.

8 large ears corn, husks and silk removed and kernels cut off (about 6 cups), cobs reserved

1 teaspoon finely chopped fresh rosemary leaves, stems reserved

1 teaspoon fresh thyme leaves, stems reserved

1 teaspoon black peppercorns

2 bay leaves

4 medium poblano or Hatch chiles

1 tablespoon cumin seeds

4 tablespoons (½ stick) unsalted butter

¼ cup chopped bacon (optional)

1 small yellow or white onion, diced (about 1 cup)

4 garlic cloves, thinly sliced

2 teaspoons salt

½ teaspoon paprika

2 ounces goat cheese, crumbled

1 cup heavy cream

3 tablespoons chopped fresh cilantro, for garnish

Lime wedges, for garnish

Place the corn cobs, rosemary stems, thyme stems, peppercorns, and bay leaves in a large stockpot and cover with 1 gallon water. Bring to a boil over high heat and boil for 30 minutes. (If the pot starts to boil over, reduce the heat to maintain a gentle boil.) Remove the pot from the heat. When cool enough to handle, strain and discard the solids. You will have 12 to 13 cups of corn stock. Set aside.

To roast the poblanos, turn the flame of a gas stovetop (or grill) to medium-high. Using tongs and an oven mitt, hold one pepper directly over the flame, turning until it is charred on all sides. Repeat with the remaining peppers. (Alternatively, you can roast the peppers under the oven broiler. Watch them carefully and turn with tongs as each side chars.) Once the peppers are charred all the way around, carefully transfer them to a plastic bag or a bowl covered with plastic wrap. Allow them to sit for about 10 minutes. The resulting steam and heat will finish cooking the peppers and make the skin easier to peel. When cool enough to handle, peel off the blistered skin. Dice the peppers, discarding the seeds and stems.

Meanwhile, toast the cumin seeds in a small, dry pan over medium heat, shaking the pan gently so that the seeds toast evenly and do not burn, about 1 minute. Remove from the heat and, when cool enough to handle, grind in a spice grinder or coffee grinder, or with a mortar and pestle. Set aside.

Melt the butter in a Dutch oven or other wide, heavy-bottomed pot over medium heat. Add the bacon (if using) and cook, stirring often, until it starts to render and crisp, about 4 minutes. Add the onion and garlic and stir. Cover and cook for 5 minutes, or until the onion

RECIPE CONTINUES

becomes translucent. Add the corn kernels, cover, and cook for an additional 5 minutes. Stir in the poblanos and enough corn stock to cover everything by ½ to 1 inch. (You will use about 10 cups of stock. Discard the remaining stock or cool completely and store, covered, in the refrigerator. Use the stock to cook grits for breakfast the next morning.) Turn the heat up to medium-high and bring to a simmer. When the mixture simmers, lower the heat to medium-low and simmer, uncovered, until the corn is very soft, 10 to 12 minutes.

Remove the pot from the heat and purée the soup with a hand-held immersion blender. (If you do not have an immersion blender, you can purée the soup in batches in a regular blender. When blending hot liquids, take care not to overfill the blender.) Strain the puréed soup through a fine-mesh strainer to remove the tough corn skins. (If you don't have a mesh strainer, you can skip this step. The soup will taste just as good; it just won't be as smooth.)

Return the soup to the heat and add the cumin, salt, paprika, goat cheese, and cream. Stir until the cheese is melted and fully incorporated. Taste and adjust for seasonings as desired. Ladle the soup into bowls and garnish with chopped cilantro and a wedge of lime.

SIMPLE PICO DE GALLO

MAKES ABOUT 2 CUPS

2 small to medium tomatoes, diced (about 1½ cups)

⅓ cup chopped fresh cilantro leaves and tender stems

¼ cup minced yellow onion

1 serrano chile, stemmed and minced

1 teaspoon minced garlic

Juice of 1 lime

1 teaspoon salt

Combine all the ingredients in a medium bowl and stir well. For best flavor, set aside at room temperature for 30 minutes before serving to allow the flavors to meld. Store leftovers in a sealed container in the refrigerator for up to 3 days.

CORN, CRAB, AND BACON GRIDDLE CAKES

SERVES 6 TO 8 AS AN APPETIZER OR SNACK

When I was growing up, my mother made griddle cakes—savory pancakes, essentially—from chickpea flour. Today, chickpea flour is relatively easy to find in US grocery stores, especially as more and more Americans adopt a gluten-free diet. But that wasn't always the case. When we lived in Bowling Green, Kentucky (where I'm pretty sure there was not a bag of chickpea flour to be found in the 1980s), Mom developed a corn-based griddle cake. She blended fresh corn kernels with a bit of yogurt, ginger, chiles, onions, and just enough flour to hold the batter together. She would scoop out portions the size of silver dollar pancakes, cook them on a griddle, and serve them with cilantro chutney. I was hooked.

Years later, I realized that corn cakes can take many forms, and I'm a fan of them all. At a restaurant in New Orleans, I had corn and crab beignets for the first time. For me, those two ingredients—the crunchy-sweet corn and the soft-sweet crab—are a perfect match. When I got home, I went to work on something similar for the Snackbar menu. One of our cooks rightly pointed out that the two sweet ingredients needed a smoky foil: How about some chopped bacon? The resulting griddle cakes were a hit, and they make frequent appearances as a special when corn is in season.

4 cups fresh corn kernels (from about 6 ears)

¾ cup all-purpose flour

¾ cup cornmeal

1 teaspoon salt

2 teaspoons cracked black pepper

3 large eggs, beaten

¾ cup half-and-half

2 medium shallots (or ½ small red onion), minced (generous ½ cup)

8 ounces fresh lump crabmeat, picked through to remove shell bits

⅓ cup chopped cooked bacon or tasso ham

1 cup shredded sharp white cheddar cheese

2 teaspoons chopped fresh flat-leaf parsley

1 teaspoon chopped fresh rosemary

¼ cup neutral oil, such as peanut or canola, or bacon fat or ghee

Simple Pico de Gallo, for serving (page 124)

NOTES: If you follow a gluten-free diet, use rice flour in place of the all-purpose flour. If you have the option, I like the texture of a medium-grind cornmeal in these griddle cakes. And if you have access to tasso ham, a Louisiana product, use it in place of the bacon. Its salty, spicy flavor is a perfect counterpoint to the sweet corn.

Place the corn kernels in the bowl of a food processor and pulse several times, until about half the kernels are broken up. If you do not have a food processor, you can chop the kernels by hand, leaving some whole. You are going for a contrast of textures.

Mix the flour, cornmeal, salt, and pepper in a large bowl. In a separate bowl, whisk together the eggs and half-and-half. Pour the egg mixture over the flour and stir to combine well, making sure there are no lumps. Fold in the chopped corn, shallots, crabmeat, bacon, cheese, and herbs. Cover and refrigerate for 20 minutes.

Heat 1 tablespoon oil over medium-high heat in a 12-inch nonstick skillet or on a stovetop griddle. Working in batches, spoon the batter onto the skillet or griddle in scoops of about ¼ cup each—think smallish pancakes. Cook the griddle cakes for 2 to 3 minutes on each side, until golden and crispy on the outside, with the center just cooked through. Transfer the cooked griddle cakes to a plate. (This is more like cooking pancakes than pan-frying, so you should not need to drain the griddle cakes on paper towels. However, you may if you like.) Or, if you like, you can keep them warm on a sheet pan in a 200°F oven while you cook the rest. Work in batches until you have used all of the batter, adding oil as needed and letting it heat up between batches. If any burned bits stick to the bottom of the skillet or griddle, scrape them off between batches.

Serve hot with pico de gallo on the side.

CORN AND COLLARD GREEN FRITTERS

MAKES ABOUT 20 FRITTERS

Like so many Southerners, I love crumbling cornbread into my stewed greens and adding a couple of dashes of hot sauce. Once, on a trip to Nashville, I had a transcendent version of this common practice at Arnold's Country Kitchen, the legendary meat-and-three. (A meat-and-three is a traditional Southern lunch restaurant, so called because the standard plate is your choice of meat accompanied by your choice of three vegetables.) For lovers of Southern food in Nashville and beyond, Arnold's is a temple. Jack and Rose Arnold opened the lunch-only restaurant in 1982, and today their son Kahlil oversees operations. I didn't want to get in his way that day, so after making my way through the cafeteria-style line, I found a seat and began to eat. Kahlil had spotted me, however, and proceeded to fill my tray with what seemed like every offering from the steam table. Among the items he delivered were light-as-a-cloud hushpuppies and a cup of rich, smoky greens. I broke the hushpuppies into the greens and ate a spoonful. Divine!

As I ate, I thought, why not add greens to a batter of fresh corn and cornmeal and fry it? Back home in north Mississippi, there is a brief period in September when corn and collards are available simultaneously. It would be just like a pakora made with corn and spinach or fenugreek leaves that I had as a child. When I returned from Nashville, I tested my theory. It was a winner.

These fritters are great as an appetizer with a little spicy Comeback Sauce (page 127) for dipping. Or serve them with Tomato-Coconut Chutney (page 99). If you don't feel like deep-frying the fritters, you can ladle the batter onto a hot griddle or skillet and cook for a couple of minutes on each side.

1 cup fresh corn kernels (from about 2 ears)

3 garlic cloves, peeled and smashed

½ cup chopped yellow onion

1 serrano or jalapeño chile, chopped

1 cup finely chopped collard green leaves (Remove ribs and stems before chopping the leaves. If you cannot find collard greens, substitute mustard greens or kale.)

1 teaspoon chaat masala (store-bought or homemade, page 8)

1 teaspoon salt

1 teaspoon freshly ground black pepper

½ teaspoon sugar

½ teaspoon ajwain seeds

½ teaspoon cumin seeds

Juice of 1 lemon

2 to 3 cups neutral oil, such as peanut or canola

½ cup cornmeal

½ cup chickpea flour

Place the corn, garlic, onion, and chile in the bowl of a food processor and pulse several times, until the corn kernels are broken up and the pepper is finely chopped. Scrape the mixture into a large bowl and add the collards, chaat masala, salt, black pepper, sugar, ajwain seeds, cumin seeds, and lemon juice. Mix well and set aside for 10 to 15 minutes.

Heat the oil in a Dutch oven or deep fryer over medium to medium-high heat.

Add the cornmeal and chickpea flour to the corn mixture and stir to incorporate fully. When the oil reaches 325°F to 350°F, drop a small spoonful of batter in. If it holds together and floats to the top, the oil is ready. Working in batches to avoid crowding, carefully drop 1-ounce portions (about a heaping tablespoon) of batter into the oil. Cook the fritters for about 90 seconds, using a slotted spoon to turn them halfway through. When one batch is cooked, remove from the oil with a slotted spoon and drain on a paper towel–lined plate. Let the oil temperature return to 325°F to 350°F between batches. If you find that the outside of the fritters is browning before the inside is cooked, lower your oil temperature. Serve immediately.

COMEBACK SAUCE

MAKES ABOUT 2 CUPS

Comeback is a popular dip, dressing, and sauce in Mississippi that's virtually unknown elsewhere. It's a little bit like a remoulade and was probably developed by Greek-American restaurateurs in Jackson. Try it as a salad dressing, spread it on a burger, or use it as a dip with anything fried, like these fritters.

- ¾ cup mayonnaise (preferably Duke's)
- ½ cup chili sauce, such as Heinz or Maggi
- ¼ cup canola oil
- 1 tablespoon Worcestershire sauce
- 1 tablespoon fresh lemon juice
- 2 tablespoons minced garlic
- 1 tablespoon grated yellow onion
- ¾ teaspoon dry English mustard, such as Colman's
- ¾ teaspoon kosher salt
- ½ teaspoon cracked black pepper

In a large mixing bowl, combine all the ingredients very well, making sure there are no lumps. Allow to sit for 30 minutes before using. Store in a tightly covered glass or plastic container in the refrigerator for up to 10 days.

CORN DHOKLAS SERVES 4 AS AN APPETIZER OR SNACK

One of my favorite snacks growing up was dhokla, a steamed cake native to Gujarat. The batter of fermented lentils (or chickpeas) and rice cooks to a soft, spongy consistency that I find irresistible. After years spent living in the South and cooking with cornmeal, I convinced myself that I could turn a cornmeal-based batter into something like a dhokla. As many times as I had eaten dhoklas growing up, I had never actually made them myself. Still, I was certain my experiment would work.

My first attempt was a failure. So I swallowed my pride and called my Aunt Janu for advice. When I explained what happened, there was silence on the other end. I began to wonder if I had stumped her, which I didn't think was possible. Then she burst out laughing. Corn dhoklas already existed, and Aunt Janu had a recipe.

Making dhoklas depends on a steaming technique that is likely new to you. Don't be daunted! It might take you more than one attempt to get the timing right, but stick with it. Properly cooked, the dhoklas will be light and fluffy, moist and delicate. If you are the sort of person who likes to be a bit of a show-off when you host a dinner party, this is the recipe for you. *Pictured served with Peanut Pesto (page 170).*

1 cup cornmeal

½ cup plain, full-fat yogurt, at room temperature (preferably Greek-style)

2 serrano chiles, stemmed and chopped

3-inch piece ginger, chopped

3 garlic cloves, peeled

1 cup fresh corn kernels (from about 2 ears)

2 teaspoons sugar

1 teaspoon salt

¼ teaspoon ground turmeric

¼ teaspoon asafoetida

2 teaspoons neutral oil, such as peanut or canola

1½ teaspoons fresh lemon juice

1 teaspoon baking soda

FOR GARNISH:

2 tablespoons neutral oil, such as peanut or canola

1 teaspoon brown mustard seeds

1 teaspoon sesame seeds

6 to 8 curry leaves

Pinch asafoetida

Mix the cornmeal, yogurt, and ¾ cup lukewarm water in a large mixing bowl; set aside in a warm spot for 30 minutes to ferment.

Meanwhile, combine the chiles, ginger, and garlic in the bowl of a food processor and pulse into a paste. Add the corn and pulse until the kernels are chopped up.

While the cornmeal-yogurt mixture continues to rest, set up your steaming apparatus. If you have four 4-ounce ramekins, you can make individual dhoklas. Otherwise you can steam one large dhokla on a plate and cut it into pieces for serving. Place a large, lidded pot on the stove but do not turn on the heat yet. Turn a pie tin or cake pan upside down in the bottom of the pot to create a platform. Grease the ramekins or, if making one large dhokla, use a greased plate with a lip or rim that fits inside the pot. Carefully add a couple of inches of water to the bottom of the pot. The water should not come up higher than the platform. (If you have prepared a water bath before, this is a little different. You want the steam to cook the dhoklas, and you do not want any boiling water to spill into the batter.)

Once the cornmeal has rested for 30 minutes, fold in the corn-ginger-chile mixture, sugar, salt, turmeric, asafoetida, oil, and lemon juice. Mix to combine into a spoonable consistency. Fold in the baking soda last, right before steaming. (The baking soda and lemon juice

RECIPE CONTINUES

create a sort of mock fermentation that makes the batter fluffy.)

Spoon the batter to fill the ramekins halfway. If using a rimmed plate, spoon or pour the batter directly onto the plate.

Turn on the heat to medium and cover the pot. Once the pot starts to steam, remove the lid. Carefully place the ramekins or plate on the platform and replace the lid. Steam for 15 to 20 minutes. Remove the lid and check to see if the cakes are completely set. If not, continue steaming for a few more minutes.

Turn off the heat. Using an oven mitt and/or tongs, carefully remove the ramekins or plate from the pot. Turn the steamed cakes out of the ramekins and onto a serving platter. If you made one large cake on a plate, cut it into four equal portions and arrange them on a serving platter. (Traditionally, dhoklas are diamond-shaped; cut into diamonds using a sharp knife or a diamond-shaped cookie cutter if you have one.)

To make the garnish, heat the oil in a small skillet. Once the oil is shimmering, add the mustard seeds and cook until they start popping, about 30 seconds. Add the sesame seeds, curry leaves, and asafoetida and cook, stirring, for 15 seconds. Remove from the heat, pour the oil mixture over the cakes, and serve immediately.

SKILLET-FRIED CORN AND OKRA SERVES 6 TO 8

Heat a cast-iron skillet and add a bit of bacon fat and a pat of butter. Sauté some onion and some sweet, fresh corn kernels cut off the cob. Season with salt and pepper and eat. This classic Southern dish was a revelation to me. After decades of living, eating, and cooking in the South, I had not had it until my mother-in-law in Paducah, Kentucky, made it for lunch one day. Where had I been? How had I missed this dish of elemental perfection?

The answer was shocking: No one wanted to cook a simple dish like that for a chef. This was a humble, everyday recipe, not one you'd serve to company. And so I had missed out. I began making the dish at home, and while it's not fancy, I believe it's absolutely worth sharing. The okra is a recent addition of mine. I tried it on a whim when we found ourselves swimming in both corn and okra after one particularly bountiful CSA share. The trick is to slice the okra very thin so that it crisps up as it fries in the fat. I like adding scallion greens and a dash or two of hot sauce just as the dish finishes cooking. This recipe is easily scaled up or down. If you have friends or family who are chefs, please invite them over and cook for them. Make something simple, just like this. They will thank you.

3 tablespoons bacon fat or neutral oil, such as peanut or canola

2 cups thinly sliced fresh okra

¾ cup thinly sliced scallion whites plus ¼ cup thinly sliced scallion greens, divided (it will take about 1½ bunches of scallions to yield ¾ cup sliced whites)

4 garlic cloves, thinly sliced

4 cups fresh corn kernels (from about 6 ears)

2 teaspoons fresh lemon juice

1 teaspoon salt

2 teaspoons cracked black pepper

2 teaspoons hot sauce

3 tablespoons fresh thyme leaves

Heat the bacon fat in a wide, heavy-bottomed skillet (preferably cast-iron) over medium heat. When the fat is hot and shimmering, add the okra and spread it out in as even a layer as possible. This will help cook the okra quickly and keep it from getting slimy. Cook until the edges of the okra start crisping up, about 5 minutes. Add the scallion whites and garlic, stir, and cook for 5 minutes. Stir in the corn and cook for an additional 5 minutes. Add the lemon juice and 1 tablespoon water. Stir and scrape up the brown bits from the bottom of the skillet and allow the liquid to evaporate. Stir in the salt, pepper, hot sauce, scallion greens, and thyme leaves. Serve immediately.

MAQUE CHOUX SERVES 6

In Louisiana, everyone makes maque choux, but no one seems to agree on its exact provenance. As a corn dish, it certainly has Native American influences. It begins with an aromatic base of bell peppers, onions, and garlic cooked in butter and bacon fat. (While the bacon is traditional, you may omit it for a vegetarian-friendly version.) According to some chefs and culinary historians, this trio actually predates the "holy trinity" of peppers, onions, and celery that forms the base of so many Louisiana dishes.

Maque choux is incredibly easy to make for a weeknight dinner, served alongside practically anything—pork, chicken, shrimp, or fish. You can also dress it up for company. Try serving it on top of a main course of redfish or spooned over sliced ripe summer tomatoes for a colorful starter. Louisiana cooks sometimes add shrimp or crawfish tails. You can do the same thing (or try crab or lobster) for a dinner party first course.

- 4 tablespoons (½ stick) unsalted butter
- 2 slices thick-cut bacon, chopped (optional)
- ½ cup minced yellow onion
- 3 garlic cloves, thinly sliced
- ½ cup small-diced green bell pepper
- 4 cups fresh corn kernels (from about 6 ears)
- 2 cups diced tomatoes (2 large or 3 medium tomatoes)
- 1 tablespoon Creole seasoning (store-bought or homemade, page 8)
- ¾ cup heavy cream
- 1 small bunch scallions, thinly sliced, green parts only (about ¾ cup)
- 1 tablespoon fresh thyme leaves
- 1 teaspoon hot sauce, or to taste
- ½ teaspoon salt, or to taste

Melt the butter in a Dutch oven or other wide, heavy-bottomed pot over medium heat. Add the bacon (if using) and cook until it begins to crisp and brown, 3 to 4 minutes. Add the onion and garlic and cook until the onion is soft and translucent, 5 to 6 minutes. Stir in the bell pepper and cook for 3 to 4 more minutes. Add the corn, tomatoes, and Creole seasoning. Stir to mix well and cook until the tomatoes release their water and it begins to evaporate, 5 to 6 minutes. Stir in the cream and simmer for 2 minutes. Remove from the heat and stir in the scallions, thyme, hot sauce, and salt. Taste and add another dash of hot sauce and/or a pinch of salt, if desired, before serving.

If you have leftovers, cool completely before storing in a covered container in the refrigerator. Reheat and enjoy the next day.

CORN KORMA SERVES 6 TO 8

This dish was born of a conversation—more of a rant, really—with my friend Cheetie Kumar, a chef and restaurateur in Raleigh, North Carolina. We both know native Southerners, including members of our own families, who love creamed corn. It's simple and sweet, and reminds folks of childhood and holidays, of grandmothers standing over a stove. But for me, it's cloying. Cheetie agreed. What if there was a way to elevate creamed corn with more time, more care, more flavor? Together we dreamed up this corn korma.

When fresh corn is gently cooked with some cream and seasoned properly, you get an unctuous dish fit for the gods. If you are a fan of chicken korma, you'll recognize a similar flavor profile here. This is a great side dish to serve with Sweet Tea-Brined Fried Chicken (page 250) or Grilled Pork Tenderloin with Tandoori Spices (page 273).

4 cups fresh corn kernels (from about 6 ears), divided

3 tablespoons unsalted butter

2 teaspoons cumin seeds

1 green cardamom pod, crushed

2 bay leaves

1 small yellow or white onion, minced (about 1 cup)

2 teaspoons minced ginger

2 teaspoons minced garlic

1 cup canned full-fat coconut milk

1 cup heavy cream

1½ teaspoons salt

1 teaspoon cracked black pepper

Put 1 cup corn kernels in the bowl of a food processor and pulse 8 to 10 times, until the kernels are broken up; set aside.

Melt the butter in a large skillet over medium heat. Add the cumin seeds and cook until they are fragrant, about 1 minute. Add the cardamom pod and bay leaves and stir. Add the onion, ginger, and garlic and cook, stirring occasionally, until the onion is soft and translucent, 5 to 7 minutes. Add the remaining 3 cups whole corn kernels. Stir to mix well and cook for 3 to 4 minutes. Stir in the chopped corn, coconut milk, cream, salt, and pepper. Increase the heat and bring to a simmer, then turn the heat down to medium-low and cook, stirring often, until the corn is cooked through and the cream is reduced and thick enough to coat the back of your spoon, about 6 minutes. Remove from the heat and serve.

If you have leftovers, let them cool completely before storing in a covered container in the refrigerator. Reheat the next day, adding a little more cream and/or coconut milk if needed.

NOT YOUR MAMA'S CORNBREAD MAKES 1 PAN/SERVES 6

I am going to be honest with you: This is not my recipe. The credit goes to my friend Farhan Momin, an Atlanta-based dentist who happens to be a very talented cook. Farhan grew up in Atlanta, the son of immigrants from Ahmedabad. His parents run a halal butcher shop and an Indian restaurant. He learned to cook from watching them, but made the smart decision to attend dental school. When Farhan is not busy being a dentist, he is part of Brown in the South, a friendly collective of chefs and cooks of South Asian descent who claim the American South as our home. Formed in 2018, we staged several dinners each year until the COVID-19 pandemic forced us take a hiatus from in-person events.

For a dinner we cooked in Raleigh, Farhan wanted to make cornbread and asked me for advice. I told him about my experiment with corn dhoklas and mentioned that I often season my cornbread batter with toasted cumin seeds, asafoetida, and curry leaves. He took all that in and made a cornbread that absolutely blew my mind. He had taken the basic technique of a traditional Southern cornbread and added elements of our shared Gujarati cuisine. The result was at once familiar and novel. I have tweaked the seasonings to my personal taste, but the soul of the recipe is his.

Roasting the corn and charring the jalapeños might seem like a lot of prep work to make a simple cornbread, but please don't skip these steps. The layers of flavors they add are well worth the effort.

2 large ears corn

2 jalapeño chiles

6 tablespoons neutral oil, such as peanut or canola, divided

1 cup yellow cornmeal

½ cup all-purpose flour

½ cup chickpea flour

⅓ cup sugar

1 tablespoon baking powder

1 teaspoon baking soda

2 teaspoons Kashmiri chili powder

1 teaspoon salt

1 teaspoon ground turmeric

1 tablespoon sesame seeds

2 tablespoons minced ginger

1 large egg

1 cup cultured buttermilk

1 tablespoon chopped fresh cilantro

1 teaspoon brown mustard seeds

1 sprig curry leaves

½ teaspoon asafoetida

1 serrano chile, stemmed and very thinly sliced

¼ cup unsweetened, shredded coconut

Preheat the oven to 400°F.

First, char or roast the corn. If charring, fold back the husks (but leave them attached) and remove the silk. Twist the husks so that each ear of corn has a "handle." Holding the handles, char the ears over a grill or gas flame on the stovetop, turning to cook evenly. If roasting, leave the husks on and roast in the oven for 5 to 6 minutes. When the corn is cool enough to handle, cut the kernels off the cobs. You should end up with 1 cup of kernels, or a little more—use it all.

To roast the jalapeños, turn the flame of a gas stovetop (or grill) to medium-high. Using tongs and an oven mitt, hold one pepper directly over the flame, turning until it is charred on all sides. Repeat with the remaining pepper. (Alternatively, you can roast the peppers under the oven broiler. Watch them carefully and turn with tongs as each side chars.) Once the peppers are charred all the way around, carefully transfer them to a small plastic bag or a small bowl covered with plastic wrap. Allow them to sit for about 10 minutes. The resulting steam and heat will finish cooking the peppers and make the skin easier to peel. Once the peppers are cool enough to handle, peel off the blistered skin. Remove and discard the seeds and stems and finely dice the peppers.

RECIPE CONTINUES

Generously brush the bottom and sides of an 8-inch cast-iron skillet or an 8 x 8-inch baking pan with 2 tablespoons oil and place it in the hot oven. Leave the pan in the oven while you mix the batter.

Combine the cornmeal, both flours, sugar, baking powder, baking soda, chili powder, salt, turmeric, sesame seeds, and ginger in a large mixing bowl. Whisk the egg and buttermilk together in a medium bowl. Pour the wet ingredients over the dry ingredients and stir to combine. Fold in the corn kernels, jalapeño, cilantro, and 2 tablespoons oil. (The batter will have some lumps.)

Using an oven mitt, remove the hot pan from the oven and carefully pour in the batter. Bake for 18 to 20 minutes, until a toothpick inserted in the center comes out clean.

Allow the cornbread to rest at room temperature for 10 minutes before serving. While it is resting, heat the remaining 2 tablespoons oil in a small skillet. Once the oil is shimmering, add the mustard seeds and cook until they start popping, about 30 seconds. Add the curry leaves, asafoetida, and serrano slices and cook, stirring, for 15 seconds. Pour the oil mixture over the resting cornbread. Sprinkle the shredded coconut on top. Cut into slices or squares and serve.

If you have any leftovers, allow them to cool completely before wrapping tightly in aluminum foil. The cornbread will keep overnight at room temperature. The next morning, toast yourself a slice and top it with a fried egg.

MAKKI KI ROTI MAKES 10 ROTIS

Simply put, makki ki roti translates to cornbread. This flatbread is a winter staple in Punjab and is almost always eaten with mustard greens, or sarson ka saag. The first time I had makki ki roti with sarson ka saag was in Lexington, Kentucky, made by my college friend Niaz Ahmed's mother. Niaz and his family were from Lahore, Pakistan. He came to Kentucky for graduate school, and his mother prepared this meal when the family visited for Niaz's graduation.

When India was divided along religious lines in 1947 to create the countries of India and Pakistan, a line was drawn through Punjab and an international border arose where there had never been one. What followed was a human migration and tragedy of untold and unseen proportions, the effects of which have left deep wounds in the psyche of both nations. And yet, we share food and language.

I love the chewy texture of makki ki roti, and it's a natural accompaniment to greens. In other words, it feels right at home in a Southern kitchen. Make a batch of your own and serve it with Kashmiri-Style Collards (page 195), Afghan-Style Spinach with Dill and Cilantro (page 187), or your grandmother's creamed collards. I've even used the rotis in place of tortillas to make tacos filled with chunks of Red Chile and Yogurt–Braised Lamb Shoulder (page 290). If serving with greens, figure two rotis per person.

3 cups corn flour, masa harina, or finely ground cornmeal

1 teaspoon salt

½ teaspoon ground cayenne pepper

2 tablespoons neutral oil, such as peanut or canola, plus about ¼ cup oil or ghee (store-bought or homemade, page 9), for cooking

¼ cup melted unsalted butter or ghee (store-bought or homemade, page 9), for brushing

Sift the flour, salt, and cayenne into a large bowl. Add 2 tablespoons oil and mix thoroughly. Slowly add ½ cup hot water, then another ½ cup, until the dough starts to come together. After you have added 1 cup, continue to add more hot water, a tablespoon at a time, kneading until you have a soft, tacky dough. (You will end up using 1¼ to 1½ cups water in all. If you have ever made corn tortillas, you are aiming for a similar consistency.) Cover the bowl and allow the dough to rest for 10 minutes. Divide the dough into 10 equal balls.

Take one dough ball and knead for 10 to 15 seconds with a few additional drops of water. Place the ball on a piece of plastic wrap and fold the plastic wrap over to cover. Press and roll the ball into a disk 4 to 5 inches in diameter and ¼ inch thick. Repeat until you have rolled all of the dough balls into disks.

Heat a griddle or skillet over medium heat. Add ½ teaspoon oil or ghee. When the oil is hot, add one roti. Cook for about 2 minutes on one side, then flip, adding a bit more oil if necessary. The roti is done when light brown blisters appear on the surface. Repeat with the remaining roti, adding oil as needed, about ½ teaspoon at a time.

Brush the cooked roti with melted butter or ghee and serve immediately.

NOTES: Roti dough lends itself to practically endless variations. Two of my favorites are radish roti and garlic-chile roti. For radish roti, add ½ cup shredded radish to the dough before you start to knead it. For garlic-chile roti, add 2 or 3 minced garlic cloves and 1 or 2 minced green chiles (such as serrano) to the dough before kneading.

GRITS UPMA SERVES 4 FOR BREAKFAST OR 6 AS A SIDE DISH

I have to admit I was always disappointed by grits until I started working at City Grocery. There, the grits are laden with butter, Parmesan, and white cheddar and seasoned with cayenne, paprika, and hot sauce. *That*, I said to myself, *is the right way to make grits.*

Then, in 2011, I watched chef Floyd Cardoz win *Top Chef Masters* with his take on upma. Eureka! Upma, that staple Indian breakfast made with semolina flour, has virtually the same texture as grits. I knew this instinctively, yet it took me more than twenty years to connect the dots. The following Sunday, I cooked grits in the style of upma, and it was a revelation. Serve these for breakfast or as a savory side dish, just as you would traditional grits. You'll notice they pop up as a suggested pairing for many of the recipes in these pages because they are just that good.

If you are new to Indian cuisine, the addition of small amounts of dry lentils (chana dal and urad dal) might be unfamiliar to you. Don't leave them out—they add nuttiness and texture.

The best grits are the ones that come from a source near you, because they are more likely to be freshly milled. Good-quality grits are usually stone-ground and labeled as such. If you are unable to source locally or regionally milled grits, you can order them online. Here in Oxford, I buy mine from Original Grit Girl. I also like the grits from Weisenberger Mill in Midway, Kentucky. Both companies do mail orders.

1 cup uncooked grits (preferably stone-ground)

3 tablespoons coconut oil, ghee (store-bought or homemade, page 9), or neutral oil, such as peanut or canola

1 teaspoon brown mustard seeds

½ teaspoon cumin seeds

Pinch asafoetida

1 teaspoon chana dal

1 teaspoon white urad dal

1 sprig curry leaves

10 to 12 cashews or 20 roasted peanuts (scant ¼ cup)

1 small red onion, minced (¾ to 1 cup)

1-inch piece ginger, minced

1 serrano chile, minced

2 teaspoons salt

1 teaspoon cracked black pepper

½ teaspoon sugar

Juice of 1 lime

2 tablespoons chopped fresh cilantro, for garnish

Toast the grits in a dry skillet over medium heat until very fragrant, about 5 minutes. Shake the pan gently so that they toast evenly. Do not let them brown. Transfer the grits to a plate or bowl.

Heat the oil in a high-sided skillet or a heavy-bottomed pot over medium-high heat. Once the oil is shimmering, add the mustard seeds and cook until they start popping, about 30 seconds. Add the cumin seeds, asafoetida, chana dal, and urad dal and cook, stirring occasionally, until the lentils are slightly toasted and fragrant, 5 to 6 minutes. Add the curry leaves and nuts and stir for 20 seconds. Add the onion, ginger, and chile and cook until the onion is soft and translucent, 6 to 7 minutes. Slowly and carefully add 3½ to 4 cups water (use more if you prefer thinner grits, less if you like them thicker) and the salt, pepper, and sugar. Once the water begins to simmer, whisk in the grits. Cook, whisking almost constantly, until the grits are cooked, about 10 minutes. (Note: Grits cooking times can vary by grind and corn variety. If you are using heirloom grits, they may take 20 minutes or longer to cook. Taste occasionally and let the texture be your guide.) Remove the pot from the heat and stir in the lime juice.

Garnish with chopped cilantro and serve.

CHAPTER SEVEN

POTATOES AND SWEET POTATOES

Potatoes are the great equalizer for many cuisines.

They are used to stretch a stew or to add a filling component to a meal. Like rice, they are inexpensive, nutritious, and substantial, but they offer even more variety in terms of cooking possibilities and the resulting textures and flavors. Potatoes are also one of the few New World foods that got absorbed into European and Indian cuisines and evolved from staple to star. I think of everything from French pommes dauphine to Indian samosas.

Sweet potatoes, in particular, became a staple in the American South—imagine a Southern sideboard without sweet potato casserole, or Thanksgiving without sweet potato pie. They are native to South America but closely related to the African yam, so they were embraced by enslaved Africans in the American South. Sweet potatoes are a major cash crop here in Mississippi. They were part of the cuisine of my Indian upbringing, too. I grew up on undhiyu, a winter dish of sweet potatoes, fresh peas, beans, and eggplant that Gujaratis revere and look forward to in much the same way as folks do a holiday ham or turkey in the United States.

My favorite way of eating sweet potatoes, though, is roasted over coals with a drizzle of ghee and sprinkles of salt and jaggery. My maternal grandmother used to prepare them this way. I once heard the North Carolina writer Randall Kenan give a lecture about Ralph Ellison's *Invisible Man*. His talk centered on a chapter in the novel in which the main character buys and eats a hot baked yam from a street vendor. Though the scene takes place in Harlem, half a world away from my grandmother's Gujarat home, it brought back a flood of memories and tears to my eyes.

CRISPY SMASHED NEW POTATOES WITH LIME, CILANTRO, AND SPICES SERVES 6 TO 8

If you are anything like me, you love potatoes in all shapes and sizes, but often end up making the same potato recipes over and over again. I used to do that with little new potatoes. I like them roasted with olive oil, a little rosemary, and salt—and that was it. That is, until I was introduced to Argentine-style smashed potatoes by John Currence. JC had gone on a trip to Argentina and came back with recipes for chimichurri and crispy new potatoes. The new potatoes are boiled in salted water until just soft, then smashed and pan-fried until they are crispy on the outside. We served them with grilled flatiron steak and chimichurri one evening at Snackbar. A couple of weeks later I found myself cooking dinner for friends and decided to try out my "new" potato recipe. As luck would have it, I was making Indian food and didn't have all the ingredients necessary to make chimichurri. I improvised and came up with this version. It has since become a regular part of my repertoire when those beautiful, freshly dug baby potatoes appear at the farmers' market. If you can't get red baby new potatoes, this recipe works well with other small potatoes such as baby Yukon Golds or fingerlings.

2 teaspoons salt, divided

2 pounds baby new potatoes (preferably red), washed

2 tablespoons coriander seeds

1 tablespoon cumin seeds

2 teaspoons fennel seeds

¼ cup olive oil

Grated zest of 2 limes (After zesting, cut the limes in half and reserve for squeezing at the end.)

1 teaspoon ground cayenne pepper

½ teaspoon ground cinnamon

½ bunch cilantro, chopped

Flaky sea salt, for sprinkling

Preheat the oven to 450°F.

Fill a large pot three-quarters full with water. Add 1 teaspoon salt and the potatoes and bring to a boil over high heat. Reduce the heat to medium-low and simmer until a knife easily pierces the largest potato, 12 to 15 minutes. Drain the potatoes in a colander and set aside to cool.

Toast the coriander seeds in a small, dry pan over medium heat for about 1 minute. Add the cumin seeds and fennel seeds and toast, shaking the pan gently so that the seeds toast evenly and do not burn, until all the spices are fragrant, about 1 more minute. Remove from the heat and, when cool enough to handle, grind in a spice grinder or coffee grinder, or with a mortar and pestle. Set aside.

Once the potatoes are dry and cool enough to handle, smash them lightly with the bottom of a small frying pan, flattening them. Do not break them up completely.

In a large mixing bowl, toss the smashed potatoes with the oil, lime zest, toasted spice mixture, cayenne, cinnamon, and remaining 1 teaspoon salt until nicely coated. Arrange in a single layer on a sheet pan and roast in the oven for 6 to 8 minutes, until the potatoes are crispy and golden brown on the outside. Transfer the potatoes to a large platter for serving, then top with a squeeze of lime juice, a sprinkle of chopped cilantro, and a few pinches of flaky sea salt.

PAN-FRIED POTATOES WITH CUMIN AND BLACK PEPPER SERVES 6

I don't know if there are any places outside of Gujarat that have a special set of recipes that one can cook and eat while "fasting." This is one such recipe. There are more traditional forms of fasting, but this version allows you to eat bland food and some root vegetables, while you give up spices, vegetables, rice, wheat, lentils and other staples. Fruit, grains like amaranth, sweet potatoes, and peanuts are allowed, but as a kid my favorite part of this day of fasting was these potatoes. I was especially fond of the crispy layer that formed at the bottom of the pan and would fight, cry, beg, and steal to get my share of it and more. Now that I have figured out how to cook these for myself, I can make sure that there are plenty of those crispy bits for me.

This is one of the easiest recipes you'll ever make, and that is a good thing because you will want to make it again and again. Serve it with just about anything.

¼ cup neutral oil, such as peanut or canola

2 tablespoons black peppercorns

2 tablespoons cumin seeds

1 sprig curry leaves (optional)

4 large russet potatoes, washed and cut into ½-inch cubes

2 teaspoons salt

Heat the oil in a large skillet (ideally large enough to fit the potatoes in a single layer) over medium-high heat. Once the oil is shimmering, add the peppercorns. Wait for them to start crackling, about 20 seconds, then add the cumin seeds and curry leaves (if using). Cook, stirring, until the cumin and curry leaves are very fragrant, 10 to 20 seconds. Add the potatoes and salt and stir to combine the potatoes with the spices. Reduce the heat to low, cover the pan, and cook for 10 minutes. Remove the lid and cook for an additional 5 minutes, or until the potatoes are cooked through and crispy. If you prefer extra-crispy potatoes, like I do, cook for a couple of minutes longer but take care not to let the potatoes burn. Serve immediately.

POTATO RAITA SERVES 6

One year, I was tasked with making a potato salad for a City Grocery Restaurant Group staff party. The problem is, I'm not much of a potato salad fan. I wanted to come up with something lighter, fresher, and more flavorful than the egg- and mayonnaise-laden versions that are so common at Southern picnics and potlucks. As I often do when faced with these sorts of challenges, I looked to my roots for ideas and came up with this recipe inspired by raita, a yogurt-based Indian condiment. The yogurt gives it a nice creamy texture with a bright tang, and the spices add a zing that is far more interesting and complex than your run-of-the-mill potato salad. Serve it at a picnic or as the perfect accompaniment to any grilled meat.

I use baby Yukon Golds or fingerling potatoes for this recipe, but larger potatoes will work as well. If you prefer a creamier potato salad, cook the potatoes by boiling them. If you want dryer potatoes with more texture, roast them instead.

- 2 pounds baby Yukon Gold potatoes, washed
- 2 teaspoons salt, divided
- 2 tablespoons olive oil (if roasting the potatoes)
- 1½ teaspoons cumin seeds
- ¼ cup canola oil
- 1 teaspoon brown mustard seeds
- 1 dried chile de árbol, stemmed
- ½ serrano chile, stemmed and seeded, and minced (about 1 tablespoon)
- 1 teaspoon minced ginger
- 1 teaspoon minced garlic
- Pinch asafoetida
- 1 sprig curry leaves (optional)
- ¼ cup minced red onion
- 1 teaspoon cracked black pepper
- ½ teaspoon chaat masala (store-bought or homemade, page 8)
- 1 cup plain, full-fat yogurt (preferably Greek-style)

If boiling the potatoes: Fill a large pot three-quarters full with water. Add 1 teaspoon salt and the potatoes and bring to a boil over high heat. Reduce the heat to medium-low and simmer until a knife easily pierces the largest potato, 12 to 15 minutes. Drain the potatoes in a colander and set aside to cool.

If roasting the potatoes: Preheat the oven to 400°F. While the oven heats, cut the potatoes in half and toss them in a medium bowl with the olive oil and 1 teaspoon salt. Arrange the potatoes in a single layer on a sheet pan and roast for 20 to 25 minutes, until they are browned and cooked. Set aside to cool.

While the potatoes cook, toast the cumin seeds in a small, dry pan over medium heat until fragrant, shaking the pan gently so that the seeds toast evenly and do not burn, about 1 minute. Remove from the heat and, when cool enough to handle, crush with a mortar and pestle or coarsely grind in a spice grinder or coffee grinder. Set aside.

To make the dressing, heat the canola oil in a medium skillet over medium-high heat. Once the oil is shimmering, add the mustard seeds and cook until they start popping, about 30 seconds. Add the dried chile, fresh chile, ginger, garlic, asafoetida, and curry leaves (if using). Cook, stirring, until the mixture is fragrant, about 20 seconds. Remove from the heat and discard the dried chile.

Combine the oil mixture, onion, cumin, remaining 1 teaspoon salt, pepper, chaat masala, and yogurt in a large bowl and mix well. When the cooked potatoes have cooled to room temperature or are just barely warm, fold them into the dressing. Serve immediately or store the potato salad in a covered container in the refrigerator for up to 3 days.

BOMBAY TOASTIES MAKES 4 SANDWICHES

Everyone has a favorite sandwich and very likely a story as to why that is so. This is mine. The summer I turned ten, my sister went off to summer camp and Dad was traveling for a conference. I spent my days being outside with friends and Mom spent hers reading, visiting neighbors, and cooking things she wouldn't if we had a full house. She even bought a new sandwich press to make us Bombay toasties. A popular roadside snack in and around Mumbai (formerly Bombay), these sandwiches are a sort of grilled cheese stuffed with mashed potato filling and spread with green chutney. I watched as Mom assembled the toasties and toasted the first one in the sandwich press over an open flame. What came out was a sight to behold—a crispy, golden brown pillow of bread, sealed at the edges but with cheese still oozing out from a spot or two. She cut it in half and we ate it right there at the kitchen counter. Since the toastie maker made only one sandwich at a time, we took turns making one for each other. It was a magical dinner, just my mother and me.

8 tablespoons (1 stick) unsalted butter, at room temperature

8 slices white bread

½ cup Peanut Pesto (page 170) or other favorite green chutney

2 cups Spicy Potato Mash (page 150)

¼ to ⅓ cup minced red onion

1 or 2 serrano chiles, stemmed and minced (optional)

1 large ripe tomato, sliced

1 beet, peeled and sliced very thin (you want at least 8 slices)

1½ cups shredded Amul cheese or sharp white cheddar cheese

2 teaspoons chaat masala (store-bought or homemade, page 8)

Generously spread butter on both sides of each bread slice. Spread one side of 4 slices with peanut pesto. Top the other 4 slices with equal amounts of potato mash, onion, chiles (if using), tomato slices, beet slices, and shredded cheese. Sprinkle with a generous pinch of chaat masala. Top each sandwich with the chutney bread slices, pesto side facing in.

Set a griddle or large skillet over medium-high heat, or heat a panini press. When the griddle or skillet is hot, add the sandwiches. If using a large griddle, you may be able to cook all four at one time. If using a skillet, you may have room for only one or two at a time. Toast the sandwiches until they are crispy and golden on the bottom, about 90 seconds. Carefully flip the sandwiches. Press them down using a grill press, a pot lid, or a smaller pan and cook for another 90 seconds, until the cheese has melted and the sandwich is golden brown on both sides. If toasting the sandwiches in a panini press, you will not need to flip them.

Serve the sandwiches immediately, topping each with one more sprinkle of chaat masala, if you like.

SPICY POTATO MASH

MAKES ABOUT 6 CUPS

For this recipe, I encourage you to seek out curry leaves for their singular flavor, which is herbaceous, nutty, and floral at once. But if you cannot find them, the mash will still be delicious. You will have enough for four Bombay Toasties (page 148) and one large Masala Potato and Cheese Omelet (page 152). You should also end up with approximately 1 cup of left-overs, which are fantastic on its own.

- 2 teaspoons salt, divided
- 4 large russet potatoes, washed
- 8 garlic cloves, roughly chopped
- ½ small red onion, roughly chopped (about ½ cup)
- 2 serrano chiles, stemmed and roughly chopped
- 2-inch piece ginger, roughly chopped
- ½ teaspoon brown mustard seeds
- 1 teaspoon chaat masala (store-bought or homemade, page 8)
- ½ teaspoon ground turmeric
- 1 pinch asafoetida
- 2 tablespoons chopped fresh cilantro leaves
- 1 sprig curry leaves (optional)

Preheat the oven to 350°F.

Fill a large pot three-quarters full with water. Add 1 teaspoon salt and the potatoes and bring to a boil over high heat. Reduce the heat to medium-low and simmer until a knife easily pierces the largest potato, about 20 minutes. Drain the potatoes in a colander.

Transfer the potatoes to a sheet pan and put them in the oven for 5 minutes to dry out the skins. Remove from the oven and, when cool enough to handle, peel the dry potatoes carefully and mash them in a large bowl. (Cooking the potatoes in their skins and peeling them afterward keeps them from getting sodden and gummy.)

While the potatoes are cooking, combine the garlic, red onion, serranos, and ginger in the bowl of a food processor or blender jar and process into a coarse paste. If you do not have a food processor or blender, chop everything very finely and combine well.

Set a small dry skillet over medium heat and add the mustard seeds. Toast until fragrant, 20 to 30 seconds. Remove from the heat. When cool enough to handle, grind coarsely in a spice grinder or using a mortar and pestle.

Add the toasted mustard seeds to the bowl of mashed potatoes, along with the garlic paste, remaining 1 teaspoon salt, chaat masala, turmeric, asafoetida, chopped cilantro, and curry leaves (if using). Mix well. If not using immediately, let the mixture cool completely, then store in a tightly sealed container in the refrigerator for up to 2 days.

MASALA POTATO AND CHEESE OMELET

SERVES 4 TO 6

The Spicy Potato Mash (page 150) that fills the Bombay Toasties (page 148) is used for all sorts of dishes in India. You have most likely had a version of it stuffed inside a dosa or a samosa. I have used it as a filling for quesadillas, formed it into patties and pan-fried them, or breaded them and deep-fried them as croquettes. I had never thought of using it for an omelet until one day I invited folks over for brunch and wanted to make dosas. Unfortunately, my dosa batter did not come out right—yes, this happens to chefs, too—and I had to scramble to put together something before the guests started arriving. We had plenty of eggs on hand, so I decided to make a Spanish tortilla-style omelet with the potato mash I had already made. I seasoned the eggs with a bit of garam masala, cayenne, and chopped cilantro and whisked them until they were frothy. I poured that mixture over the potatoes in a nonstick skillet, sprinkled sharp white cheddar over the top, and stuck the whole thing into a 350°F oven until the eggs were just set and the cheese melted. I slid the omelet out onto a cutting board, cut it into wedges and served it with buttered toast, a side of salsa, and some Maggi Hot and Sweet sauce. It was a hit at my brunch, and it will be at yours, too. It's just as good for dinner, served with a simple green salad on the side.

8 large eggs

2 tablespoons finely chopped fresh cilantro leaves

1 teaspoon garam masala (store-bought or homemade, page 8)

½ teaspoon salt

½ teaspoon ground cayenne pepper

1 tablespoon ghee (store-bought or homemade, page 9)

3 cups Spicy Potato Mash (page 150)

½ cup sharp white cheddar cheese

Preheat the oven to 350°F.

Crack the eggs into a large bowl and add the cilantro, garam masala, salt, and cayenne. Whisk until very frothy and light.

Heat the ghee in an 8-inch ovenproof nonstick skillet over medium heat. (An 8-inch skillet is the best size to give you the proper thickness. If you use a larger one, you will end up with a thinner omelet.) Once the ghee is shimmering, add the potato mash to the skillet and cook for 2 minutes, or until the potatoes are lightly browned. Add the egg mixture to the potatoes, give everything a gentle stir, sprinkle the cheddar on top, and put the whole thing in the oven until the eggs are set, 5 to 6 minutes. Carefully remove the skillet from the oven, then gently slide the omelet out onto a cutting board. Cut into wedges and serve immediately.

COAL-ROASTED SWEET POTATOES, TWO WAYS

The best way to cook sweet potatoes is by burying them under the embers of a campfire, drinking whiskey (or chai) while they cook. My grandmother's house had two outdoor wood-burning "stoves" that were used to heat a big drum of water and to cook large pots of stews or make gallons of chai or to heat even more water when needed. My grandmother was usually the one who would start the fire early and it would be down to smoldering embers when we kids were finally up. To tide us over until lunch and to keep us out of the house, Grandma would give us a small sweet potato each and send us out to cook them in the embers. Those sweet potatoes eaten in Grandma's yard with a dollop of fresh whipped butter are one of my favorite food memories.

Those memories came flooding back on a college camping trip to the Red River Gorge. For our post-hike dinner, my friend EJ Bunzendahl (she of the Green Tomato Pie, page 100) placed sweet potatoes directly in the embers of the campfire to roast. Half a world away, I felt like a kid at my grandmother's house once again.

If you don't have a charcoal grill, you can bake the sweet potatoes in a very hot oven. They won't have that smoky flavor, but they are still delicious. You can season them any way you like—here are my two favorite preparations. Both of them can be scaled down for smaller crowds and up for larger ones.

COAL-ROASTED SWEET POTATOES WITH GHEE, CLOVES, BLACK PEPPER, AND NUTMEG

SERVES 6

6 medium sweet potatoes, washed

½ cup ghee (store-bought or homemade, page 9), divided

2 to 3 tablespoons coarse kosher salt

36 to 40 whole cloves

1 tablespoon freshly ground black pepper

1 teaspoon freshly grated nutmeg

Heat the grill to medium-high or preheat the oven to 500°F.

Rub or brush each sweet potato with 2 teaspoons ghee and season them generously with coarse kosher salt, as you would a baked potato. Poke 5 or 6 cloves into the skin of each potato and wrap each potato individually in aluminum foil. Roast directly on the charcoal or on wood embers or in the oven until a skewer or fork inserted into the foil pierces the potato without resistance, about 20 minutes. (A skewer is a better tester than a fork since it will go all the way through.) Using tongs, carefully remove the sweet potatoes from the heat, transfer to a platter, and let them rest for 5 minutes, still wrapped in the foil.

Meanwhile, set a small saucepan over medium heat. Add the remaining ghee, remaining 5 or 6 cloves, ground pepper, and nutmeg and cook until the spices are very fragrant, 20 to 30 seconds. Remove the pan from the heat. Cut a slit through the foil into each sweet potato and gently push the ends toward each other (like you would for a baked potato) to open the potato along the slit, exposing the flesh inside. Be careful not to let the escaping steam burn you. Add a spoonful of the spiced ghee and a pinch of salt to the inside of each potato. Dig in.

COAL-ROASTED SWEET POTATOES WITH ROSEMARY-CHILE-LIME BUTTER

SERVES 6

6 medium sweet potatoes, washed and quartered lengthwise

2 sticks (1 cup) unsalted butter

3 tablespoons chopped fresh rosemary

Grated zest and juice of 2 limes

2 chipotle chiles in adobo, finely chopped
(or 2 jalapeño chiles, finely chopped, if you prefer the fresh chile taste)

1 tablespoon salt

1 teaspoon light brown sugar

Heat the grill to medium-high heat or preheat the oven to 500°F.

Meanwhile, cut six 10-inch squares of heavy-duty aluminum foil and lay them out on your work surface. Place the sweet potato wedges in a large bowl.

Melt the butter in a small saucepan over low to medium-low heat. Add the rosemary, lime zest and juice, chiles, salt, and sugar and stir. Cook until the mixture is very fragrant, 30 seconds to 1 minute. Pour the butter mixture over the sweet potato wedges and toss to coat.

Place four potato wedges in the center of each foil square. Bring two sides of the foil together and fold over the top. Fold the opposite sides in, crimping them closed. Repeat with the remaining foil and potatoes until you have made six packets.

Place the foil packets on the charcoal or on wood embers and cook for about 20 minutes, until the potatoes are completely soft and the butter is nutty and fragrant. If cooking the potatoes in the oven, place the foil packets on a sheet pan to minimize leakage. Using tongs, carefully remove the packets from the heat. Serve immediately.

SWEET POTATO, HAM, AND CHEDDAR BISCUITS MAKES ABOUT 12 BISCUITS

Every year at Thanksgiving my father-in-law makes a sweet potato casserole with lots of butter, cinnamon, and brown sugar. My mother-in-law always has ham as well as turkey on the table. During one of these family gatherings my wife made biscuits for breakfast and we warmed up the leftover ham to serve with it. I did what almost anyone presented with ham and biscuits in the South would do—I made a ham and cheese biscuit. That's when the light bulb went off. What if I were to put the ham and cheese in the biscuit, thereby making an all-in-one tasty morsel? I wrote out a recipe for a ham and cheese biscuit, then quickly realized that it needed a touch of sweetness to counteract the salty ham and the salty cheese. That is when my father-in-law's sweet potatoes came to mind. Voilà! I had exactly what I was looking for: a savory biscuit that perfect married salty and sweet.

1 medium to large sweet potato

1¾ cups all-purpose flour, plus extra for rolling dough

1 tablespoon light brown sugar

1 tablespoon baking powder

1 teaspoon salt

½ teaspoon baking soda

1 tablespoon chopped fresh thyme or rosemary leaves

6 tablespoons unsalted butter, chilled and cubed

½ cup finely diced good country ham (I use Benton's.)

1 jalapeño chile, seeded and minced

½ cup shredded Gruyère or sharp white cheddar cheese

1 tablespoon grated orange zest

1 large egg

⅓ cup cultured buttermilk

Pepper jelly, preserves, or Tomato-Coconut Chutney (page 99), for serving

NOTE: You may roast and mash the sweet potato the day before you plan to make the biscuits. Let it cool to room temperature, then store in a covered container in the refrigerator.

Preheat the oven to 400°F. Line a sheet pan with parchment.

Pierce the sweet potato a few times with the tines of a fork, wrap it in aluminum foil, and bake until tender when poked with a fork or skewer, about 45 minutes. When cool enough to handle, cut the sweet potato in half, scrape the flesh into a bowl, and mash with a fork. Measure ¾ cup mashed sweet potato. Once cooled to room temperature, set aside in the refrigerator to chill.

In a large bowl, combine the flour, brown sugar, baking powder, salt, baking soda, and thyme or rosemary. Using your fingertips or a pastry cutter, mix the butter into the flour until it resembles a coarse meal. Stir in the ham, jalapeño, cheese, and orange zest. Chill the flour mixture for 10 minutes. (When making biscuits, you will get the best results if all your components are cold. If it is a hot day, chill the mixture in the freezer. On a cold day, the refrigerator will do.)

In a small bowl, whisk together the chilled sweet potato, egg, and buttermilk. Fold this into the chilled flour mixture to form a dough. The dough will be soft and fairly moist.

Turn out the dough onto a lightly floured work surface and roll it into a rectangle (it does not have to be perfect). Fold the dough into thirds as if you were folding a letter to put in an envelope. Turn the piece of dough 90 degrees, roll it back out, and fold into thirds again. Repeat these steps, folding, turning, and rolling a total of six to eight times. This process is what creates

the biscuit's layers. Finally, roll the dough to ½-inch thickness and cut into 2½-inch rounds with a biscuit cutter, cookie cutter, or the rim of a glass. Gather the scraps, reroll, and cut again. (You will not repeat the folding process at this point.) Repeat a third time, if needed, until all the dough is used. You should end up with 12 biscuits. (Be aware that the second and third rerolls will not rise as much as the batch you cut first.) Or, if you prefer, you can cut the biscuits into 12 squares using a sharp knife.

Place the biscuits on the prepared sheet pan just touching each other. Bake for 10 to 12 minutes, until light golden brown. Transfer to a rack to cool slightly, then serve with your favorite topping.

SWEET POTATO PURÉE WITH SORGHUM AND CAYENNE SERVES 6 TO 8

Some Southern cooks have a tendency to gild the lily by over-sweetening sweet potato dishes, at least to my taste. This silky purée, at once savory and sweet, is the perfect antidote. Elegant and versatile, it can be served with Sweet Tea-Brined Fried Chicken (page 250), Whole Grilled Okra (page 60), grilled pork chops, or smoked duck.

Do seek out sorghum syrup for this recipe—its minerally sweetness is a perfect foil for the earthy sweetness of the sweet potato. That said, you can substitute maple syrup for an equally delicious glaze if sorghum is hard to find where you live.

6 medium sweet potatoes, washed

1 cup heavy cream

8 garlic cloves, peeled

2-inch piece ginger, minced

4 tablespoons (½ stick) unsalted butter, at room temperature

¼ cup sour cream

2 teaspoons sorghum syrup

2 teaspoons salt

1 teaspoon ground cayenne pepper

Preheat the oven to 400°F. Line a sheet pan with parchment or aluminum foil.

Pierce each sweet potato a few times with the tines of a fork, place on the prepared sheet pan, and bake until tender when poked with a fork or skewer, about 45 minutes. Remove from the oven and set aside to cool.

Meanwhile, combine the cream, garlic, and ginger in a small saucepan and simmer over medium heat until the garlic is very soft, 10 to 12 minutes. Remove from the heat and set aside.

When the sweet potatoes are cool enough to handle, cut each one in half, scrape out the flesh, and transfer it to a mixing bowl. Add the cream mixture, butter, sour cream, sorghum, salt, and cayenne and purée using a handheld blender, or transfer to a food processor and mix until it is very smooth. Taste and add a pinch more cayenne and/or salt, if desired. Serve warm. Store leftovers in the refrigerator and reheat to enjoy the next day, or use for Leftover Sweet Potato Pound Cake with Sorghum Glaze (page 162).

SWEET POTATO AND PEANUT SALAD SERVES 8

This sweet potato salad will become your new favorite picnic item. The flavors and textures are far more interesting than a standard-issue potato salad, with a dressing that is at once creamy, spicy, acidic, and sweet. If you cannot find cane or sorghum syrup, use maple syrup instead.

3 pounds sweet potatoes, peeled and cut into 1-inch cubes (about 8 cups before cooking)

3 tablespoons olive oil

1½ teaspoons salt

FOR THE DRESSING:

1 teaspoon cumin seeds

¼ cup Creole or other grainy mustard

2 tablespoons creamy peanut butter (preferably an all-natural peanut butter with no added salt or sugar)

1 tablespoon fresh lime juice

1 teaspoon hot sauce

1 teaspoon cane syrup, sorghum syrup, or maple syrup

1 teaspoon ground cinnamon

½ teaspoon freshly grated nutmeg

½ teaspoon ground cayenne pepper

FOR THE SALAD:

1 small red onion, minced (¾ to 1 cup)

½ cup sliced scallion greens

1 small red bell pepper, stemmed, seeded, and minced (about ¾ cup)

1 serrano chile, stemmed, seeded if desired, and minced

1 cup roasted lightly salted peanuts, chopped

½ cup dried unsweetened cranberries or seedless raisins, chopped

Preheat the oven to 350°F degrees. Line a sheet pan with parchment.

Combine the sweet potato cubes, olive oil, and salt in a large bowl and toss to coat. Spread them in a single layer on the prepared sheet pan and bake for 25 to 30 minutes, until just soft. Remove from the oven and set aside to cool.

Meanwhile, make the dressing. Toast the cumin seeds in a small, dry pan over medium heat, shaking the pan gently so that the seeds toast evenly and do not burn, about 1 minute. Remove from the heat and set aside until cool enough to handle. Combine the mustard, peanut butter, lime juice, hot sauce, cane syrup, cinnamon, nutmeg, cayenne, and toasted cumin in a bowl and whisk until well blended; set aside.

When the sweet potatoes have cooled to room temperature, combine them with the red onion, scallions, bell pepper, serrano, chopped peanuts, and dried cranberries or raisins in a large bowl. Pour the dressing over the salad and gently mix to distribute and coat the vegetables. Taste and add salt to your liking. Serve at room temperature. Store leftovers in a covered container in the refrigerator for up to 2 days. If making the salad in advance, leave out the peanuts. Stir them in just before serving so that they retain their crunch.

LEFTOVER SWEET POTATO POUND CAKE WITH SORGHUM GLAZE

MAKES ONE 12- TO 14-CUP BUNDT CAKE

My Sweet Potato Purée with Sorghum and Cayenne (page 159) makes a generous amount, and you may find that you have some left over. Enter this easy pound cake. The flavors land in that perfect place where you can get away with it at brunch or with afternoon chai—or it can be a dessert worthy of a dinner party.

The golden milk seasoning is a great way to underscore the flavors in the leftover purée and is worth ordering from Spicewalla. (Otherwise, you may substitute a mixture of ½ teaspoon pumpkin pie spice, ¼ teaspoon ground ginger, and ¼ teaspoon ground white pepper.) Sorghum syrup is worth seeking out for the glaze, especially as it will complement the sorghum in the sweet potato purée. That said, you can substitute maple syrup for an equally delicious glaze. If you prefer, you can replace the pecans with walnuts, or use a combination. You could even swap out the nuts for golden raisins or dark chocolate chips—this is a flexible and forgiving recipe. Serve each slice with a heaping scoop of vanilla ice cream.

I like a thicker glaze that will just blanket the top of the cake and start to run down the sides but not fully coat the whole cake. You can adjust the consistency of the glaze and even the amount you use to suit your taste.

3 cups all-purpose flour, plus more for dusting

2 teaspoons baking powder

1 teaspoon Spicewalla golden milk seasoning

¾ teaspoon salt

¾ teaspoon ground cinnamon

½ teaspoon baking soda

8 tablespoons (1 stick) unsalted butter or ghee (store-bought or homemade, page 9), at room temperature

½ cup coconut oil

1 cup granulated sugar

1 cup packed light brown sugar

4 large eggs, at room temperature

1½ cups Sweet Potato Purée with Sorghum and Cayenne (page 159)

1½ teaspoons vanilla extract

½ cup cultured buttermilk

1½ cups chopped pecans, plus more for the top (optional)

1 recipe Sorghum Syrup Glaze (page 164)

Preheat the oven to 350°F with a rack in the bottom third. Butter or spray a Bundt pan and dust with flour.

Sift the flour, baking powder, golden milk seasoning, salt, cinnamon, and baking soda into a large bowl; set aside.

In a stand mixer, or in a large bowl with a handheld mixer, beat the butter, coconut oil, granulated sugar, and brown sugar on medium speed until fluffy. Add the eggs, one at a time, beating well after each addition.

In a small bowl, combine the sweet potato purée and vanilla and mix until well blended. Add to the batter in the mixing bowl and beat on medium speed until thoroughly combined.

Reduce the speed to low and add half of the dry ingredients, mixing until you have a cohesive blend. With the mixer still running, slowly pour in the buttermilk and mix until combined, then add the rest of the dry ingredients and mix until just blended. Do not overbeat.

Fold in the pecans by hand with a large silicone spatula, being sure to scrape the bowl so there are no streaks of unmixed flour. Spoon the batter into the prepared pan, being sure to fill all the grooves, and smooth the top with a small offset spatula or knife,

RECIPE CONTINUES

pressing down to make sure there are no air pockets. It is a thick batter and will self-level in the pan.

Bake for 50 to 60 minutes, until a tester inserted all the way into the cake comes out clean. (I like to test the cake in three spots to make sure it is evenly done.) Place the pan on a cooling rack for about an hour. When the cake is just warm to the touch, remove it from the pan.

Spoon or pour the warm sorghum glaze over the still-warm cake. If you like, sprinkle the top of the cake with more chopped nuts, pressing gently to get them to stick to the glaze.

Cool completely before slicing and serving. The cake can be stored, covered, at room temperature for up to 2 days or in the refrigerator for up to 4 days. If storing in the refrigerator, allow it to sit on the counter for at least an hour to come to room temperature before serving.

SORGHUM SYRUP GLAZE

MAKES ABOUT 1¼ CUPS

⅓ cup sorghum syrup

3 tablespoons unsalted butter

1½ to 2 cups confectioners' sugar

Salt

In a small saucepan, combine the syrup and butter and cook over medium heat until the butter is melted. Remove from the heat. In a bowl, whisk together 1½ cups confectioners' sugar and a generous pinch of salt. Add the syrup mixture and whisk to combine. If you want a thicker glaze, add up to ½ cup more sugar until you get the texture you like.

SWEET POTATO TURNOVERS WITH CARDAMOM AND BLACK PEPPER

MAKES 12 TURNOVERS; SERVES 6 FOR DESSERT

There are two types of pie people in this world: those who eat the pie for the filling, and those who eat the pie for the crust. I fall in the latter category, which is why I am a big fan of turnovers, empanadas, hand pies, and the like.

When I think of a handheld pastry, I immediately think of a samosa, so this dough has savory leanings, even though I serve the turnovers for dessert or a sweet snack. I love the way the dough plays off the sweet, spicy, and peppery filling.

FOR THE SWEET POTATO FILLING:

3 large sweet potatoes, peeled and cut into 1-inch cubes

¼ cup ghee (store-bought or homemade, page 9)

¾ cup seedless raisins

1½ tablespoons cracked black pepper (These should be fairly large pieces—you can achieve this texture by cracking black peppercorns in a mortar and pestle or with the back of a spoon.)

¾ teaspoon cardamom seeds, crushed (Crush enough green cardamom pods to yield ¾ teaspoon seeds—4 to 5 pods. Then, crush the seeds themselves with a mortar and pestle.)

4 tablespoons cane sugar crystals, divided (You want a sugar with crystals that are larger than granulated sugar. This can be coarse sugar, sanding sugar, or turbinado.)

FOR THE DOUGH:

½ teaspoon salt

3½ to 4 cups all-purpose flour, sifted, plus more for dusting

1 teaspoon cracked black pepper

1 teaspoon fennel seeds, crushed

4 cups plus 6 tablespoons neutral oil, such as peanut or canola, divided

NOTE: If you do not want to deep-fry, you could place the turnovers on a parchment-lined sheet pan and bake them in a 375°F oven for about 15 minutes, until golden. The flavors will be just as good, but the crust will not have the same texture.

Preheat the oven to 350°F. Line a sheet pan with parchment paper.

To make the filling, in a medium bowl, toss the sweet potatoes with the ghee. Spread them out in a single layer on the prepared sheet pan and bake for 20 minutes, or until cooked through.

While the potatoes are cooking, put the raisins in a small bowl and add enough water to cover them. Soak for 20 minutes to plump, then drain.

When the potatoes are done, return them to the bowl. Toss immediately with black pepper, cardamom, raisins, and 2 tablespoons sugar. Mash the mixture lightly with the back of a spoon. Allow to cool to room temperature. The filling can be made up to a day ahead; allow it to cool completely before storing in a covered container in the refrigerator.

To make the dough, dissolve the salt in 1 cup warm water; set aside. Combine the flour, pepper, and fennel seeds in the bowl of a food processor and pulse until well blended. Continue to pulse the flour mixture while slowly adding 6 tablespoons oil through the feed tube. Remove the lid and scrape down the sides of the food processor. Cover again and, with the motor running, slowly add the salt water through the feed tube until the dough comes together. Scrape the dough out onto a lightly floured work surface. Knead the dough (moisten your hands if necessary) until it is smooth. Shape into a ball or disk, wrap in plastic wrap, and chill for 10 to 15 minutes or up to overnight in the refrigerator.

Divide the chilled dough into 12 equal portions, each slightly smaller than a golf ball. Roll out one portion at

a time on a lightly floured surface into a 5-inch circle. Spoon 2 to 3 tablespoons filling in the middle of the circle. Fold the dough in half over the filling to make a semicircle and crimp the edges with a fork to seal. Repeat the process with the remaining portions of dough, until you have 12 turnovers.

Heat 4 cups oil to 350°F in a cast-iron skillet, Dutch oven, or electric fryer. If you don't have a deep-fry thermometer, drop in a scrap of dough to test the temperature. If it sizzles and floats to the top, your oil is ready. If it sinks to the bottom of the pot, the oil still needs to heat up more.

While the oil is heating, line a sheet pan with paper towels and place it near the stove or fryer.

Once the oil is ready, carefully add three or four turnovers, depending on the size of your pot or fryer. If the pot is too crowded, it will bring down the temperature of the oil, resulting in soggy, undercooked turnovers. Watch the turnovers as they fry, carefully turning them with a slotted spoon until they are golden brown on both sides. If you see that the crust is burning, your oil is too hot, and you need to reduce the heat slightly. Carefully remove the turnovers and place on the prepared sheet pan. Sprinkle with some of the remaining 2 tablespoons sugar. When all of the turnovers from the first batch are finished, let the oil temperature return to 350°F before adding more. Serve hot or at room temperature.

CHAPTER EIGHT

PEANUTS

There is a photograph of me when I was two or three years old, standing up in the back seat of my parents' white Ford Galaxy. I'm holding a brown bag of roasted peanuts, my shoulder turned away from my older sister's outstretched hand.

My sister looks angry, and our mother is turned around in the front seat, no doubt trying to firmly talk me into sharing. That photograph was taken at a roadside stand somewhere near Oak Ridge, Tennessee. We lived there for three years while my father worked at the Oak Ridge National Laboratory. When we traveled, I remember we'd stop at rural produce stands for peaches, corn, and peanuts. These farm stands used to be a fixture of the rural landscape; sometimes they were nothing more than a farmer selling fruit from the bed of his pickup truck.

On these family car trips, we'd stop at roadside picnic spots to eat our lunches or snacks. I don't remember going to many restaurants. It was just recently that I guessed why. The time period between 1966 and 1969 when we lived in Tennessee was during the height of the Civil Rights Movement. We were Indian, not African American. But my parents might have thought—or known—that we would be unwelcome at small-town Southern restaurants. I brought that up with my father when he visited Mississippi recently, but he didn't want to discuss it. He did say that he once turned down an offer to give a seminar at Tulane University in New Orleans, because his white colleagues cautioned him against the interstate road trip it would entail.

Shortly after that photo was taken, Mom and Dad decided to move our family back to India. If they had stayed, this could have been a very different Southern cookbook.

Back in Ahmedabad, peanuts were a staple in my mother's pantry. Peanut-cilantro chutney was on the table every day. At the movie theater, we snacked on roasted peanuts instead of popcorn. Once, my mother's brother tried his hand at growing peanuts. He then invited his nieces and nephews to help with the harvest. I remember all of us being dead tired that evening, our hands black from the dirt and blistered from pulling up the peanut plants. That same night, I also remember my mother making the best boiled peanuts I have ever had. The whole family sat around a big mound of steaming, spicy boiled peanuts, laughing and telling stories. I don't think I'll ever attempt to grow peanuts like my uncle, but I'll happily eat them whenever I have the chance.

Another reason I love peanuts: They are inexpensive and widely available. That said, if you're having trouble finding the kind of peanut a recipe calls for, do as I do and browse Nuts.com.

PEANUT PESTO MAKES ABOUT 2 CUPS

This is a recipe for the peanut chutney that I grew up eating at home with practically every meal. If my mother were still around, she would ask me why I was calling it pesto. Allow me to explain—to her and to you.

The peanut chutney my mother made followed virtually the same format as a pesto, in that it combined green herbs, garlic, and nuts. So, when I first came across Italian-style pesto in the United States, I recognized it as a variation on one of the many chutneys I'd known growing up. In the American South, chutneys are popular as well. But the term tends to refer to a cooked fruit relish. So the first time I served this spread on a fried chicken sandwich for lunch at City Grocery, I called it peanut pesto. I'm sorry, Mom.

Since you'll be blending everything together, the chile and ginger can be roughly chopped. Use this as you would any pesto—stir it into pasta dishes or mix it with a little mayonnaise for a sandwich spread.

For a slightly different flavor, try replacing one bunch of cilantro with equal parts mint and basil leaves. I often use this variation for my Collard-Wrapped Catfish (page 235).

1½ cups raw unsalted peanuts (Roasted will also work, although I prefer the earthiness of raw peanuts for this recipe.)

1 serrano chile, stemmed and chopped

2-inch piece ginger, chopped

4 garlic cloves, peeled

1 teaspoon granulated sugar

2 bunches cilantro, leaves and tender stems

1 teaspoon salt

Juice of 2 lemons

Combine all the ingredients in the bowl of a food processor and process until well combined and mostly smooth. If necessary, add water a couple of teaspoons at a time to thin the mixture slightly. You're looking to achieve a spoonable consistency, similar to any other pesto you'd make or buy.

PEANUT AND OLIVE SPREAD MAKES ABOUT 2 CUPS

At Snackbar, we frequently offer a happy hour special called "Things in Jars." We serve our homemade flatbread crackers with a rotating selection of spreads, both classic and unexpected, like pimento cheese, deviled ham, and Kentucky beer cheese. I am constantly looking to make these offerings more interesting and often experiment with flavor combinations at home. Teresa and I always put out olives and nuts to nosh on when we have company, so I thought about ways to combine the two. I landed on this peanut-olive spread, which I serve with crackers or as the filling for a finger sandwich.

- 8 ounces cream cheese, softened
- ⅓ cup chopped roasted unsalted peanuts
- 1 tablespoon peanut butter (preferably an all-natural peanut butter with no added salt or sugar)
- ⅓ cup chopped pitted green olives jarred in brine, plus 1 tablespoon olive brine
- 1 teaspoon Sriracha
- ½ teaspoon garlic powder

Combine all the ingredients in the bowl of a food processor and process until evenly mixed. The spread will be thick and not completely smooth—you are looking to achieve a texture akin to chunky peanut butter. Store in an airtight container in the refrigerator for up to 1 week.

BOILED PEANUT CHAAT

SERVES 10 AS A COCKTAIL SNACK (ABOUT ½ CUP PER PERSON)

I grew up eating boiled peanuts, so when I rediscovered them at a roadside stand in rural South Carolina, I was over the moon. Though less common than they used to be, boiled peanut stands still dot the roadsides of the rural South. A few years ago, a friend and fellow boiled peanut lover challenged me to incorporate boiled peanuts into a dinner menu. My mind went to chaat, the catch-all term for savory snacks in India, and here is the preparation I dreamed up. I recommend making the boiled peanuts first and prepping the rest of the ingredients while the boiled peanuts cool. Since this is such a perfect cocktail party food, the recipe serves 10 people. It's the kind of thing you'll want to serve right away rather than saving leftovers, so you can certainly cut it in half for a smaller gathering.

2 tablespoons neutral oil, such as peanut or canola

½ teaspoon cumin seeds

1 sprig curry leaves

1 recipe Boiled Peanuts (page 174), drained and cooled

1 cup roasted, salted peanuts

1 small red onion, minced (¾ to 1 cup)

1 serrano chile, stemmed and minced

2 Roma tomatoes, seeded and diced small

½ English cucumber, seeded and diced small (¾ to 1 cup)

⅓ cup chopped fresh cilantro leaves and tender stems

¼ cup chopped fresh mint leaves

1½ teaspoons chaat masala (store-bought or homemade, page 8)

¼ teaspoon ground cayenne pepper

Juice of 2 limes

1 teaspoon honey or cane syrup

Salt

Heat the oil in a large skillet over medium heat. When the oil is shimmering, add the cumin seeds and curry leaves and stir until they crackle and become very fragrant, about 30 seconds. Add the boiled peanuts and stir to coat, then remove from the heat. Transfer the peanuts to a large bowl and stir in the roasted peanuts, onion, chile, tomatoes, cucumber, cilantro, mint, chaat masala, cayenne, lime juice, and honey. Combine everything well and season with salt to taste. Portion individual servings of about ½ cup each in small bowls or paper cones.

NOTES: If you can't find raw, shelled peanuts at your grocery store, they are almost always available at Indian markets. I recommend MDH brand Chunky Chat Masala, available online or at your favorite Indian market, or Spicewalla brand. For most home cooks, it's more economical to buy prepared chaat masala than to make your own. If you do want to make your own chaat masala, see the recipe on page 8.

BOILED PEANUTS

MAKES ABOUT 4 CUPS

3 cups raw unsalted peanuts

2 lemons, sliced into ¼-inch-thick rounds

5 garlic cloves, thinly sliced

2 tablespoons minced ginger

2 tablespoons salt

½ teaspoon ground turmeric

½ teaspoon ground cayenne pepper

2 bay leaves

Fill a large pot with water and add all the ingredients. Bring to a boil over high heat, cover, and boil for 25 to 30 minutes, until the peanuts are soft but not mushy. (You may need to turn the heat down slightly so that the pot does not boil over.) Drain and set aside to cool. Remove and discard the lemon slices, garlic slices, and bay leaves. Served warm, these are a great snack on their own.

BOILED PEANUT CHOW-CHOW MAKES ABOUT 8 CUPS

Folks who have eaten at my house know that I am a fan, and even a collector, of condiments. This is very likely the result of growing up in a household where there were always a couple of chutneys and two or three pickles on the table at every meal.

One of my favorite "Southern" condiments is chow-chow, a kind of relish. There is some debate as to whether it is even Southern at all. I've heard that it might be from Pennsylvania, or that it made its way down to what is now Louisiana with the Acadians in the eighteenth century. All you and I need to know is that chow-chow is delicious and versatile.

Generally chow-chow is made with just vegetables. I have come across a couple of versions that incorporated field peas. I really like the texture and flavor the boiled peanuts provide. Chow-chow will last a long time in a sealed container in your fridge. It also makes a great gift, if you are inclined to give some away.

4 cups apple cider vinegar

½ cup turbinado sugar

2 teaspoons salt

4 or 5 whole cloves

2 teaspoons ground turmeric

2 teaspoons yellow mustard seeds

1 teaspoon coriander seeds

1 teaspoon celery seeds

1 teaspoon ground cayenne pepper

2 cups diced green tomatoes

1 cup diced sweet onion

½ cup diced red bell pepper

1 tablespoon minced jalapeño chile

2 cups shredded green cabbage

1½ cups Boiled Peanuts (page 174)

⅓ cup prepared yellow mustard (I use French's.)

¼ cup thinly sliced scallion greens

In a heavy-bottomed pot, heat the vinegar, sugar, and salt over medium heat, stirring frequently, until the sugar is completely dissolved. Continue to simmer until the liquid is reduced by half, 20 to 25 minutes. Stir in the cloves, turmeric, mustard seeds, coriander seeds, celery seeds, and cayenne and simmer for 5 minutes. Stir in the green tomatoes, onion, bell pepper, jalapeño, and cabbage. Raise the heat to medium-high and simmer for an additional 15 minutes. Stir in the boiled peanuts and prepared mustard. Remove from the heat and cool to room temperature. When cool, stir in the scallion greens. The chow-chow will keep in a covered container in the refrigerator for up to a month.

PEANUT CURRY SERVES 6

My maternal grandmother grew up in what is now Maharashtra. Her father, my great-grandfather, was a doctor who made frequent house calls to his patients in the countryside. Often, these families would send him home with homemade candy or milk or other edible treats.

When I was in my early teens, my uncle decided to grow peanuts on a small piece of land he had leased from a farmer friend. All the nieces and nephews were invited to celebrate the harvest—which meant that we were there to help with the hard work of digging the peanuts. After a long day, we returned to my grandmother's house to clean up and have supper.

That evening, predictably, peanuts featured heavily in the meal. Grandma made a peanut curry, which was new to my cousins and me. When we asked her about it, she told us about her father bringing back treats from his house calls when she was a young girl. It turns out that this peanut curry was one such treat. My uncle's first peanut harvest was the perfect occasion for her to revisit this dish. Decades later and halfway across the world, I thought of my grandmother's peanut curry when I developed this recipe. It calls for two kinds of peanuts for a pleasing contrast of textures.

In India, a curry like this would be part of a thali. You can also serve it as a vegetarian main dish with steamed rice or a flatbread such as chapati.

- 3 cups raw unsalted, shelled peanuts, skins removed
- 2 teaspoons salt, divided
- 1 cup roasted unsalted peanuts
- ½ teaspoon coriander seeds
- 2 tablespoons neutral oil, such as peanut or canola
- 2 teaspoons cumin seeds
- 1 sprig curry leaves (optional)
- 1 large red onion, minced (about 1¾ cups)
- 1 teaspoon garam masala (store-bought or homemade, page 8)
- ½ teaspoon ground turmeric
- ½ teaspoon ground cayenne pepper
- ½ cup canned full-fat coconut milk
- 2 teaspoons fresh lime juice
- ½ teaspoon light brown sugar
- ¼ cup chopped fresh cilantro leaves, for garnish
- 1 serrano chile, stemmed and thinly sliced, for garnish
- Steamed rice or flatbread, for serving

Fill a large pot with water and add the raw peanuts and 1 teaspoon salt. Bring to a boil over high heat, cover, and boil for 25 to 30 minutes, until the peanuts are soft but not mushy. (You may need to turn the heat down slightly so that the pot does not boil over.) Drain the peanuts, reserving 1½ cups boiling liquid.

Put the roasted peanuts in the bowl of a food processor and pulse until you have as fine a powder as possible. Set aside.

Toast the coriander seeds in a small, dry pan over medium heat, shaking the pan gently so that the seeds toast evenly and do not burn, until fragrant, about 2 minutes. Remove from the heat and, when cool enough to handle, grind in a spice grinder or coffee grinder, or with a mortar and pestle. Set aside.

Heat the oil in a Dutch oven or other heavy-bottomed pot over medium heat until shimmering. Add the cumin seeds and cook until fragrant, about 10 seconds. Add the curry leaves (if using) and onion. Reduce the heat to medium, cover, and cook until the onion is very soft, about 15 minutes. Stir in the garam masala, turmeric, cayenne, and ground coriander. Cook until the spices become fragrant and darken slightly, about 2 minutes. Add the roasted peanut powder and cook for 1 minute, stirring constantly. Slowly add the coconut milk and the liquid reserved from the boiled peanuts. Bring to a simmer and cook until you have a thick, gravy-like sauce, 5 to 7 minutes. Stir in the boiled peanuts, lime juice, sugar, and remaining 1 teaspoon salt. Cover and simmer for 5 more minutes.

Turn off the heat and allow the curry to sit for 5 to 6 minutes before serving so that it thickens up and the flavors have a chance to meld. Garnish each serving with chopped cilantro and serrano slices. Serve with rice or flatbread.

PEANUT-CRUSTED FISH SERVES 6

Spanish mackerel has a wonderful flavor, with a texture that's slightly oily and not too dense. In my opinion, it is underutilized compared to some of the more popular Gulf fish, like grouper and redfish. This recipe was a hit at Snackbar; we sold more mackerel when it was on the menu than I would have thought possible. It works just as well in a home kitchen—easy enough for a weeknight dinner, yet special enough for a dinner party. If you can't find Spanish mackerel, try black bass, trout, or drum.

In addition to fish, this crust works just as well with pork chops, duck breasts, or chicken breasts. It's fine to roughly chop the shallot, ginger, and chiles since you will be using a food processor to make the peanut crust.

You'll see that this recipe calls for crusting the skin side of the fish. With most fish, including mackerel, there's no reason not to eat the skin. However, this recipe will also work with skinless fish fillets. If you're able to tell which side had the skin, that's the side you should crust.

1 small shallot, roughly chopped

2-inch piece ginger, roughly chopped

2 Fresno or jalapeño chiles, stemmed and roughly chopped

12 to 14 mint leaves

6 to 8 sprigs cilantro, leaves and tender stems chopped

3 teaspoons light brown sugar, divided

Grated zest and juice of 2 limes

3 tablespoons fish sauce, divided

2 cups lightly salted roasted peanuts

6 (5- to 6-ounce) Spanish mackerel fillets

Salt

Freshly ground black pepper

4 large eggs

3 tablespoons neutral oil, such as peanut or canola

1 teaspoon Sriracha

Steamed rice, for serving

Combine the shallot, ginger, chiles, mint, cilantro, 1 teaspoon brown sugar, lime zest, and 1 tablespoon fish sauce in the bowl of a food processor and process to a paste. Add the roasted peanuts and pulse 8 to 10 times, until the peanuts are chopped evenly but not completely pulverized. Pour the mixture out onto a plate. Taste and add salt if desired, starting with ½ teaspoon.

Season each fish fillet with a pinch each of salt and pepper.

In a bowl, whisk the eggs with a pinch each of salt and pepper and the juice of ½ lime (about 1 tablespoon). Pour the egg mixture into a wide, shallow bowl or baking dish. From left to right on the counter to the left of the stove, line up the fish fillets, then the egg mixture, then the crust.

Heat the oil in a large nonstick pan or cast-iron skillet over high heat. When the oil is shimmering, take one fish fillet and dip the skin side in the egg mixture, then press the eggy side into the peanut crust. Carefully place the fish in the pan, crust-side down. Repeat with the remaining fillets. You may need to cook the fish in two batches depending on how wide your skillet is.

Cook the fish on the crust side for 3 minutes. Lower the heat to medium, gently flip the fillets, and cook for another 4 minutes, or until cooked through. The fish will flake easily all the way through when it is finished.

While the fish is cooking, whisk together the remaining 2 tablespoons fish sauce, remaining 2 teaspoons brown sugar, remaining 3 tablespoons lime juice, Sriracha, and a pinch of salt in a small bowl. Set aside.

Transfer the cooked fish to a serving platter and drizzle a spoonful of sauce over each fillet. Serve with steamed rice.

PEANUT SOUP SERVES 6

Dr. Jessica B. Harris's work has greatly contributed to our understanding of the foodways of the African diaspora in the Caribbean and the United States. I first saw her speak when I was a student in culinary school, and I was in awe of her commanding presence and the depth and breadth of her knowledge. Years later, I found her holding court at the City Grocery bar one evening during the Southern Foodways Alliance symposium in Oxford. Fortified by rum, I was finally brave enough to strike up a conversation. I've considered Dr. Harris a friend and mentor ever since.

It's her recipe for West African peanut stew that inspired this soup. From her book *High on the Hog*, I learned that peanuts were a staple in West African cuisine, just as they had been in my native Gujarat. I combined Jessica's recipe for peanut stew with elements of my mother's dal as a way to honor two women who have taught me so much.

2 teaspoons coriander seeds

2 teaspoons cumin seeds

3 tablespoons neutral oil, such as peanut or canola

1 large yellow or white onion, minced (1½ to 1¾ cups)

2 tablespoons minced ginger

2 tablespoons minced garlic

2 tablespoons tomato paste

1 cup raw unsalted peanuts

1 small sweet potato, peeled and diced (about 1½ cups)

1 habanero pepper, stemmed, seeded if desired, and minced

1 teaspoon hot paprika

1 teaspoon ground turmeric

½ teaspoon ground cayenne pepper

8 cups unsalted vegetable stock, Chicken Bone Stock (page 247), or store-bought unsalted chicken stock

1 cup canned full-fat coconut milk

½ cup good-quality creamy peanut butter (preferably an all-natural peanut butter with no added salt or sugar)

1½ teaspoons salt

1 tablespoon fresh lime juice, plus lime wedges, for serving

1 cup roasted salted peanuts, chopped, for garnish

Toast the coriander seeds in a small, dry pan over medium heat for about 1 minute. Add the cumin seeds and toast, shaking the pan gently so that the seeds toast evenly and do not burn, until both spices are fragrant, about 1 more minute. Remove from the heat and, when cool enough to handle, grind in a spice grinder or coffee grinder, or with a mortar and pestle.

Heat the oil in a Dutch oven or other wide, heavy-bottomed pot over medium-high heat until shimmering. Add the onion and cook until translucent, 5 to 6 minutes. Add the ginger and garlic and cook until fragrant, 2 to 3 minutes. Stir in the tomato paste and cook for an additional 2 to 3 minutes, until the tomato paste becomes a few shades darker in color. Stir in the peanuts, sweet potato, habanero, coriander and cumin mixture, paprika, turmeric, and cayenne. Add the stock, stirring to scrape up any bits of tomato paste that may have stuck to the bottom of the pot.

Lower the heat to medium or medium-low, cover, and simmer until the peanuts are very soft and the sweet potato is falling apart, 15 to 20 minutes. In a bowl, whisk together the coconut milk, peanut butter, and ¼ cup hot liquid from the pot to create a thick slurry. Pour this mixture in the pot and stir to incorporate. Cover and simmer for another 15 minutes. Add the salt and lime juice. Stir and taste, adjusting the seasonings to your liking.

Blend the soup with a hand-held immersion blender until smooth. If you do not have an immersion blender, you can blend the soup in batches in a regular blender.

Ladle into bowls and garnish each serving with chopped roasted peanuts. Serve with lime wedges on the side for squeezing as desired.

PEANUT CHIKKI MAKES ABOUT TWELVE 2-INCH SQUARES

In Gujarat, peanut and sesame seed chikkis are especially common around Uttarayan, a winter festival celebrated by flying kites and eating lots of good food. Traditionally, cooks in India begin with raw peanuts, then roast them and remove the peanut skins. I cheat and use roasted lightly salted peanuts partly because I am lazy and partly because I like how the slight saltiness plays with the minerally sweetness of the jaggery. Do seek out jaggery for this recipe rather than substituting regular sugar. Most Indian markets sell jaggery in blocks as well as in powder form. For the quantity called for in this recipe, it's much easier to work with the powder. And be forewarned: Once you've tried peanut chikki, a Snickers bar will never taste quite as good. Forget about regular peanut brittle.

You need a candy thermometer to make this recipe. You will cook the syrup to the hard ball stage, or 255°F to 265°F. If the syrup gets too hot, the brittle will be far too hard, and I can't be responsible for your dentist bill. If it is not hot enough, the chikki will be too soft. My mother and aunts never used a candy thermometer. Instead, they would drop a few drops of the hot syrup into a bowl of cold water. If it sank and solidified into a brittle ball, the jaggery was at the right (hard ball) stage. If you make candy often, or if you learned how to do so from an elder like your grandmother, you may know the same trick. Otherwise, rely on the thermometer.

¾ cup jaggery

2 teaspoons ghee (store-bought or homemade, page 9)

1 cup lightly salted roasted peanuts

½ teaspoon cardamom seeds, crushed (Crush enough green cardamom pods to yield ½ teaspoon of seeds—about 3 pods. Then, crush the seeds themselves with a mortar and pestle.)

Line a sheet pan with parchment and grease lightly with cooking spray, butter, or neutral oil. Don't skip this step; if you do, it will be extremely difficult to remove the chikki from the pan.

Combine the jaggery, ghee, and 1 tablespoon water in a stainless steel pot and attach a candy thermometer. Heat over medium-low heat. The jaggery will melt and start bubbling away. Watch the thermometer. When it reaches 260°F, gently stir in the peanuts and cardamom using a wooden spoon. Make sure all the peanuts are evenly coated with the syrup. Carefully pour the mixture onto the prepared sheet pan. Lay another piece of parchment on top and, while the mixture is still hot and pliable, roll it out with a rolling pin to a uniform thickness of about ¼ inch. Remove the top parchment and score the brittle with a sharp knife or rolling pizza cutter, making 2-inch squares. You want to cut most of the way through, but not all the way down to the pan. Allow the brittle to completely cool and set before breaking it into squares. Store in an airtight container at room temperature for up to a week.

AUSTIN'S NESHOBA COUNTY FAIR PEANUT PIE

SERVES 8

There is a lot of turnover in the restaurant business, especially in a small college town like ours. Once in a while, we get an employee we hope will never leave—someone whose talent and drive raises the bar in the kitchen and motivates all their colleagues to be better. Our former pastry chef Austin Agent was one such person.

Austin got off to a rocky start in the Snackbar kitchen. He was impatient, and his desserts didn't always complement the rest of the menu. We weren't sure he would last very long. Then, seemingly overnight, he found his groove and turned our pastry program around. Austin discovered that there was great value in the recipes and techniques he had learned from his grandmother in Neshoba County, Mississippi. You don't see this much anymore, but farmers and laborers across the region used to purchase a bottle of cola (Coke, Pepsi, or RC) and a sleeve of salted peanuts at convenience stores or farm commissaries. They'd pour the peanuts into the soda and drink it, crunching the peanuts as they sipped. The snack was cheap and portable, and provided an energy-boosting hit of sugar, salt, caffeine, and protein. I borrow Austin's inventive reimagining of this iconic working-class snack here, and remain sad that he left Snackbar in 2019 for Las Vegas. This recipe works well with a homemade or store-bought pie crust.

2 (12-ounce) cans cola

1 (9-inch) pie crust (store-bought or homemade, page 101)

1½ cups lightly salted roasted peanuts

3 large eggs

1 cup light corn syrup

1 cup granulated sugar

2 tablespoons melted unsalted butter

1 teaspoon pure vanilla extract

½ teaspoon ground cayenne pepper

Salt

Vanilla ice cream, for serving

Pour the cola into a saucepan on the stove. Wait for the bubbles to subside, then turn the heat to low. Slowly reduce the cola to a syrup, stirring occasionally, 30 to 40 minutes. You want to end up with about ½ cup thick syrup. Remove the pan from the heat. If you have more than ½ cup syrup, reserve the excess for drizzling on top of the finished pie.

Preheat the oven to 350°F.

If using homemade pie crust, roll the dough between two sheets of parchment or waxed paper to a 10-inch circle about ⅛ inch thick. Fit the circle into a 9-inch pie pan.

Spread the peanuts in an even layer in the bottom of the pie shell.

In a large mixing bowl, lightly beat the eggs. Add the corn syrup, cola syrup, sugar, butter, vanilla, cayenne, and a pinch of salt in a large mixing bowl. Stir well to combine.

Spoon or gently pour the filling mixture into the pie shell. You want the peanut layer to remain intact at the bottom.

Bake on the center rack of the oven for 60 to 70 minutes, until the top is just set. Allow to rest for 20 to 25 minutes.

To serve, cut the pie in eight slices. Drizzle each slice with reserved cola syrup if you have it and serve with a scoop of vanilla ice cream.

CHAPTER NINE GREENS

My relationship with greens is a late-blooming love story.

As a child, I didn't like greens. My parents, however, loved them. Every winter, spinach, mustards, kohlrabi, fenugreek, and occasionally collards would show up on the table. The arrival of greens generally coincided with that of some of my favorite vegetables: peas, eggplant, cabbage, and cauliflower. My mother would employ a parenting strategy that must be universal: I had to eat my greens first, and then I could have a serving of what I really wanted.

As I grew older, I developed a liking for some greens, especially a dish my mother used to make with split moong (mung) beans and spinach. Around the same time, I discovered that our Punjabi neighbor cooked mustard greens that were nothing like my mother's. Hers were rich with butter and seasoned with onions and ginger. I began to understand that ingredients can bridge divides of geography and culture. Our neighbors were from a different region and spoke a different language, yet our kitchens had something in common.

When we moved to France in my late teens, I came across kale, chard, and escarole—greens I had never seen in India. I tasted French salad with arugula and frisée, and hearty Italian minestra with greens and beans.

By the time I moved to Kentucky, I knew my turnips from my mustards. And I had developed a full-blown addiction to collards, their slight bitterness giving way to sweetness. On coming to Mississippi, I discovered gas station cafés that served simple, satisfying plate lunches. Greens of some sort were always on offer. I saw how their appeal transcended differences of race, class, and culture. That is when the light bulb went on for me: Dishes including greens were born of thrift. They are hardy, cheap, and nutritious. This is as true in Gujarat and Punjab as it is in France and Mississippi. The better I understood greens, the more I came to love them, and to love cooking them. They are a humble reminder of homes both old and new.

NOTE: When a recipe calls for sliced or chopped sturdy greens such as collards, I remove the stems as well as the tough, woody part of the rib toward the bottom of each leaf. At the restaurant, we sometimes add those ribs to stocks. And sometimes we dice and pickle the stems, as you can do using the recipe in this chapter (page 196). Always wash, rinse, and drain greens thoroughly to remove soil and sand before proceeding with a recipe.

CABBAGE, KALE, CARROT, AND PEANUT SALAD SERVES 6 TO 8

Even though I grew up in a vegetarian household, we never really ate salads. My mother did serve kachumber, a common preparation of fresh vegetables that falls somewhere between a relish, a salsa, and a chopped salad. Her version included carrots, cucumbers, and sometimes beets and radish, dressed with lemon juice and garnished with chopped peanuts. But until we moved to France, and then the United States, we were unfamiliar with lettuce-based salads. Then, all of a sudden, as vegetarians in omnivorous lands, we couldn't escape them. I quickly grew to love salads, and I was delighted by the sheer variety of lettuces available.

Still, from time to time, I missed the texture and flavor of my mother's kachumber. So a few years ago, I set out to recreate it, with a few twists inspired by the autumn offerings at our local farmers' market. I use kale because I have come to like it as an adult, and cabbage because that is what I grew up with. If you prefer, you can substitute thinly sliced Brussels sprouts for the cabbage. The Honeycrisp apple adds a tart-sweet crunch.

This is a great dish if you are looking for something raw, crunchy, and fresh to make in the late fall or early winter. Serve it as a first course or as a light accompaniment to a hearty cold-weather dish such as Pork Indad (page 281).

FOR THE DRESSING:

3 tablespoons canola oil

1 teaspoon brown mustard seeds

⅓ cup fresh lime juice

1 tablespoon light brown sugar

1 teaspoon salt

1 teaspoon chaat masala (store-bought or homemade, page 8)

FOR THE SALAD:

2 cups thinly sliced green or red cabbage (about ½ small head)

2 cups thinly sliced kale, such as Lacinato or Red Russian (Do not use the curly kind.)

2 cups carrots, peeled and cut into matchsticks (3 or 4 carrots)

1 small red onion, thinly sliced

1 Honeycrisp or other tart-sweet apple, unpeeled, cored, and cut into matchsticks

⅓ cup chopped fresh cilantro leaves and tender stems

⅓ cup chopped fresh mint leaves

1 jalapeño chile, stemmed and minced

1 cup chopped roasted peanuts

1 small to medium beet, peeled and shredded (about ½ cup; optional)

First, make the dressing. Heat the oil in a small skillet over medium-high heat. Once the oil is shimmering, add the mustard seeds and cook until they start popping, about 30 seconds. Remove the pan from the heat and allow the oil to cool completely. Once the oil has cooled, whisk it together with the lime juice, brown sugar, salt, and chaat masala, until the sugar and salt are completely dissolved. Set the dressing aside while you chop the salad components. If you are making the dressing in advance, allow it to cool completely before storing it in a covered container in the refrigerator.

In a large bowl, combine all of the salad ingredients except the beet, if using. Give everything a toss to combine. Pour in the dressing and toss again. Allow the dressed salad to sit for 15 minutes before serving so that the flavors meld and the cabbage and kale soften slightly. If using the beet, toss it in just before serving to avoid turning the whole salad purple.

AFGHAN-STYLE SPINACH WITH DILL AND CILANTRO SERVES 6

My senior year in college, I became friends with a Turkish classmate named Oksuz Celebi, whose family had lived and traveled all over the world thanks to his father's job with the United Nations. Over our spring break, we traveled to Washington, DC, to visit some friends of his family. The Durranis were Afghan and, like the Celebis, had traveled and worked all over the world. Mr. Durrani, it turned out, had done some of his schooling in India and had worked for a time in Delhi. His Hindi was better than mine. On the first night of our visit, while Mr. Durrani entertained us, Mrs. Durrani, her daughter, and their housekeeper were busy in the kitchen cooking up an Afghan feast.

Of the many wonderful dishes we enjoyed that night, I was blown away by the spinach. It had been cooked long and slow, concentrating its flavors. The pleasantly bitter taste of the spinach itself was complemented by brightly herbal dill and the tangy funk of cilantro. This was spinach as I had never known it before. It showed me what spinach could be.

This recipe, which makes an elegant side for a dinner party, calls for 3 pounds of fresh spinach, which is going to look like a lot before it cooks. Trust me, you will need all of it.

1 tablespoon coriander seeds

1 teaspoon fennel seeds

⅓ cup olive oil

4 bunches scallions, chopped

1 tablespoon minced garlic

1 teaspoon ground fenugreek seeds

3 pounds fresh, tender spinach (large stems removed, if any)

3 cups unsalted vegetable stock, Chicken Bone Stock (page 247), or store-bought unsalted chicken stock, divided

¾ cup chopped fresh cilantro leaves and tender stems

¼ cup chopped fresh dill or 1 tablespoon dried dill (may be labeled dill weed)

3 tablespoons fresh lemon juice

1 teaspoon honey

2 teaspoons salt

1½ teaspoons cracked black pepper

Toast the coriander seeds in a small, dry pan over medium heat for about 1 minute. Add the fennel seeds and toast, shaking the pan gently so that the seeds toast evenly and do not burn, until both spices are fragrant, about 1 more minute. Remove from the heat and, when cool enough to handle, grind in a spice grinder or coffee grinder, or with a mortar and pestle. Set aside.

Heat the oil in a Dutch oven or other wide, heavy-bottomed pot over low heat. Add the scallions and garlic and cook, stirring occasionally, until the scallions are very soft, 6 to 8 minutes. Add the fenugreek and stir. Begin adding the spinach in batches, stirring and adding handfuls as it wilts. Once all the spinach has been added, stir in the coriander-fennel mixture and 1½ cups stock. Cover the pot and cook for 15 to 20 minutes, until the spinach is very tender. Remove the lid and stir in the cilantro, dill, and remaining 1½ cups stock. Cook uncovered for 12 to 15 minutes, until most of the liquid has evaporated. The cooked spinach should look smooth, almost melted. Stir in the lemon juice, honey, salt, and pepper. Serve hot.

KALE (OR CHARD) FRITTERS MAKES 25 TO 30 FRITTERS

By now you have probably figured out that I like frying things. I blame this vice on my Gujarati childhood—almost all of our savory snacks are fried, and I love all of them. Every Gujarati I know can wax nostalgic about eating fritters by the roadside with a cuppa chai as the rain clouds roll in. My favorite of these fried concoctions were methi na bhajiya—fritters made with fresh fenugreek leaves. Fresh fenugreek leaves are not readily available in the States, so I substitute whatever greens I have on hand. Kale or Swiss chard will offer that ideal hint of bitterness.

You would not find cheese in a traditional Gujarati fritter, but I love the slight creaminess and the salty tang of cheddar. (Omit the cheese if you prefer a vegan fritter.)

These fritters make a great snack or finger food for a party—this recipe will serve a small crowd of 6 to 8. They are also an excellent accompaniment for Stewed Gujarati-Style Black-Eyed Peas (page 49).

2 cups chickpea flour

¾ cup cornmeal (a coarse grind works best)

1 teaspoon crushed coriander seeds (Crush whole seeds with a mortar and pestle or coarsely grind in a coffee grinder. For this recipe, there is no need to toast the seeds.)

1 teaspoon ajwain seeds

1 teaspoon salt

½ teaspoon ground cayenne pepper

½ teaspoon sugar

½ teaspoon baking soda

Pinch asafoetida

1 tablespoon minced ginger

1 cup shredded sharp white cheddar cheese

2 cups finely chopped kale or chard (from 1 bunch)

2 cups neutral oil, such as peanut or canola

Chaat masala (store-bought or homemade, page 8), for sprinkling

In a large bowl, mix the chickpea flour, cornmeal, crushed coriander seeds, ajwain seeds, salt, cayenne, sugar, baking soda, and asafoetida. Add 1 cup water and whisk until you have a smooth paste. Fold in the ginger, cheese, and greens. Mix well, making sure that all the greens are evenly covered in the batter. If the mixture is too dry or stiff, add water a tablespoon at a time. The batter should be thick and dense but still spoonable.

Heat the oil to 350°F in a Dutch oven, cast-iron skillet, or electric fryer. If you don't have a deep-fry thermometer, drop in a small spoonful of batter to test the temperature. If it sizzles and floats to the top, your oil is ready. If it sinks to the bottom of the pot, the oil still needs to heat up more. If the oil is too hot, your batter will burn on the outside while the center of the fritter will be raw. In that case, lower the heat and wait a couple of minutes before you start to fry a batch.

While the oil is heating, line a large plate with paper towels and set it near the stove.

Gently drop tablespoon-size balls of batter in the oil, five or six fritters at a time, being careful not to let the hot oil splash you. Cook the fritters for 1 to 1½ minutes, turning with a slotted spoon so that they cook evenly. On the first batch, you might want to break open one of the fritters to make sure it is cooked all the way through before taking the rest out of the oil. Transfer the cooked fritters to the paper towel–lined plate and sprinkle immediately with chaat masala. When all of the fritters from the first batch are finished, let the oil temperature return to 350°F before adding more. Repeat until you have used all of the batter. Transfer the fritters to a platter and serve immediately.

COLLARD GREENS GARNI SERVES 6 TO 8

This dish is loosely inspired by Alsatian choucroute garni, the hearty winter staple of cabbage and sausage. Although I spent a year in Strasbourg with my parents when I was eighteen, I had never tried choucroute garni until I returned to the Alsace region with Teresa a few years ago. When we got back home, I developed this dish for the menu at Snackbar as a way to transplant the tastes of Alsace to the American South. Spicy, sweet, tart, and rich at once, it makes a satisfying one-pot meal and is even better with a pan of cornbread on the side.

Feel free to substitute another hardy green such as kale or chard for the collards.

- 4 tablespoons (½ stick) unsalted butter
- 1 cup chopped bacon (about 6 thick-cut strips)
- 1 large yellow onion, thinly sliced from root to tip
- 1 tablespoon minced garlic
- 1 cup thickly sliced andouille or other spicy sausage
- 3 pounds collard greens (about 5 small bunches), stems and tough ribs removed, leaves finely chopped
- 1 cup Chicken Bone Stock (page 247) or store-bought unsalted chicken bone stock
- 3 cups peeled and sliced peaches, pears, or apples
- 3 tablespoons apple cider vinegar
- 2 teaspoons salt
- 1 teaspoon red pepper flakes
- 1 teaspoon brown sugar
- 2 tablespoons fresh thyme leaves

Melt the butter in a Dutch oven or other wide, heavy-bottomed pot over medium-high heat. Add the chopped bacon and render until it is crispy, 3 to 5 minutes. Add the onion and garlic and cook, stirring, until the onion is very soft, about 8 minutes. Stir in the andouille, greens, and stock. Turn the heat down to medium, cover, and cook for 8 to 10 minutes, until the greens are beginning to soften. Stir in the peaches, vinegar, salt, red pepper flakes, and brown sugar. If the mixture is at a full boil, turn the heat down to low. Cover and cook for another 8 to 10 minutes, until the peaches are soft and the greens are cooked through. Stir in the thyme leaves. Taste and adjust for salt as needed before serving.

NOTE: Since this is a fall-winter dish, pears or apples might be easier to find than peaches. But preserved peaches (*not* in syrup!), which we keep on hand at Snackbar, complement the flavors wonderfully. I've even made this dish at home with frozen sliced peaches with excellent results.

COLLARD GREEN SLAW SERVES 6 TO 8

I have served this slaw time and again for a decade, and it is always a hit. The thinly sliced collards make for an unexpected and flavorful twist on cabbage slaw, and the dressing hits all the right notes: acidic, creamy, spicy, and sweet. It is an easy recipe to put together, perfect for a potluck.

Two important things to remember when making this are to cut the collards as thin as you can and to use your hands to mix in the dressing, massaging and bruising the collard leaves. This technique, along with letting the dressed slaw sit before serving, will allow the dressing to stick to the collards and help break them up so that they aren't tough to chew. If you like kale salads, you might already be familiar with this technique. It works equally well for collards and other sturdy, leafy greens.

FOR THE DRESSING:

⅓ cup apple cider vinegar

¼ cup mayonnaise (preferably Duke's)

2 tablespoons Creole or other grainy mustard

1 tablespoon sorghum syrup, maple syrup, or cane syrup

1 tablespoon hot sauce

2 teaspoons paprika

1 teaspoon celery seed

1 teaspoon salt

1 teaspoon freshly ground black pepper

FOR THE SLAW:

¾ cup chopped pecans

2 cups chiffonade collard green leaves (about ½ bunch; remove the tough stems before slicing the leaves)

2 cups thinly sliced green or red cabbage (about ½ small head)

2 medium shallots, thinly sliced from root to tip (½ to ⅔ cup)

First, make the dressing: Whisk together all the dressing ingredients in a small bowl. If making in advance, store the dressing in a covered container in the refrigerator until ready to use.

Toast the pecans in a small, dry skillet over medium heat until fragrant, 2 to 3 minutes, shaking the pan gently so that the nuts toast evenly and do not burn. Remove from the heat and allow to cool to room temperature.

Combine the collards, cabbage, shallots, and pecans in a large bowl. Pour the dressing over the slaw and mix vigorously with your hands. Taste and season with a pinch more salt and/or pepper, if desired.

Allow the slaw to stand for 30 minutes before serving.

SAAG-STYLE COLLARDS SERVES 4 TO 5

If you have ever eaten at an Indian buffet, there is a good chance you have had saag, a generic Hindi word for greens. Too often, at Indian restaurants in the United States, it translates as little more than overcooked spinach. A few years ago, when my good friend Meherwan Irani invited me to cook with him for a video segment at the *Southern Living* test kitchen, we decided to make a proper saag. Since we were in Birmingham, Alabama, we used readily available collard greens. We served our saag with Meherwan's makki ki roti for a play on greens and cornbread—as fine a Southern lunch as you can have.

This recipe calls for two ingredients that might be new to you: amchur (dried mango powder) and mustard oil. Both are available at Indian grocery stores, or you can order them online.

1 teaspoon coriander seeds

½ teaspoon cumin seeds

2 tablespoons ghee (store-bought or homemade, page 9)

2 cups minced yellow onion (1 to 1½ large onions)

1 tablespoon minced ginger

1½ teaspoons minced garlic

1 tablespoon tomato paste

2¼ teaspoons garam masala (store-bought or homemade, page 8)

¼ teaspoon ground turmeric

2½ pounds collard greens, tough ribs and stems removed, leaves finely chopped (8 to 10 cups, from about 2 bunches)

1½ teaspoons salt

1 cup heavy cream

1 teaspoon mustard seed oil or peanut oil

½ teaspoon amchur (dried mango powder)

½ teaspoon sugar

Toast the coriander seeds in a small, dry pan over medium heat for about 1 minute. Add the cumin seeds and toast, shaking the pan gently so that the seeds toast evenly and do not burn, until both spices are fragrant, about 1 more minute. Remove from the heat and, when cool enough to handle, crush with a mortar and pestle or grind coarsely in a spice grinder or coffee grinder. Set aside.

Heat the ghee in a Dutch oven or other wide, heavy-bottomed pot over medium-low heat until fragrant, 1 to 2 minutes. Add the onions and cook, stirring occasionally, until they are caramelized, about 20 minutes. Cooking the onions low and slow until they caramelize is the key to this recipe; be patient and do not rush this step. You are looking for most of the liquid to cook out and for the onions to take on a caramel-brown color. They will break down to more of a paste consistency than individual pieces.

Once the onions have caramelized, add the ginger and garlic and cook, stirring, for 3 to 4 minutes. Add the tomato paste, stir, and cook for 3 to 4 minutes more. Stir in the crushed coriander and cumin, garam masala, and turmeric and cook for 2 to 3 more minutes, until fragrant. Add ¾ cup water and stir, scraping up any bits that may have stuck to the bottom. At this point, you should have a richly fragrant brown paste in the bottom of the pot. Stir in the greens and salt. Mix very well to coat the greens in the onion and spice paste. Turn the heat down to low, cover, and cook until the greens have begun to soften and are no longer crunchy, about 20 minutes. They will wilt and reduce substantially. Stir in the cream, cover, and cook for 8 to 10 minutes, until the cream has thickened and the greens are cooked through. You may need to add a touch more water if the greens appear too dry. Stir in the mustard oil, amchur, and sugar. Taste and season with additional salt if needed. Indian restaurants in the United States often serve a very smooth saag. If you prefer that smooth texture, blend the greens with an immersion blender before serving. (I do not blend my saag.) Serve hot.

STEWED TURNIP GREENS AND ROOTS WITH MUSTARD SEEDS, GINGER, AND LEMON

SERVES 6 TO 8

I use the humble turnip often, especially in the winter, when we get beautiful ones from our friends at Native Son Farm in nearby Tupelo, Mississippi. I'm certainly not the first to cook turnip greens and roots together, but it's less common than you might think. I suspect this is because the bulbs last much longer than the greens, so traditionally, home cooks would have cooked the greens first and stored the bulbs for later use in roasts and stews. If your local farmers' market operates year-round, you'll be able to find turnips with the greens attached during the winter season. If not, look for the greens and the bulbs near each other at the grocery store.

This technique will work for most root vegetables with edible greens, like radishes, kohlrabi, or even beets. I like to serve these with a Simple Herb and Lemon Roasted Chicken (page 248) for a humble, hearty winter supper. This dish also pairs well with Grilled Pork Tenderloin with Tandoori Spices (page 273).

Because the whole point is to use the greens attached to the turnips, you'll have a lot more turnip than greens in this recipe. If you love turnip greens, feel free to add an extra bunch, or even two, to even out the ratio of turnips to greens (there is no need to adjust anything else if you do this).

8 medium turnips (2 to 2½ pounds) with greens attached, or 8 medium turnips and 2 bunches of turnip greens

2 tablespoons neutral oil, such as peanut or canola

1 tablespoon brown mustard seeds

2 to 3 dried chiles de árbol, stemmed and broken in half

2-inch piece ginger, minced (2 heaping tablespoons)

6 to 8 garlic cloves, thinly sliced

2 teaspoons chopped fresh rosemary

½ teaspoon ground turmeric

2 to 3 cups Chicken Bone Stock (page 247) or store-bought unsalted chicken stock

2 teaspoons salt

Grated zest and juice of 2 lemons

Cut the greens from the turnip roots. Wash, peel, and dice the roots into ½-inch pieces. Chop and wash the greens thoroughly, discarding the hard, woody part of the stems and ribs.

Heat the oil in a Dutch oven or other wide, heavy-bottomed pot over medium heat. Once the oil is shimmering, add the mustard seeds and cook until they start popping, about 30 seconds. Add the diced turnips and cook until they begin to brown slightly, 4 to 5 minutes. Stir in the dried chiles, ginger, garlic, rosemary, and turmeric. Add the greens and stock (use more or less stock depending on how soupy you like the finished dish). Give everything a stir, then lower the heat, cover, and cook until the turnips are just soft and the greens are wilted and bright green, 10 to 12 minutes. Stir in the salt, lemon zest, and lemon juice. Cover again and cook for 5 minutes more, until the turnips are tender but not mushy.

KASHMIRI-STYLE COLLARDS (Haaq)

SERVES 8 AS A SIDE DISH OR 4 AS A MAIN COURSE

Haaq is Kashmiri for greens, and it most often refers to collards. I have a vivid memory of eating this dish for the first time at age seven or eight. My father had a Kashmiri Hindu student named Dhar, and a colleague of his in the physics department had a Kashmiri Muslim student named Haq. Dhar and Haq often came to our house for dinner. Normally, when they joined us for a meal, Mom would cook her usual Gujarati dishes. But on this particular day when I came home from school, Uncle Dhar and Uncle Haq were sitting at the table on either side of my mother with a pile of greens between them.

Dhar explained to my mother that his Hindu family seasoned their greens with asafoetida. Haq said that his Muslim family used shallots and garlic, and sometimes his mother added kohlrabi greens to the collards. That evening we had haaq for dinner with steamed basmati rice.

We opened Snackbar in April 2009, soon after my mother passed away. Around that same time, the Kashmir region, which is no stranger to conflict and tragedy, suffered an earthquake. As excited as I was about the new restaurant, I was feeling down. When a farmer showed up at the back door that morning to deliver a box of young, tender collard greens, I decided to make haaq for that evening's special. Drawing on the happy memory of Dar and Haq at my family's table, I prepared a version that combined both Kashmiri traditions. Now, I cook these often as a reminder that a simple recipe has the power to bring us together and that food is a great way to build bridges and break down barriers.

Haaq is as flavorful as it is easy to prepare. Serve it as a side dish or eat it as a simple vegetarian meal with steamed rice.

3 tablespoons ghee (store-bought or homemade, page 9)

1 tablespoon cumin seeds

3 or 4 dried chiles de árbol, stemmed

1½ teaspoons asafoetida

2 tablespoons minced ginger

3 small shallots, thinly sliced from root to tip

5 garlic cloves, sliced very thin

5 bunches tender collard greens (4 to 5 pounds), stemmed, washed, and torn into bite-size pieces

2 teaspoons salt

1 teaspoon light brown sugar

1 teaspoon fresh lemon juice

Heat the ghee in a Dutch oven or other wide, heavy-bottomed pot over medium heat until fragrant, 1 to 1½ minutes. Add the cumin seeds and cook for 30 seconds. Stir in the dried chiles and asafoetida. Add the ginger, then the shallots, then the garlic, stirring well with each addition. Reduce the heat to low, cover, and cook until the shallots are just beginning to brown, 3 to 4 minutes. Add 2 cups water, the greens, salt, brown sugar, and lemon juice and stir to mix well. Cover and cook for 20 minutes, or until the greens are tender. Serve hot.

PICKLED COLLARD GREEN STEMS MAKES 1½ QUARTS

I learned this technique from my friend Todd Richards, who has a recipe for pickled collard green stems in his wonderful cookbook, *Soul*. It reminded me of how my mother always found a way to use every part of the vegetable in our kitchen when I was growing up.

Inspired by Todd, and my mother, I developed my own version of pickled collard green stems, which get an extra element of sweet-tart crunch from the addition of Granny Smith apple. These pickled collard stems add a nice bright flavor to relishes and slaws, or can be served on their own as a condiment. The recipe works just as well with mustard green stems. Next time you find yourself wondering what to do with the stems after you have trimmed a mess of greens, take the time to make this easy pickle. You will be glad you did.

4 cups diced (½-inch) tender collard stems (4 to 5 bunches)

1 cup diced (½-inch) Granny Smith apple

2 cups apple cider vinegar

¾ cup apple juice

¼ cup thinly sliced garlic (8 to 10 cloves)

¼ cup light brown sugar

1 tablespoon salt

1 teaspoon ground cayenne pepper

1 tablespoon coriander seeds

6 whole cloves

3 bay leaves

2 teaspoons hot sauce

Bring a large pot of salted water to a boil over high heat. While the water is heating, fill a large bowl with cold water and ice cubes. When the water boils, add the collard stems. After 1 minute, transfer the stems to the ice bath. Drain and pat dry. This blanching and shocking step cooks out some of the toughness of the stems and sets the color. Mix the collard stems with the diced apple in a large nonreactive bowl; set aside.

Combine the vinegar, apple juice, garlic, brown sugar, salt, cayenne, coriander seeds, cloves, bay leaves, and hot sauce in a medium saucepan and bring to a boil over high heat. Once the sugar and salt are completely dissolved, remove the pan from the heat and let cool for 5 minutes. Pour the liquid over the stems and apple and stir to combine. Allow the mixture to cool completely, then store in an airtight container in the refrigerator. The pickled stems will keep in the refrigerator for about 2 weeks.

MUSTARD GREEN AND FIELD PEA MINESTRA

SERVES 4 TO 6 AS A MAIN COURSE

Here in Mississippi, it might be November before the weather turns pleasantly cool and crisp. When it finally does, there is nothing I would rather have for supper than a steaming-hot bowl of soup, a piece of hearty bread for sopping, and perhaps a nice glass of wine. I developed this soup one fall to feed a delegation of Italian guests who were traveling through Mississippi to study blues music and Southern literature. I wanted something that would be familiar to them, yet rooted in Mississippi. I came up with this warming, filling soup, which plays on Italian minestra but employs a quintessentially Southern combination of peas and greens.

I prefer the spiciness of mustard greens here, but feel free to use whatever greens you like. Swiss chard works well, as does escarole. Since I make this soup in the fall or winter, I use dried peas. I use the smallest variety I can find, such as lady peas or crowder peas, because they cook faster. Black-eyed peas are easy to find and also work well. Remember to soak the peas the day before you plan to make the soup.

If you're an omnivore who finds yourself stumped when feeding vegan or vegetarian guests, this is a great solution. It pairs especially well with a piece of crusty bread drizzled with good olive oil.

- 3 cups dried field peas
- 2 tablespoons olive oil
- 1 large yellow or white onion, thinly sliced from root to tip
- 2 cups peeled, diced carrots
- 2 cups diced celery
- ¼ cup thinly sliced garlic (8 to 10 cloves)
- 12 cups unsalted vegetable stock
- 4 cups chopped mustard greens (2 to 3 bunches)
- 2 tablespoons balsamic vinegar
- 1½ tablespoons chopped fresh rosemary
- 1 tablespoon salt
- 1 tablespoon red pepper flakes

Put the dried peas in a bowl or pot and add enough water to cover them by 1 to 2 inches. Cover the bowl with a kitchen towel or plate and let the peas soak overnight at room temperature. When ready to begin cooking, drain the peas, rinse them, and drain again. Set aside.

Heat the oil in a Dutch oven or stockpot over medium-high heat. Add the onion and cook until it starts to sweat, about 6 minutes. Add the carrots, celery, and garlic. Cook, stirring occasionally, until the onion starts to turn golden, 8 to 9 minutes. Add the soaked peas and stock, cover, and simmer over low heat until the peas are just beginning to soften, 12 to 15 minutes. Stir in the greens, vinegar, rosemary, salt, and red pepper flakes, cover, and cook until the peas are cooked through and the greens are soft, 10 to 12 minutes. Taste and adjust the seasonings, if desired, before serving.

CHAPTER TEN

SHRIMP

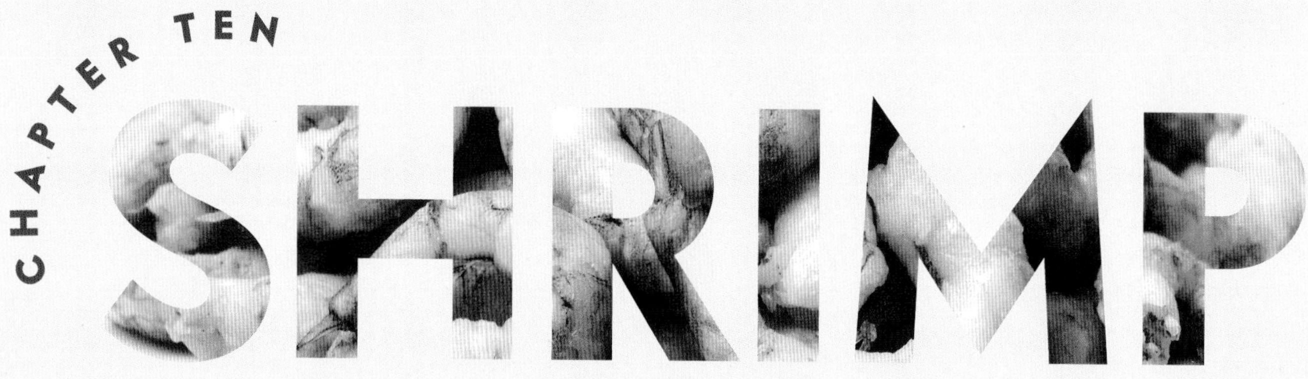

My mother's hometown of Jafarabad, Gujarat, is on the Arabian Sea. To visit her relatives, we took a long bus ride from Ahmedabad, much of it along the coast.

The bus passed through old fishing towns and villages. In the summer, the small fishing villages would smell pungent with shrimp and fish that were drying by the beach or on rooftops. They would be stored in preparation for monsoon season, when the rains came, the seas got rough, and all fishing stopped for four months.

Jafarabad itself had a fairly large community of fisherfolk and shrimpers called Kharvas. Almost all were Muslim, many of Yemeni or Abyssinian descent. They were and are hard-working folks. When we visited, my grandparents would often hire a boat to take us out to a nearby island for a picnic. Sometimes, if my grandmother (a strict vegetarian) was not sailing with us, the captain would pull out shrimp or bait fish from their hold and allow me to feed the seagulls that inevitably followed the boat.

Most of the shrimpers working on the Gulf Coast today are of Vietnamese descent. They are immigrants, or the children (in some cases, grandchildren) of immigrants. For a while I was an ambassador for Wild Caught Mississippi Shrimp, promoting their product as superior to shrimp imported from Asia. So I, an immigrant, was supporting shrimp caught mostly by immigrants. But at the same time, I was implying that the shrimp caught by people like the Kharvas—people I had grown up admiring, whom I knew worked very hard—was somehow inferior to that being caught and sold here. Being caught between one's old home and the new is a burden that immigrants often bear.

Shrimp has been on every menu I've written for the last fifteen years. Many of the recipes in this chapter make perfect starters or cocktail snacks. Whenever possible, look for domestic shrimp from the coast closest to you. Always buy shrimp in their shells! Packaged shrimp that is already peeled and deveined (usually sold frozen) is almost certainly going to be of inferior quality. That said, many shrimpers do freeze their catch right on the boat, so there's no shame in using frozen shrimp, as long as it is good quality, responsibly sourced, and still in the shell. If you are working with frozen shrimp, an overnight thaw in the refrigerator is best. In a pinch, you can run frozen shrimp under cold tap water to thaw it quickly and safely. If you're shopping at a seafood market or another store with a large selection, you'll probably have size options. At a smaller market, you may not. If you do have a choice, most of the recipes here will work best with large (U16/20) or medium (U21/25) shrimp unless otherwise noted. The number range refers to the number of shrimp per pound at that size. In general, you can plan on about a quarter pound of shrimp per guest for appetizers, or a third of a pound per person for a main course. (Shellfish lovers with a hearty appetite might put away closer to half a pound—and I don't blame them!) All of these recipes assume that you are working with headless shrimp.

POACHED SHRIMP

SERVES 6 TO 8 AS AN APPETIZER OR 4 TO 6 AS A MAIN COURSE

In cooking, sometimes the simplest things are the hardest to get right. Take poaching shrimp, for example. In theory, there is really nothing to it: Season the water, heat it up, chuck a few nice shrimp in it for a minute, take them out and dunk them in an ice bath, and voilà!

But too often, the shrimp end up over- or undercooked. What gives? For years, I did not have the answer. Eventually, I sought the advice of three chefs who have poaching shrimp down to a science—John Currence at City Grocery, Ashley Christensen of Poole's Diner in Raleigh, and Mike Lata of the Ordinary in Charleston. What were those chefs doing that I wasn't? It turns out, there are three keys to poached-shrimp success. First, use the best-quality shrimp you can find. Second, season your poaching liquid well. That is where the flavor is, so don't cut corners with this step. And third, do *not* boil the shrimp—a gentle poach will give you the perfect texture and doneness.

Once you've mastered this technique, you'll want to make poached shrimp again and again. Serve them as an appetizer or cocktail snack with cocktail sauce or French Remoulade (page 203) for dipping.

2 pounds domestic shrimp (preferably U16/20)

1 cup dry white wine, such as sauvignon blanc or Chablis

2 lemons, cut in half

4 sprigs flat-leaf parsley

4 sprigs thyme

6 garlic cloves, sliced

1 celery stalk, chopped

1 tablespoon salt

1 tablespoon black peppercorns

1 teaspoon Old Bay seasoning

1 teaspoon hot sauce

French Remoulade (page 203), for dipping

Using kitchen shears or scissors, cut along the back of each shrimp, through the shell and just deep enough into the flesh to expose the vein. Leave the shells on but remove the veins and rinse the shrimp under cold running water. Drain and set aside.

In a large pot, combine the wine, lemon halves, parsley, thyme, garlic, celery, salt, peppercorns, Old Bay, and hot sauce with 12 cups water. Bring to a boil over medium-high heat, then lower the heat and simmer for 12 to 15 minutes. Remove the pot from the heat and stir in the shrimp. Cover and allow to stand for exactly 3 minutes. This allows the shrimp to cook to perfect doneness. Meanwhile, fill a large bowl with cold water and ice cubes.

After 3 minutes, use a slotted spoon to transfer the shrimp to the ice bath. Chill for 2 minutes, then drain the ice water. Peel the shrimp and serve with the remoulade.

FRENCH REMOULADE

MAKES ABOUT 1⅓ CUPS

1 cup good mayonnaise (preferably Duke's)

2 teaspoons fresh lemon juice

1½ teaspoons Dijon mustard

¼ cup minced cornichons

1 anchovy fillet, minced to a paste (about 1½ teaspoons)

2 teaspoons chopped fresh flat-leaf parsley leaves

1 teaspoon chopped fresh tarragon leaves

1 teaspoon minced fresh chives

1 teaspoon salt

1 teaspoon freshly ground black pepper

Combine all the ingredients in a bowl and stir to mix well. Cover and refrigerate for at least 1 hour before using. The remoulade will last for up to 5 days in a sealed container in the refrigerator.

PICKLED SHRIMP MAKES ABOUT 2 POUNDS

Pickled shrimp are especially beloved along the coast of South Carolina and Georgia. My favorite way to serve them is on rye toast with a smear of cream cheese and a thin slice of cucumber. They also make a great starter or light lunch when served on a salad with Bibb lettuce, some shaved celery, charred corn, and a simple herb vinaigrette.

The key to this recipe is to begin with perfectly poached shrimp—turn back to page 202 for the proper technique.

2½ cups apple cider vinegar

1 small red onion, thinly sliced

10 garlic cloves, thinly sliced

2 tablespoons minced ginger

1 lemon, sliced into ¼-inch-thick rounds

1½ teaspoons coriander seeds

1 tablespoon black peppercorns

3 bay leaves

½ teaspoon Old Bay seasoning

½ teaspoon ground turmeric

1 teaspoon hot sauce

2 pounds Poached Shrimp (page 202), peeled and deveined

In a saucepan, combine the vinegar, red onion, garlic, ginger, lemon, coriander seeds, black peppercorns, bay leaves, Old Bay, turmeric, hot sauce, and 1 cup water. Bring to a boil over high heat, then lower the heat and simmer for 5 minutes. Remove the pan from the heat and allow the pickling liquid to cool to lukewarm. (You do not want the pickling liquid to overcook the shrimp.)

Put the shrimp in a large bowl. Pour the pickling liquid over the shrimp and stir gently. When the pickling liquid has cooled to room temperature, transfer the shrimp and liquid to airtight containers, such as large mason jars, and refrigerate for at least 4 hours before serving. The pickled shrimp will keep for up to 4 days in the refrigerator.

SHRIMP SALAD MAKES ABOUT 2 POUNDS

Teresa and I were scheduled to go to Maine for our honeymoon. Unfortunately, the terrorist attacks of September 11, 2001, kept us from flying there that year. It was more than a decade before we finally made it to Maine, the first visit for both of us. One of our primary objectives for the long weekend was to eat as much lobster as possible. Of all the lobster variations we tried, my favorite was a lobster roll—a buttered, toasted bun full of lobster salad simply dressed with mayonnaise.

That got me thinking—back home, we have lovely yeast rolls, beautiful shrimp, and the world's best mayonnaise (that would be Duke's). Why had I never seen a shrimp roll? When Teresa and I returned home, I set about creating a lobster roll–style salad with Royal Red shrimp from the Gulf. The result is perfect on a buttered roll or atop a bed of lettuce. I later found out that a handful of Southern restaurants and chefs, such as the Ordinary in Charleston, already served shrimp rolls. But developing my own was the fun part. This recipe makes enough for 8 to 10 shrimp rolls. You may, of course, cut it in half.

1 cup mayonnaise (preferably Duke's)

1 tablespoon Sriracha

⅓ cup minced fennel bulb

¾ cup minced celery

1 cup minced sweet onion

⅓ cup minced red bell pepper

2 teaspoons minced jalapeño chile

2 teaspoons minced ginger

⅓ cup chopped fresh mint

¼ cup chopped fresh basil

Grated zest and juice of 2 lemons

1 teaspoon salt

2 pounds Poached Shrimp (page 202), peeled and deveined

NOTE: Any time I can get my hands on Royal Red shrimp, I use them for this recipe. I have also used wild-caught Argentine Red shrimp. Both of these varieties are delicate and sweet, almost lobsterlike in taste and texture. (In fact, at Snackbar, we replaced a longstanding lobster mac and cheese with shrimp to show off Royal Reds from the Gulf.)

Combine the mayonnaise, Sriracha, fennel, celery, onion, red bell pepper, jalapeño, ginger, mint, basil, lemon zest and juice, and salt in a large bowl. Mix the ingredients well.

Cut the shrimp according to how you plan to serve the salad. To make shrimp rolls, chop the shrimp into small pieces. If you'll be serving the salad over lettuce, butterfly the shrimp in half lengthwise (head to tail) so that you have two flat pieces.

Fold the shrimp into the dressing mixture, making sure that all ingredients are well combined. Cover and chill for an hour before serving for the best flavor. This salad will keep refrigerated for up to 2 days.

SHRIMP AND BLACK-EYED PEA FRITTERS (Accara) MAKES 25 TO 30 FRITTERS

My friend Guelel Kumba grew up in Senegal and lived in Paris before coming to the United States. For a time he operated Afrissippi, a food truck in Oxford where he served dishes like mafé and chicken yassa. Guelel is an excellent cook as well as a griot—a musician and storyteller in his native Fulani tradition. While we worked together at City Grocery, we bonded over our shared love for music and spicy food—and the fact that he could talk to me in French.

As our friendship grew, I learned more about Senegal and realized that the coastal communities of that west African nation lived much like the coastal communities in Gujarat. The subsistence fishermen face many of the environmental and economic challenges to their maritime culture. I learned that the Fulani tradition of storytelling through song is a direct ancestor of blues and rap and that many of the ingredients and dishes I loved, from both India and the American South, had African origins.

Black-eyed pea fritters were one food we had in common. I learned to make the Gujarati version, dal vada, from my grandmother. Guelel grew up eating accara, the West African equivalent. This is not a traditional Senegalese recipe, nor is it a traditional Gujarati one. I like to think of it as a Mississippi creation.

- 2 cups dried black-eyed peas
- 1 pound domestic shrimp (preferably U16/20)
- 1 small yellow onion, minced (about 1 cup)
- 3 tablespoons minced ginger
- 1 jalapeño, stemmed and minced
- 3 tablespoons chopped fresh cilantro leaves and tender stems
- 2 teaspoons salt
- 2 teaspoons garam masala (store-bought or homemade, page 8)
- ½ teaspoon ground cayenne pepper
- 1 tablespoon hot sauce
- Grated zest and juice of 1 lime
- 2 cups neutral oil, such as peanut or canola

Put the dried peas in a bowl or pot and add enough water to cover them by 1 to 2 inches. Cover with a kitchen towel or plate and let the peas soak overnight at room temperature. When ready to begin cooking, drain the peas, rinse them, and drain again. Set aside.

Using kitchen shears or scissors, cut along the back of each shrimp, through the shell and just deep enough into the flesh to expose the vein. Remove and discard the shells and veins. Rinse the shrimp under cold running water and pat dry. Chop the shrimp into small pieces.

In a large bowl, combine the peas, onion, ginger, jalapeño, cilantro, salt, garam masala, cayenne, hot sauce, lime zest and juice, and shrimp; mix well.

Add the mixture in batches to the bowl of a food processor, cover and pulse until the mixture resembles a coarse meal. Transfer to a large mixing bowl, cover, and chill for 30 minutes. (This step helps the fritters hold together as they fry.)

Heat the oil to 350°F in a Dutch oven, cast-iron skillet, or electric fryer. If you don't have a deep-fry thermometer, drop in a small spoonful of batter to test the temperature. If it sizzles and floats to the top, your oil is ready. If it sinks to the bottom of the pot, the oil still needs to heat up more. If the oil is too hot, your batter will burn on the outside while the center of the fritter will be raw. In that case, lower the heat and wait a couple of minutes before you start to fry a batch.

While the oil is heating, line a large plate with paper towels and set it near the stove.

Before frying all of the accara, cook one as a test to check the seasonings. Gently drop a piece of the mixture the size of a marble into the oil and fry for 3 to 4 minutes, turning occasionally with a slotted spoon until it is evenly cooked on all sides and the shrimp are cooked through. Remove from the oil and let it cool slightly before tasting. If you are happy with the taste, proceed with frying the rest of the accara. If you think the mixture needs salt (or anything else), add it as desired, being sure to incorporate well.

Gently drop large marble-size balls of batter into the oil, 6 to 8 at a time, being careful not to let the hot oil splash you. Fry for 3 to 4 minutes, turning with a slotted spoon so that they cook evenly. Transfer the cooked accara to the paper towel–lined plate. When all of the accara from the first batch are finished, let the oil temperature return to 350°F before adding more. Repeat until you have used all of the batter. Transfer to a platter and serve immediately.

GRILLED SHRIMP WITH MANGO CHUTNEY GLAZE SERVES 4 TO 6

I moved to the United States just as Paul "Crocodile Dundee" Hogan implored Americans to "put a shrimp on the barbie" in a series of television commercials for Australian tourism. I had never eaten shrimp before, but every time I passed the seafood case at a grocery store, the commercial would start playing in my head. Finally, in the summer of 1994, I gave in. I bought some shrimp as my contribution to a cookout with a large group of friends. I knew that I would need to season or marinate the shrimp in some way and then skewer them for cooking. The only things I had in my fridge besides beer, milk, and ketchup were a jar of Major Grey's chutney and a wilted bunch of cilantro. So I made a marinade with chutney, ketchup, and chopped cilantro. I know, I know—but remember, this was *very* early in my cooking life.

I over-grilled the shrimp, but the marinade had potential. Over the years, I kept tinkering (the ketchup had to go!) until I landed upon this version. It is easy to put together and it tastes fantastic—sweet, sour, and hot. The stickiness from the chutney caramelizes on the grill, creating a sweet-bitter char. So crack open a can of Foster's and put some shrimp on the barbie. What are you waiting for, mate?

2 pounds domestic shrimp (the largest size you can find—ideally U15)

2 teaspoons salt

1 tablespoon black peppercorns

2 teaspoons cumin seeds

1 tablespoon sesame seeds, divided

1 cup Major Grey's style mango chutney

2 teaspoons Sriracha

1 tablespoon soy sauce

Grated zest of 2 limes, plus lime wedges, for serving

2 tablespoons neutral oil, such as peanut or canola

Chopped fresh cilantro, for garnish

NOTE: If you don't have an outdoor grill, you can broil the shrimp in the oven for 3 to 4 minutes.

Using kitchen shears or scissors, cut along the back of each shrimp, through the shell and just deep enough into the flesh to expose the vein. Remove and discard the shells and veins. Rinse the shrimp under cold running water. Pat dry. Toss the shrimp with the salt in a large bowl and set aside while you make the glaze.

Toast the black peppercorns in a small, dry pan over medium heat for about 1 minute. Add the cumin seeds and toast, shaking the pan gently so that the seeds toast evenly and do not burn, until both spices are fragrant, about 1 more minute. Remove from the heat and, when cool enough to handle, crush with a mortar and pestle. (You do not want too fine a grind here. If you're using a spice grinder or coffee grinder, keep it brief to achieve a texture that is more crushed than ground.) Set aside.

Set the same dry skillet over low heat; add the sesame seeds and toast until fragrant. Transfer 2 teaspoons to a small bowl to make the glaze and reserve the remaining 1 teaspoon for serving.

For the glaze, to the bowl with the 2 teaspoons sesame seeds, add the ground pepper and cumin, chutney, Sriracha, soy sauce, and lime zest and juice and whisk until smooth and well combined. Set aside ⅓ cup of the glaze for serving. Add the remaining glaze to the bowl with the salted shrimp and toss to coat the shrimp evenly. Allow to marinate for 10 to 15 minutes.

Heat the grill to medium-high.

Skewer the shrimp on wooden or metal skewers. (If using wooden skewers, soak them in water for 15 to 20 minutes first so that they do not catch fire on the grill.) Brush the oil on the grill grates so the shrimp do not stick. Place the shrimp skewers on the grill, making sure that the shrimp are lying flat. Grill for 2 minutes on each side. Transfer the cooked shrimp to a platter and brush on the reserved glaze. Sprinkle on the chopped cilantro and reserved 1 teaspoon toasted sesame seeds and serve with lime wedges for squeezing.

STIR-FRIED SHRIMP WITH BLACK PEPPER AND CORIANDER SERVES 4

One of my all-time favorite shrimp recipes is in chef Floyd Cardoz's cookbook *One Spice, Two Spice*. The first time I made his grilled black pepper shrimp, I was blown away by how something so simple and quick to cook could taste so good. I've adapted it here as an even simpler stir-fry. The longer I've spent in the kitchen, the more I'm convinced that simple preparations often lead to the best dishes.

These shrimp pair well with a simple Khichadi (page 21), or tuck them into tortillas with Collard Green Slaw (page 190) for the best shrimp tacos you've ever had.

- 1 pound domestic shrimp (U16/20)
- Grated zest and juice of 1 lemon, plus lemon wedges, for serving
- 1 teaspoon salt
- ½ teaspoon ground turmeric
- 2 tablespoons coriander seeds
- 2 tablespoons black peppercorns
- ¼ cup cornmeal (preferably medium grind)
- 3 large egg whites
- 3 tablespoons neutral oil, such as peanut or canola
- 1-inch piece ginger, thinly sliced
- 1 sprig curry leaves

Using kitchen shears or scissors, cut along the back of each shrimp, through the shell and just deep enough into the flesh to expose the vein. Remove and discard the shells and veins. Rinse the shrimp under cold running water. Pat dry.

Combine the lemon zest and juice, salt, and turmeric in a medium nonreactive bowl. Add the shrimp and toss to coat. Refrigerate for 15 to 20 minutes.

Meanwhile, toast the coriander seeds and black peppercorns in a small, dry pan over medium heat, shaking the pan gently so that they toast evenly and do not burn, until both spices are fragrant, 1 to 2 minutes. Remove from the heat and, when cool enough to handle, crush coarsely with a mortar and pestle. (You do not want too fine a grind here. If you're using a spice grinder or coffee grinder, keep it brief to achieve a texture that is more crushed than ground.)

Combine the ground coriander and pepper with the cornmeal on a rimmed plate or pie tin.

Beat the egg whites until frothy in a medium bowl.

Remove the shrimp from the refrigerator. Assemble, from left to right on your work space: the shrimp, then the egg whites, then the cornmeal mixture, then a sheet pan or large plate lined with parchment. Remove a shrimp from the marinade, shaking any excess liquid back into the bowl. Dip the shrimp in the beaten egg whites, then dredge it in the cornmeal mixture, turning to coat. Set the shrimp on the parchment-lined sheet pan. Repeat with the remaining shrimp. When you have coated all the shrimp, let them sit for 5 more minutes. The egg whites will begin to dry, which will allow the crust to adhere through cooking.

RECIPE CONTINUES

Heat the oil in a large sauté pan over medium-high heat. When it begins to shimmer, add the ginger, curry leaves, and shrimp. Cook the shrimp for about a minute, then gently turn and cook for 1 more minute. If you do not have a pan large enough to cook all the shrimp in a single layer at once, you may do so in two batches. Remove from the pan and serve immediately with lemon wedges for your guests to squeeze over their shrimp as desired.

PARSI-STYLE SWEET, SOUR, AND SPICY SHRIMP (Kolmi no Patio) SERVES 6

I adapted this recipe from the Parsis, an Indian community of Persian descent. More than one thousand years ago, followers of Zoroastrianism fled religious persecution in what is now Iran. They settled in present-day Gujarat, and many eventually made their way south to Mumbai. It is unclear whether the Parsis brought a taste for shrimp with them from Persia, or whether they adopted it as part of their cuisine in coastal Gujarat or later in Mumbai.

This dish is served in Parsi homes and in the famous Parsi cafés of Mumbai, where it is known as kolmi no patio and can be made with either shrimp or prawns. The flavors are fantastic—first, you get the vinegar tanginess, then heat from the chiles and cayenne, then sweetness from the jaggery. For a hearty meal, serve the shrimp with Khichadi (page 21).

2 pounds domestic shrimp (U16/20)

Juice of 1 lemon

2 teaspoons ground turmeric, divided

1½ teaspoon ground cayenne pepper

2 teaspoons coriander seeds

2 teaspoons cumin seeds

10 medium tomatoes

¼ cup neutral oil, such as peanut or canola

2 small yellow onions, minced (about 2 cups)

1½ tablespoons minced garlic

1½ tablespoons minced ginger

2 serrano chiles, stemmed and minced

2 teaspoons salt, divided

2 tablespoons jaggery or light brown sugar

3 tablespoons apple cider vinegar

½ bunch cilantro, leaves and tender stems chopped, divided

Using kitchen shears or scissors, cut along the back of each shrimp, through the shell and just deep enough into the flesh to expose the vein. Remove and discard the shells and veins. Rinse the shrimp under cold running water. Pat dry. Combine the lemon juice, 1 teaspoon turmeric, and cayenne in a large nonreactive bowl and mix well to blend. Add the shrimp, toss to coat, and refrigerate for 30 minutes.

Meanwhile, toast the coriander seeds in a small, dry pan over medium heat for about 1 minute. Add the cumin seeds and toast, shaking the pan gently so that the seeds toast evenly and do not burn, until both spices are fragrant, about 1 more minute. Remove from the heat and, when cool enough to handle, grind in a spice grinder or coffee grinder, or with a mortar and pestle. Set aside.

Dice 4 of the tomatoes; you should have 4 to 5 cups diced. Roughly chop the other 6 tomatoes and then purée them in a food processor or blender. You should have 4 to 5 cups of puréed tomatoes.

Heat the oil in a wide skillet over medium heat. When the oil begins to shimmer, add the onions and cook slowly until they are very soft and golden, 10 to 12 minutes. Add the garlic and ginger and cook for 5 minutes. Add the puréed tomatoes and cook until most of the water has evaporated, about 10 minutes. You should have a nice thick paste with a concentrated tomato flavor. Stir in the diced tomatoes, serranos, remaining 1 teaspoon turmeric, ground coriander and cumin, and 1 teaspoon salt. Cook until the diced tomatoes start to break down, about 5 minutes. Stir in the jaggery and vinegar cook for an additional 2 to 3 minutes. Add the marinated shrimp and stir until the shrimp are just cooked through, about 3 minutes. Stir in half the cilantro and the remaining 1 teaspoon salt. Garnish with the remaining chopped cilantro and serve.

SHRIMP WITH OKRA AND COCONUT MILK

SERVES 6

This dish is incredibly easy and flavorful. You can serve it as a first course with crusty bread or as a main course with steamed rice, Grits Upma (page 140), or Khichadi (page 21).

- 2 pounds domestic shrimp (U16/20)
- Juice of 1 lemon
- 2 teaspoons salt, divided
- 2 teaspoons cracked black pepper, divided
- 1 habanero pepper
- 4 allspice berries
- 4 star anise pods
- 1 teaspoon coriander seeds
- 2 bay leaves
- 6 sprigs thyme
- 1 stalk lemongrass, roughly chopped
- 2 teaspoons neutral oil, such as peanut or canola
- 4 small shallots, thinly sliced from root to tip
- 2 large tomatoes, diced (about 2½ cups)
- ½ cup dry vermouth
- 4 cups Shortcut Shrimp Stock
- 1 (13.5 ounce) can full-fat coconut milk
- 1 pound tender okra pods, cut into 1-inch pieces

SHORTCUT SHRIMP STOCK

MAKES ABOUT 5 CUPS

Shells from 2 pounds shrimp

Place the shrimp shells in a saucepan over medium-high heat and toast them until they turn opaque and become fragrant, 1 to 2 minutes. Add 8 cups water and bring to a boil. Reduce the heat to low and simmer for 25 to 30 minutes. Strain and discard the shells.

Using kitchen shears or scissors, cut along the back of each shrimp, through the shell and just deep enough into the flesh to expose the vein. Remove the shells and veins, reserving the shells to make the shrimp stock. Rinse the shrimp under cold running water. Pat dry.

Put the shrimp in a large bowl and add the lemon juice and 1 teaspoon each salt and pepper; refrigerate for 30 minutes.

Make a sachet using a paper coffee filter or an 8-inch square of doubled cheesecloth. Using a toothpick or skewer, poke a couple of holes in the habanero pepper. This will allow it to release some heat but not too much. Place the habanero, allspice, star anise, coriander, bay leaves, thyme, and lemongrass in the filter or the center of the cheesecloth. Gather the corners together and tie securely with a piece of kitchen twine to hold the spices inside. Set aside. Wash your hands after handling the habanero.

Heat the oil in a Dutch oven or other wide, heavy-bottomed pot over medium heat. When the oil begins to shimmer, add the shallots and cook until very soft, 6 to 7 minutes. Add the tomatoes and cook until they break down and release all their water, 3 to 5 minutes. Add the vermouth and cook until it has completely evaporated, about 4 minutes. Add the shrimp stock, coconut milk, okra, and the aromatic sachet. Bring to a boil, then reduce the heat and simmer for 20 minutes, or until the okra is just soft. Drain the shrimp in a colander, add to the pot, and cook for 2 to 3 minutes. Turn off the heat and season with the remaining 1 teaspoon each salt and pepper. Discard the herb sachet and serve.

SHRIMP, CORN, AND SUMMER SQUASH FRICASSEE SERVES 4

Fricassee is a cross between a quick sauté and long stewing. The most common fricassee you might have heard of is the classic French chicken fricassee. As the French colonized the Caribbean and parts of what is now the American South, such as New Orleans, the fricassee method was adapted to suit local ingredients. Here, shrimp takes the place of chicken for a dish that's a bit lighter and comes together more quickly. This particular recipe is inspired by a dish my friend Nina Compton served us for dinner one night at her New Orleans restaurant Compère Lapin, where the menu draws on culinary influences from her native Saint Lucia. Seafood with some sweetness to it, whether shrimp, crab, or lobster, pairs beautifully with corn. (For further proof, try the Corn, Crab, and Bacon Griddle Cakes on page 125.) And corn, in turn, plays beautifully with summer squash when both are in season. So my adaptation of Nina's shrimp fricassee becomes a celebration of peak summer produce.

You'll see that the recipe calls for habanero pepper. Although habaneros can be extremely hot, they add a beautiful floral note to the finished dish. (If you were to substitute a different pepper, you'd lose that element.) Depending on your preference for heat, you may want to remove some or all of the habanero's seeds to temper the fire. Be sure to wash your hands, knife, and cutting board after handling the habanero.

This is a weeknight-friendly supper paired with simple steamed rice or grits.

1 pound domestic shrimp (U16/20)

2 tablespoons olive oil

2 bunches scallions, sliced, whites and greens separated

6 garlic cloves, thinly sliced

2 bay leaves

1½ cups fresh corn kernels (from about 2 ears)

1 to 2 habanero peppers, seeded and minced

1 pound summer squash, diced small (about 1½ cups)

1 tomato, diced (about ¾ cup)

2 tablespoons fresh thyme leaves

3 tablespoons chopped fresh flat-leaf parsley

½ cup dry white wine, such as sauvignon blanc or Chablis

Juice of 1 lemon

2 teaspoons salt

1 teaspoon freshly ground black pepper

2 tablespoons unsalted butter

Using kitchen shears or scissors, cut along the back of each shrimp, through the shell and just deep enough into the flesh to expose the vein. Remove the shells and veins, reserving about one-quarter of the shells to make the shrimp stock. Rinse the shrimp under cold running water. Pat dry.

To make the stock, place the shrimp shells in a saucepan over medium-high heat and toast them until they turn opaque and become fragrant, 1 to 2 minutes. Add 1 cup water and bring to a boil. Turn down the heat to low and simmer for 10 to 15 minutes, until the volume is reduced by about half. Strain and discard the shells. Measure out ½ cup of the stock and set aside.

Heat the oil in a Dutch oven or other wide, heavy-bottomed pot over medium-high heat. When it begins to shimmer, add the scallion whites, garlic, and bay leaves and cook until the scallions are just soft, about 3 minutes. Add the corn and cook for another minute. Add the shrimp, habanero, and shrimp stock and cook, stirring, for 3 to 4 minutes. The shrimp will begin to curl. Stir in the squash, tomato, thyme, parsley, wine, lemon juice, salt, and pepper. Cook for an additional minute, or until the shrimp are opaque. Add the butter and stir vigorously until it melts into the liquid in the pot and makes a creamy sauce.

Remove the pot from the heat and stir in the scallion greens. Serve immediately.

SHRIMP RECHEADO SERVES 6

Recheado is a Portuguese dish that made its way to Goa, a former Portuguese colony on India's western coast. The name means "stuffed" in Portuguese, and by the time the concept arrived in Goa, it had picked up a taste for hot chiles in Mozambique, and notions of toasting and grinding nuts from Oman via the spice trade. Goans added ginger, cinnamon, and cardamom to the mix. The result is a spicy, flavorful paste that works well with many kinds of seafood. I love using it with large shrimp, as they are easy to source and easy to cook. Serve shrimp recheado with steamed white rice, or with Grits Upma (page 140) for a twist on shrimp and grits.

- 10 to 12 dried whole Kashmiri, guajillo, or New Mexico chiles, stemmed
- ½ cup raw unsalted cashews
- 1 large yellow onion, roughly chopped
- 1-inch piece ginger, roughly chopped
- 8 to 10 garlic cloves, peeled
- 2 teaspoons black peppercorns
- 1 tablespoon coriander seeds
- 3 to 4 green cardamom pods
- 1 cinnamon stick
- 2 teaspoons cumin seeds
- 2 pounds domestic shrimp (U15 or U16/20 count)
- ¼ cup olive oil
- 1 teaspoon ground turmeric
- ⅓ cup red wine vinegar
- 2 teaspoons light brown sugar
- 2 teaspoons salt
- Chopped fresh cilantro, for garnish

Soak the dried chiles and cashews in a bowl of warm water until soft, about 10 minutes. Drain the chiles and cashews and transfer to the bowl of a food processor, along with the onion, ginger, and garlic, and process into a smooth paste.

Toast the black peppercorns, coriander seeds, cardamom pods, and cinnamon stick in a small, dry pan over medium heat for about 1 minute. Add the cumin seeds and toast, shaking the pan gently so that the spices toast evenly and do not burn, until everything is fragrant, about 1 more minute. Remove from the heat and, when cool enough to handle, grind in a spice grinder or coffee grinder, or with a mortar and pestle. Set aside.

Using kitchen shears or scissors, cut along the back of each shrimp, through the shell and just deep enough into the flesh to expose the vein. Remove and discard the shells and veins. Rinse the shrimp under cold running water. Pat dry. Using a sharp paring knife, butterfly the shrimp: Cutting from top to tail, cut along the back of each shrimp, almost but not all the way through. You should end up with two attached halves that open like a book. Set aside.

Heat the oil in a large skillet over medium heat. When the oil begins to shimmer, add the onion-chile-cashew mixture and cook, stirring frequently, until the onions are completely cooked through and you have a dark, rust-colored paste, 8 to 10 minutes. Add the toasted ground spices and turmeric, stir, and cook until they are very fragrant, 1 to 2 minutes. Lower the heat to medium-low and carefully stir in the vinegar, sugar, salt, and 2 cups water. Scrape up any bits that may have stuck to the bottom. Continue to cook until the water is almost all evaporated and you have a nice, smooth, thick paste. Stir in the butterflied shrimp and cook for 3 to 4 minutes, until the shrimp are cooked through. Garnish with the chopped cilantro and serve.

CHAPTER ELEVEN

EAT OR WE BOTH STARVE. That is the sign that greets you as you climb the steps to the front porch of Taylor Grocery, a legendary catfish restaurant just outside Oxford, Mississippi.

While the sign may seem like a cute play on words, the message rings true in Mississippi. The state is poor by virtually all economic measures. And the region along the Mississippi River known as the Delta is the poorest part. Beyond low-paying agricultural work, there are few jobs available. The public education system offers little in the way of opportunity, and I often feel that state politicians are not inclined to fix it. The large African American population in the Delta has seen its share of hardships over the years, and they still face inequities with regards to education, healthcare, and economic opportunity. One bright spot, a money maker and a job creator, is the catfish industry. Virtually all domestic farm-raised catfish comes from Mississippi, Arkansas, Alabama, and Louisiana. The industry employs some ten thousand men and women and contributes billions of dollars to the economies of states that need it most. For that reason, I'm inclined to heed Taylor Grocery's call.

Catfish is mild, versatile, healthy, and inexpensive. The industry's best practices are environmentally responsible. Criticisms that catfish is a muddy-tasting bottom feeder do not apply to the farm-raised variety. (I suspect those criticisms are leveled by folks who've never had the pleasure of eating catfish.) Many years ago, John Currence told me something that has stayed with me. He said, "It is easy to impress people with fancy ingredients. It is difficult to transfer humble, often forgotten ingredients into something that people want—but doing exactly that is the mark of a good chef." Over the years at Snackbar, I have taken that advice to heart and applied to it to catfish. While I'm cooking a Mississippi product, I often apply the flavors and techniques of South and East Asia. Many Asian countries employ similar fish in their cuisines—think of the Vietnamese cha ca la vong, which uses a close relative of the North American channel catfish.

I don't often recommend that folks buy frozen fish, or that they make an effort to seek out a particular species. But in the case of Mississippi farm-raised catfish, I am going to make an exception. Some very fine people's livelihoods depend on our eating what they produce.

When catfish is the centerpiece of a meal, figure one 5- to 7-ounce fillet per person. If your fillets are smaller, remember that they will cook more quickly, and you may want to scale up to 1½ or even 2 fillets per guest. Smaller, thinner fillets are especially good for frying—and I promise, your family and friends will want seconds. For all recipes in this chapter, if you have difficulty sourcing catfish, feel free to use the best available mild and flaky option, ideally one that comes from waters near you. Depending on where you live, this might be drum, redfish, flounder, or cod. That said, several catfish farms do ship frozen fish nationwide, including Simmons Farm Raised Catfish in Yazoo City, Mississippi.

SMOKED CATFISH PÂTÉ MAKES 2½ TO 3 CUPS

You can find smoked fish dips across the South, and especially along the Gulf Coast. In the Florida Panhandle, the fish is likely to be mullet. Here in Mississippi, it's catfish. The smoked catfish dip at Ajax Diner in Oxford inspired this recipe, which also borrows from the classic Florida version. I generally make a large batch of this around the holidays, put it in small Weck or Ball jars, and distribute it to our neighbors with nice crackers.

Smoking the fish is the most complex part of this recipe, but it's really not hard once you get the hang of it. Stovetop smoking is a great trick to have in your repertoire. My wife is not a fan of smoky flavor, so when I make this dip at home, I bake the fish instead. Feel free to do the same if you prefer.

As with all other recipes in this chapter, if you have difficulty sourcing catfish, feel free to use the best local option of mild and flaky fish, such as drum, redfish, flounder, or cod.

1 pound Smoked Catfish (page 226), broken up into 2-inch pieces

8 ounces cream cheese

¼ cup sour cream

¼ cup mayonnaise (preferably Duke's)

2 tablespoons unsalted butter, at room temperature

2 tablespoons minced yellow onion

2 tablespoons minced celery

2 tablespoons pickle relish, such as Mt. Olive or Heinz

2 teaspoons Worcestershire sauce

1 teaspoon hot sauce

½ teaspoon minced garlic

½ teaspoon Creole seasoning (store-bought or homemade, page 8)

Grated zest and juice of 1 small lemon

Salt

Crackers, for serving

Combine all the ingredients in a food processor and blend until smooth. Taste and add salt as desired. Transfer to a bowl and serve with crackers. If not using immediately, transfer the pâté to airtight containers and refrigerate for up to 5 days.

SMOKED CATFISH

MAKES 1 POUND

For this recipe you will need two disposable 9 x 13-inch aluminum baking pans, one 2 inches deep and one 4 inches deep. Look for these at the supermarket near the baking ingredients; most stores carry a variety of sizes. You will also need wood chips for smoking, which can be found at the supermarket or hardware store. Hickory tends to be the most commonly available, but you might see apple, cherry, or mesquite. Any of these will work. You can also use this method to smoke other types of fish, such as trout.

1 pound catfish fillets

Preheat the oven to 350°F. Turn on your stove's vent hood. You may also want to crack open a window or door.

Using a toothpick or skewer, poke approximately 24 holes in the bottom of the shallower aluminum pan. Place the fish fillets in a single layer in the perforated pan and cover loosely with aluminum foil. (If the pan came with an aluminum lid, you may use that instead.)

Place the nonperforated pan directly on the stovetop. Form a piece of aluminum foil into a shallow bowl to hold the wood chips and place in the middle of the pan. Turn the heat to medium-low. Using a long-reach lighter, light the chips until they start smoke vigorously. Carefully place the perforated pan on top of the pan holding the wood chips, taking care not to let the bottom of the perforated pan touch the wood chips. Allow the fish to smoke on the stovetop for 30 seconds to 1 minute, then turn off the heat.

Transfer the entire apparatus to the oven and bake for 5 to 6 minutes. The catfish will continue to smoke in the oven as it cooks through. Allow to cool to room temperature.

CATFISH AND POTATO CROQUETTES

MAKES 10 TO 12 CROQUETTES

I love tapas, especially croquetas—Spanish croquettes. However, I am not a big fan of the bacalao (salt cod) ones usually served at tapas bars. I find them too salty and fishy. Fear not, the humble catfish comes to the rescue! I personally like the nonsmoked version, but many prefer the smoked fish. Try both and see which one you prefer.

1 pound catfish fillets

2½ teaspoons salt, divided

2½ teaspoons freshly ground black pepper, divided

¼ to ½ teaspoon Creole seasoning (store-bought or homemade, page 8)

2 large russet potatoes, washed

2 teaspoons cumin seeds

2 teaspoons fennel seeds

2 shallots, minced (about ⅔ cup)

1 serrano chile, stemmed and minced

3 tablespoons chopped fresh flat-leaf parsley

2 large egg yolks, plus 2 whole eggs

Grated zest and juice of 1 lemon, plus lemon wedges, for serving

1½ cups bread crumbs

¼ to ½ cup neutral oil, such as peanut or canola

If smoking the catfish, follow the method on page 226.

If baking, preheat the oven to 350°F. Line a sheet pan with parchment or aluminum foil. Place the catfish fillets on the prepared sheet pan. Sprinkle the fillets with ½ teaspoon each salt and pepper and the Creole seasoning. Bake for 8 to 10 minutes, until cooked through; set aside.

Increase the oven temperature (or turn it on, if you smoked the catfish) to 400°F. Pierce the potatoes several times with the tines of a fork. Wrap the potatoes in foil and place them directly on an oven rack. After 45 minutes, check the potatoes for doneness. If a fork or skewer goes in easily, the potatoes are done. (A skewer is a better tester than a fork since it will go all the way through.) If not, continue baking for another 15 minutes. Test again for doneness. When the potatoes are done, remove and discard the foil and set the potatoes aside to cool.

While the potatoes are cooling, toast the cumin seeds and fennel seeds in a small, dry pan over medium heat, shaking the pan gently so that the seeds toast evenly and do not burn, about 1 minute. Remove from the heat and set aside.

When the potatoes are cool enough to handle, peel them, cut them into chunks, and mash them in a large bowl. A potato masher will do the job, but running them through a potato ricer is ideal for creating a smooth, uniform texture. Flake the catfish with a fork and add it to the bowl, along with the shallots, serrano, cumin and fennel, parsley, egg yolks, remaining 2 teaspoons each salt and pepper, and the lemon zest and juice. Mix well. If the mixture is too loose to hold together, add a tablespoon or two of bread crumbs to bind it. Roll into portions the size of golf balls and flatten out into pucks about 1 inch thick. You will have 10 to 12 croquettes.

RECIPE CONTINUES

Set the croquettes on a large plate or sheet pan. Whisk the whole eggs with 1 cup water in a shallow bowl. Pour the bread crumbs into a shallow dish or pie tin.

Heat ¼ cup oil to 350°F in a cast-iron skillet, Dutch oven, or electric fryer. While the oil is heating, set up your frying station. From left to right on the counter to the left of the stove, line up the croquettes, then the bowl of egg wash, then the dish of bread crumbs. On the other side of the stove, place a large plate or sheet pan lined with paper towels.

When the oil is sizzling hot, you are ready to begin breading and pan-frying. Use one hand to handle the croquettes, keeping the other hand clean. Working one at a time, dip the croquette in egg wash, turning to coat. Then press it into the breadcrumb mixture, turning and rolling to coat on all sides. Gently place the croquette in the oil. Repeat with 3 to 5 more croquettes. Do not crowd the pan—depending on the size of your skillet, you will probably cook four to six croquettes at a time. Cook the croquettes for 2 to 3 minutes, until golden and crispy on the bottom. Using a slotted spatula, carefully flip the croquettes and cook for 2 to 3 minutes on the other side, until golden, crispy, and warmed all the way through. Transfer the cooked croquettes to the paper towel–lined plate to drain. Add more oil, if needed, between batches and let it come up to temperature before adding more croquettes to the pan. Continue until all the croquettes are cooked.

Serve immediately with lemon wedges for guests to squeeze over their croquettes as desired.

CORNMEAL-FRIED CATFISH SERVES 8

About nine miles south of downtown Oxford sits Taylor, Mississippi, a tiny community with an outsize reputation as the home of the South's best catfish. If catfish is a religion in Mississippi, Taylor Grocery is its high church. Lynn Hewlett, his wife, Debbie, and their daughter, Sarah Margaret, have owned and operated the restaurant since the late 1990s. They're open for dinner Thursday through Sunday, and hungry folks from near and far tailgate on the porch and in the parking lot while they wait for an open table.

Now, I won't pretend that I can fry catfish better than Lynn Hewlett does, but I *can* pass along what I've learned from him. First, season the fish itself as well as the dredge. Second, use peanut oil for frying. Third, fry the fish at a relatively low temperature—325°F is ideal—to achieve a crispy crust and a moist, flaky inside. Fourth, and this one is the most important, remember that a fish fry is a social event. Invite as many family and friends as you can, and scale this recipe up accordingly. The more you share, the better the fish will taste. Kale (or Chard) Fritters (page 188) and Cabbage, Kale, Carrot, and Peanut Salad (page 186) make excellent accompaniments.

2 large eggs

2½ cups cultured buttermilk

1 teaspoon Worcestershire sauce

1 teaspoon hot sauce

1½ cups cornmeal (preferably medium grind)

½ cup rice flour

2 teaspoons salt, divided

2 teaspoons freshly ground black pepper, divided

1 tablespoon Creole seasoning (store-bought or homemade, page 8), divided

8 (5- to 7-ounce) catfish fillets

4 cups peanut oil

Tartar sauce, for serving (optional)

Lemon wedges, for serving

To make the batter, whisk together the eggs, buttermilk, Worcestershire sauce, and hot sauce in a shallow bowl; set aside.

To make the dredge, combine the cornmeal, rice flour, 1 teaspoon each salt and pepper, and ½ tablespoon Creole seasoning in a shallow baking dish or pie tin.

Pat the catfish fillets dry and season on both sides with the remaining 1 teaspoon each salt and pepper and remaining ½ tablespoon Creole seasoning; set aside on a large plate or sheet pan.

Heat the oil to 325°F in a cast-iron skillet, Dutch oven, or electric fryer. Use a deep-fry thermometer to check and maintain even oil temperature. Try to keep the oil as close to 325°F as possible throughout frying, and do not let it go above 350°F.

While the oil is heating, set up your frying station. From left to right on the counter to the left of the stove, line up the plate of seasoned fish fillets, then the bowl of batter, then the dish of dredge. On the other side of the stove, place a large plate or sheet pan lined with paper towels. Keep a slotted spatula or a spider strainer by the stove for removing the fish from the oil.

Once the oil has come to temperature, you're ready to begin battering, dredging, and frying. Depending on the size of your vessel and how many fillets you are using, you will probably need to fry the catfish in two or three batches. (If the pot gets too crowded, it will

RECIPE CONTINUES

bring down the temperature of the oil, resulting in soggy fish that is undercooked on the inside.) Use one hand to handle the fish, keeping the other hand clean. Take one seasoned fillet and place it in the bowl of batter, submerging it or flipping to coat. As you lift the fillet out of the batter, gently shake the excess back into the bowl. Next, place the fish in the dredge, flipping to coat. Then, gently lower the fish into the hot oil, being careful not to splash yourself. Repeat with two or three more fillets. Unless your pot or fryer is very large, fry no more than four fillets at a time.

After 4 minutes, use a slotted spatula or similar tool to gently turn the fillets in the oil. Cook for another 4 minutes, or until the fillets are golden brown and crispy and the fish is cooked through. Carefully transfer the fried fish to the paper towel–lined plate. If working in batches, repeat the battering and frying steps with the remaining fillets. Make sure the oil temperature returns to 325°F between batches. If you want to wait until all of the fish is fried before serving your guests, you may transfer the drained fillets to a sheet pan in a 200°F oven to keep them warm.

Once all the fish is fried, serve with tartar sauce, if desired, and lemon wedges for squeezing.

PUNJABI-STYLE FRIED CATFISH SERVES 6

One Sunday afternoon, I was watching YouTube videos of Indian street food vendors and came across one of a man serving fried fish in Amritsar. The city is located in the northern Indian state of Punjab, near the border with Pakistan. I watched the chunks of carp fry in sizzling oil dyed golden by turmeric. I wanted to learn more. I called two chef friends who have roots in Punjab, Maneet Chauhan of Nashville and Sunny Baweja of Richmond, Virginia. Both told me that river fish, dredged in a spiced chickpea-flour batter and deep-fried, is a very popular roadside snack in Punjab. (The state's name means "Land of Five Rivers," after all.) You'll rarely find this kind of fish on the menu in sit-down restaurants, because it is considered a food of the poor and working class.

This made me think—where else in the world is there a tradition of frying fish that has long been considered food for poor, working-class people, not fit to be served at fine restaurants? Where else would you find a shack serving up delicious fried fish on makeshift tables with plastic chairs, or packed to-go in Styrofoam clamshells? The answer, of course, is all over the world. Vietnam. Great Britain. And my home state of Mississippi, where catfish is king.

I asked chefs Chauhan and Baweja to share their recipes with me, and I tried my own adaptation with catfish. Catfish took to the spicy chickpea-flour batter like a fish to water, and I had a dining room full of happy guests.

The method here is a little different than for the Cornmeal-Fried Catfish (page 229) because so much of the flavor and texture comes from a thick coating of batter. Dusting the marinated fillets with rice flour or cornstarch before dipping them in the batter helps the batter adhere to the fish and stay on as it fries.

- 2 teaspoons turmeric
- 3 teaspoons salt, divided
- 1 teaspoon ground cayenne pepper
- 3 tablespoons fresh lemon juice
- 6 (5- to 7-ounce) catfish fillets
- 1 teaspoon coriander seeds
- 2 teaspoons cumin seeds
- ½ cup chickpea flour
- 1 tablespoon minced garlic
- 1 tablespoon minced ginger
- 1 tablespoon minced cilantro stems, plus chopped cilantro leaves, for garnish
- 2 teaspoons minced serrano chile
- 1 tablespoon paprika
- 1 teaspoon ajwain seeds
- 2 cups neutral oil, such as peanut or canola
- ½ cup rice flour or cornstarch
- Chaat masala (store-bought or homemade, page 8), for garnish
- Thinly sliced red onion, for serving
- Lime wedges, for serving

To make the marinade, combine the turmeric, 2 teaspoons salt, cayenne, and lemon juice in a nonreactive bowl. Add the fish fillets and flip to coat. Refrigerate for 20 to 30 minutes.

To make the batter, toast the coriander seeds in a small, dry pan over medium heat for about 1 minute. Add the cumin seeds and toast, shaking the pan gently so that the seeds toast evenly and do not burn, until both spices are fragrant, about 1 more minute. Remove from the heat and, when cool enough to handle, grind in a spice grinder or coffee grinder, or with a mortar and pestle. Transfer the ground coriander and cumin to a shallow bowl. Add the chickpea flour, garlic, ginger, cilantro stems, serrano, paprika, ajwain seeds, and remaining 1 teaspoon salt. Add ½ cup water and whisk to combine everything well. If the batter seems too thick, add another ¼ cup water and whisk again. It should be a thick, almost waffle batter consistency.

Heat the oil to 350°F in a cast-iron skillet, Dutch oven, or electric fryer. Use a deep-fry thermometer to check and maintain even oil temperature.

While the oil is heating, set up your frying station.

RECIPE CONTINUES

Take the fish out of the refrigerator. Put the rice flour or cornstarch in a shallow baking dish or pie tin. From left to right on the counter to the left of the stove, line up the marinated catfish, then the dish of rice flour or cornstarch, then the bowl of batter. On the other side of the stove, place a large plate or sheet pan lined with paper towels. Keep a slotted spatula or a spider strainer by the stove for removing the fish from the oil.

Once the oil has come to temperature, you're ready to begin dusting, battering, and frying. Depending on the size of your vessel, you will probably need to fry the catfish in two batches. (If the pot gets too crowded, it will bring down the temperature of the oil, resulting in soggy fish that is undercooked on the inside.) Use one hand to handle the fish, keeping the other hand clean. Take one fillet out of the marinade, gently shaking off any excess liquid. Place it in the dish of rice flour or cornstarch, turning to coat it lightly and/or using your fingers to sprinkle a light dusting all over the fish. This step helps the batter adhere. Next, dip the fish in the batter, turning to coat. Then, gently lower the fish into the hot oil, being careful not to splash yourself. Repeat with two or three more fillets. Unless your pot or fryer is very large, fry no more than three or four fillets at a time.

After 3 to 4 minutes, use a slotted spatula or similar tool to gently turn the fillets in the oil. Cook for another 3 to 4 minutes, until the fillets are golden brown and crispy and the fish is cooked through. Carefully transfer the fried fish to the paper towel–lined plate. If working in batches, repeat the battering and frying steps with the remaining fillets. Make sure the oil temperature returns to 350°F between batches. If you want to wait until all of the fish is fried before serving your guests, you may transfer the drained fillets to a sheet pan in a 200°F oven to keep them warm.

Before serving, sprinkle the fried fish with chaat masala and chopped cilantro leaves. Serve with sliced red onion and lime wedges for squeezing.

ENGLAND
STAINLESS

COLLARD-WRAPPED CATFISH SERVES 8

I am a big fan of cooking fish en papillote, the French technique of baking fish and vegetables in a pouch made of folded parchment paper. In India, as well as in many other places, cooks employ a similar technique using leaves rather than paper. One of my favorite preparations is the Parsi patra ni machhi—"fish wrapped in leaf"—in which the fish is coated in green chutney, wrapped in banana leaves, and steamed. For years, I used this technique with pompano and flounder. Then, I tried a version of patra ni macchi with catfish and collard leaves. Between the Gujarati-style green chutney and the Mississippi staples of catfish and collards, I was able to reference my roots and my home in a single recipe.

This is an easy recipe, easily halved for a family of four, but the unexpected presentation also makes it worthy of a dinner party. While I developed this dish with catfish in mind, you can substitute another mild, flaky fish such as cod, flounder, or redfish.

8 (5- to 7-ounce) catfish fillets

1 tablespoon salt

1 teaspoon ground turmeric

Juice of 2 limes

16 large collard green leaves, stemmed

1 cup Peanut Pesto (page 170) or other favorite green chutney

2 to 3 tablespoons ghee (store-bought or homemade, page 9) or neutral oil, such as peanut or canola

NOTE: You'll need kitchen twine to tie up the "packets."

Place the catfish fillets in a nonreactive shallow dish and sprinkle evenly with the salt, turmeric, and lime juice. Refrigerate for 30 minutes.

Preheat the oven to 375°F.

While the catfish is marinating, bring a large pot of salted water to a boil over high heat. While the water is heating, fill a large bowl with cold water and ice cubes. When the water boils, add the collard leaves and cook for 30 seconds. Using tongs, remove the leaves and transfer to the ice bath. This will stop the cooking process. Drain the blanched collard leaves and pat them dry.

Remove the catfish from the refrigerator. Lay 2 collard leaves one on top of the other in a cross. Spread 1 tablespoon peanut pesto in the middle. Place a catfish fillet on top and spread a second tablespoon of peanut pesto on top of the fish. Fold the leaves over the fish to make a packet and secure with kitchen twine. Repeat the process with the remaining collard leaves, catfish fillets, and peanut pesto until you have 8 packets.

Heat the ghee or oil in a large skillet over medium heat. When it is shimmering, add the fish packets and sear for 45 seconds. Flip and sear on the other side for about 45 seconds more. You want to get a slight crisp on the collard leaves before baking. Depending on the size of your skillet, you may need to sear the fish packets in two batches. Transfer the seared packets to a sheet pan and bake for 8 to 10 minutes, until the fish is cooked through. Before serving, carefully cut and discard the twine.

TANDOORI-SPICED BAKED CATFISH SERVES 4 TO 6

As a Mississippi chef, it is my responsibility and my pleasure to highlight Mississippi products, including farm-raised catfish. There are several places around Oxford to get a great fried catfish plate, so I try to think up new ways to feature catfish on the menu at Snackbar. Most Mississippians are used to eating simple, cornmeal-battered fried catfish fillets, so I wasn't sure how our customers would take to baked catfish with a decidedly Indian profile. But the dish is full of flavorful spice and not too much heat, so it pleases a variety of palates. And while not all restaurant dishes are the kind of thing you'd want to make on a weeknight, this one absolutely is—it comes together easily and cooks quickly. And, it turns out, the marinade is versatile: It's the same one I use for the Grilled Pork Tenderloin with Tandoori Spices (page 273).

- 1 cup plain, full-fat yogurt (preferably Greek-style)
- 1 teaspoon honey
- 1 tablespoon minced ginger
- 1½ teaspoons minced garlic
- ½ teaspoon fresh lemon juice
- 1 teaspoon salt
- ¾ tablespoon tandoori masala (I use Spicewalla brand.)
- ½ teaspoon Kashmiri chili powder or hot paprika
- ¼ teaspoon ground cayenne pepper
- 4 to 6 (5- to 7-ounce) catfish fillets
- Chopped fresh mint or scallions, for garnish

To make the marinade, whisk the yogurt, honey, ginger, garlic, lemon juice, salt, tandoori masala, Kashmiri chili powder, and cayenne in a large bowl until smooth. Add the fish to the marinade and mix gently until all the fillets are fully covered. Refrigerate the marinated fish for at least 1 hour but no more than 4 hours.

When the fish is almost finished marinating, preheat the oven to 450°F. Line a sheet pan with aluminum foil. Spray the foil with nonstick cooking spray or brush it with oil or ghee.

Shake the excess marinade off the fish fillets and lay them out on the prepared pan in a single layer. Make sure they are not touching each other.

Bake for 6 to 7 minutes. The fillets should be slightly browned at the edges. Garnish with chopped mint leaves or scallions. Serve hot.

INDO-CHINESE CHILE CATFISH

SERVES 6 AS AN APPETIZER OR 4 AS A MAIN COURSE

India is a vast and diverse place. The coexistence of many religions, races, and cultures make the country what it is. There was once a significant population of Chinese migrants living in Indian metros, especially Calcutta. Today, Indo-Chinese cuisine is popular in restaurants across India. On the menu at such restaurants you'll find noodles, stir-fries, and deep-fried chunks of vegetables or meat tossed in a fiery chile sauce. It is very much a hybrid, neither fully Chinese nor Indian. For instance, a single dish might be flavored with soy sauce and garam masala.

If you've had Chicken 65—chunks of battered and deep-fried chicken tossed in a spicy sauce—you'll get the idea for how this dish comes together. While the catfish is marinating in a simple seasoning of salt, pepper, and ginger, you'll make the batter and the sauce. You'll batter and fry the catfish pieces and then toss them in the sauce to coat. I like to serve the catfish as an appetizer or finger food, albeit a slightly messy one, with cocktails. Alternatively, you can serve over rice for a main dish.

FOR THE CATFISH:

- 1 pound catfish fillets, cut into bite-size pieces
- 1 tablespoon minced ginger
- 1 teaspoon salt
- 1 teaspoon freshly ground black pepper

FOR THE BATTER:

- ½ cup all-purpose flour
- ½ cup cornstarch
- 1 teaspoon baking soda
- 1 teaspoon freshly ground black pepper
- 2 large eggs, beaten
- 2 tablespoons minced celery
- 1 tablespoon soy sauce

FOR THE SAUCE:

- 2 tablespoons canola oil
- 1 tablespoon minced ginger
- 1 tablespoon minced garlic
- 4 scallions, thinly sliced, whites and greens separated
- 1 serrano chile, stemmed and minced
- ¼ cup soy sauce
- ⅓ cup chili sauce, such as Heinz or Maggi
- 2 teaspoons Sriracha
- 2 teaspoons sesame seeds
- 1 tablespoon cornstarch whisked with ¼ cup water to make a slurry
- 1 teaspoon light brown sugar

FOR FRYING:

- 2 cups neutral oil, such as peanut or canola

RECIPE CONTINUES

Toss the catfish pieces with the ginger, salt, and pepper in a bowl. Refrigerate for 20 to 30 minutes to allow the catfish to absorb some of the seasonings.

To make the batter, combine the flour, cornstarch, baking soda, pepper, beaten eggs, celery, and soy sauce in a medium bowl with 1 cup water; mix well and set aside.

To make the sauce, heat the oil in a skillet over medium heat. When the oil is shimmering, add the ginger, garlic, scallion whites, and serrano and cook, stirring, for about 1 minute. Stir in the soy sauce, chili sauce, Sriracha, and sesame seeds. Add the cornstarch slurry, turn the heat up to medium-high, and bring the mixture to a boil. Boil for 1 minute, then turn off the heat and stir in the sugar. Set aside. When cool enough to handle, transfer to a large measuring cup.

Heat the oil to 350°F in a cast-iron skillet, Dutch oven, or electric fryer. If you don't have a deep-fry thermometer, drop in a spoonful of batter to test the temperature. If it sizzles and floats to the top, your oil is ready. If it sinks to the bottom of the pot, the oil still needs to heat up more.

While the oil is heating, set up your frying station. Remove the catfish from the refrigerator. Place it next to the bowl of batter. On the other side of the stove, place a large plate or sheet pan lined with paper towels. Next to that, place a large bowl, the sauce, and a serving platter. Keep a slotted spoon or a spider strainer by the stove for removing the fish from the oil.

Once the oil has come to temperature, you're ready to begin battering and frying. Depending on the size of your vessel, you may need to fry the catfish pieces in two batches. (If the pot gets too crowded, it will bring down the temperature of the oil, resulting in soggy fish that is undercooked on the inside.) Use one hand to handle the fish, keeping the other hand clean. Transfer half of the fish to the bowl of batter, submerging the pieces to coat them completely. Remove the pieces one at a time, shaking the excess batter back into the bowl. Gently lower the fish into the hot oil, being careful not to splash yourself. Fry the fish pieces, turning them with a slotted spoon as needed until golden brown and crispy on all sides, 3 to 4 minutes. Carefully transfer the fried fish to the paper towel–lined plate using a slotted spoon or spider strainer. If working in batches, repeat the battering and frying steps with the remaining fish pieces. Once all the fish is fried, transfer it to the mixing bowl. Pour half the sauce over the fish and gently toss to coat evenly, adding a little more sauce if needed. If you are serving the fish on its own as an appetizer, you want it to be coated but not soaking in the sauce. If serving the fish as a main dish over rice, spoon additional sauce over each serving; it'll be wonderfully absorbed by the rice. Garnish with the scallion greens.

CATFISH IN SPICY COCONUT SAUCE SERVES 4

I find few things better to eat than a light yet flavor-packed stew. This recipe, influenced by Keralan meen moilee (a coconut milk–based fish curry) and Thai yellow curry, is a personal favorite. It's a reminder that a dish can be balanced with spices without being spicy-hot. The flavors of lime, ginger, cloves, curry leaves, and toasted black pepper in coconut milk give the stew a beautiful depth and brightness. If you want more heat, you can increase the black pepper.

I like to serve this dish with steamed aromatic rice and Whole Grilled Okra (page 60) or Peanut Masala–Stuffed Baby Eggplant (page 112) in summer. In the cooler months, I pair it with Sprouted Red Pea Stir-Fry (page 54) and Afghan-Style Spinach with Dill and Cilantro (page 187). This sauce works well with shrimp, chicken, tofu, and even beef.

1 tablespoon black peppercorns

2 tablespoons ghee (store-bought or homemade, page 9) or coconut oil

½ teaspoon brown mustard seeds

2 sprigs curry leaves

½ teaspoon ground turmeric

3 whole cloves

2 shallots, sliced thinly lengthwise

2-inch piece ginger, minced (2 heaping tablespoons)

3 large ripe tomatoes, diced, or 1 (14-ounce) can crushed tomatoes

1 (13.5 ounce) can full-fat coconut milk

4 (5- to 7-ounce) catfish fillets, cut into thirds

Grated zest and juice of 2 limes

1 teaspoon salt

¼ cup chopped fresh cilantro or torn basil leaves

Steamed rice, for serving

Toast the black peppercorns in a small, dry skillet over medium heat, shaking gently so that they toast evenly and do not burn, until fragrant, about 1 minute. Remove from the heat. When cool enough to handle, crush the peppercorns with a mortar and pestle or coarsely grind in a spice grinder or coffee grinder. Set aside.

Heat the ghee in a Dutch oven or other wide, heavy-bottomed pot over medium heat. Once it is shimmering, add the mustard seeds and cook until they start popping, about 30 seconds. Add the curry leaves, turmeric, cloves, and ground pepper. Cook for 30 seconds, stirring constantly. Add the shallots, stir, and cook until softened, about 5 minutes. Add the ginger and tomatoes, mix well, cover, and cook for 5 minutes. Remove the lid, add the coconut milk and ¾ cup water, stir, and bring to a simmer. Simmer for 6 to 8 minutes. Add the fish, lime zest and juice, and salt. Simmer, uncovered, for 5 to 6 minutes more, until the fish is cooked through. Taste and adjust the seasonings as needed. Gently stir in the cilantro or basil. Serve over steamed rice.

KUNG PAO CATFISH SERVES 6 TO 8

My first exposure to American Chinese food was while I was in college. My friends and I would go out for a cheap dinner on the weekends to save our money for beer. One of our regular haunts was a Chinese restaurant called Golden Wok. I worked my way through the vegetarian options on the menu: vegetable fried rice, broccoli with garlic sauce, vegetable lo mein. Then, one night, a friend suggested that I try the kung pao tofu. I had never had tofu before, and to me it tasted like poorly made paneer. But I was hooked on the rest of the flavors—the heat of the chiles, the tangy bite of the ginger, and the crunch of the peanuts. I've been a fan of kung pao anything ever since. Eventually I had a more authentic version made with mouth-numbing Sichuan peppercorns, which took my appreciation to a new level.

Unfortunately, I live hundreds of miles from a true Sichuan restaurant, so I have to satisfy my kung pao craving at home. I like using catfish here because it takes on the flavor of the sauce so nicely. Do seek out Sichuan peppercorns for that numbing effect. They are available online from several spice purveyors, including La Boîte. If you don't have the Sichuan peppercorns, proceed without them—you'll end up with more of a Golden Wok version, but it will still satisfy.

I usually serve the catfish with steamed rice, but I have also served it as an unexpected taco filling.

FOR THE MARINADE:

2 teaspoons salt

2 teaspoons cracked black pepper

3 tablespoons soy sauce

1 tablespoon dry sherry

1½ tablespoons cornstarch

6 (5- to 7-ounce) catfish fillets, cut into ½-inch pieces

FOR THE SAUCE:

1½ tablespoons sugar

2 teaspoons cornstarch

2 tablespoons soy sauce

2 tablespoons apple cider vinegar

2 teaspoons sesame oil

FOR THE STIR-FRY:

¼ cup neutral oil, such as peanut or canola

12 to 15 small dried chiles de árbol, stemmed

1 teaspoon Sichuan peppercorns

4 star anise pods

3-inch piece ginger, sliced into very thin matchsticks

6 to 8 garlic cloves, sliced thinly

10 to 12 scallion whites, cut into ½ inch pieces

1½ cups roasted unsalted peanuts or cashews

Steamed white rice, for serving

To make the marinade, whisk together the salt, pepper, soy sauce, sherry, cornstarch, and 2 tablespoons water in a shallow bowl or dish. Add the catfish pieces and marinate for 30 minutes in the refrigerator.

Meanwhile, make the sauce. Whisk together the sugar, cornstarch, soy sauce, cider vinegar, sesame oil, and 2 tablespoons water in a bowl; set aside.

Remove the catfish from the refrigerator. Heat the oil in a wok or a heavy sauté pan over high heat until shimmering but not smoking. Add the chiles, Sichuan peppercorns, and star anise. Stir-fry until very fragrant, about 20 seconds, being careful not to burn the spices. Add the ginger and garlic and sauté for 15 seconds. Add the marinated catfish and cook, gently tossing and stirring until the catfish is dry and almost cooked through, about 5 minutes. Add the sauce, scallion whites, and peanuts. Toss gently to make sure everything is evenly coated in the sauce and cook for about 2 more minutes, until the catfish is cooked through. Serve hot with steamed white rice.

CATFISH PARMESAN SERVES 8

You have probably had chicken, veal, or eggplant Parmesan. I love all three. There is a sizable Italian community in the Mississippi Delta, and more than once, while eating with Delta Italian friends, I wondered aloud if they had ever thought of making catfish Parmesan. I inevitably received a raised eyebrow or a "Bless your heart." I finally decided to try the combination myself, and I am here to tell you that the idea is far from crazy. Catfish, as you already know, is perfect when breaded and fried—in this case, pan-fried. Topped with a simple tomato sauce (I always use Marcella Hazan's classic recipe of slow-simmered tomatoes, onions, and butter) and melted provolone cheese, it is even better. You can serve it as a main dish with a simple green salad on the side, and save leftovers for a parm sandwich.

8 (5- to 7-ounce) catfish fillets

½ teaspoon salt

½ teaspoon freshly ground black pepper

1½ cups plain bread crumbs

1 cup grated Parmesan

2 teaspoons dried oregano

1 teaspoon dried thyme

1 teaspoon red pepper flakes

½ teaspoon freshly grated nutmeg

2 large eggs

1 cup whole milk

½ cup olive oil or canola oil

2 cups tomato sauce

8 slices good-quality provolone cheese

¼ cup chopped fresh flat-leaf parsley, for garnish

Preheat the oven to 375°F.

Pat the catfish dry, place on a large plate or sheet pan, and season with the salt and pepper. Set aside.

Mix the breadcrumbs, Parmesan, oregano, thyme, pepper flakes, and nutmeg together in a shallow baking dish or pie tin.

Whisk the eggs and milk together in a shallow bowl.

Heat the oil in a skillet over medium heat. While the oil is heating, set up your frying station. From left to right on the counter to the left of the stove, line up the catfish, then the bowl of egg wash, then the dish of bread crumb mixture. On the other side of the stove, place a 9 x 13-inch baking pan lined with nonstick aluminum foil or parchment.

When the oil is sizzling hot, you are ready to begin breading and pan-frying the catfish. Use one hand to handle the catfish, keeping the other hand clean. Working with one fillet at a time, dip the catfish in the egg wash, turning to coat. Then press it into the breadcrumb mixture, turning to coat. Gently lower the breaded fish into the oil. Repeat with one or two more fillets. Do not crowd the pan—depending on the size of your skillet, you will probably cook two or three fillets at a time. Cook the fish for 2 minutes on one side, then use a slotted spatula to flip and cook for two minutes more. When the fish is crispy and golden on both sides, transfer to the prepared baking pan. Repeat until all the fillets are breaded and pan-fried, arranging them in a single layer in the baking pan. Top generously with the tomato sauce, followed by the provolone slices.

Bake for 5 to 6 minutes, until the cheese is melted and the tomato sauce bubbly. Garnish with chopped parsley and serve hot.

CHAPTER TWELVE

CHICKEN

My first attempt at eating chicken was a complete failure.

I was seventeen and, like most of my neighbors and classmates, I'd grown up in a vegetarian household. We had friends who ate "non veg," but my parents explained that it was just something we Bhatts didn't do. The summer before our senior year in high school, a few of us decided that we were going to rebel. We were going to eat meat. We didn't dare try to cook it for ourselves at one of our houses, and we were too afraid to ask the mothers of our meat-eating friends. We didn't want to impose, but more importantly, we didn't want them to tell our mothers.

So I came up with a brilliant scheme. We would go to a restaurant and order chicken. My friend Mumtaz Ali's parents owned a famous non-veg restaurant in Ahmedabad, so I asked him if he could get us in. Of course he could. How about Wednesday night? Perfect!

We told our parents we were going to see the new Amitabh Bacchan movie, the 9 p.m. show at Ropalee Cinema. We took the bus into town and showed up at the restaurant twenty minutes early. Mumtaz greeted us outside and led us into a private, air-conditioned dining room. As soon as we sat down, a waiter entered with glasses of icy rose sherbet. After all, we were Master Ali's guests, and this was his family's restaurant. We were living large.

Soon, the food began to arrive. First came a massive platter of pilaf with cashews and figs, followed by green mango slaw, potatoes cooked in yogurt, stuffed baby eggplants, cucumber chaat, two types of lentils, and baskets of warm, buttered tandoori. Finally, the maître d' came in bearing a large bowl. "The specialty of the house and young Master Ali's favorite dish," he announced, "the Paramount Hotel's famous Butter Chicken."

This was it! We looked at one another, and if we had known how to back then, we would have chest-bumped, or at least high-fived. The waiter continued, "made especially for Master Ali's friends by your hostess, his mother, Mrs. Fatima Ali."

My jaw hit the floor. Mrs. Ali? Fatima Aunty? We exchanged nervous glances, and the rebellion was crushed before it even started.

Mrs. Ali came in just as we were all properly squirming. "Hi boys, I told your mothers that I am feeding you tonight," she said. "I even told them that you will stay the night at our house after the late picture show. Relax, dig in, and make yourselves at home."

I ate a lot that night, but I couldn't bring myself to try the chicken. I did scoop some of its rich, fragrant sauce onto my plate. I spent the next year and a half thinking that chicken tasted like onions and tomatoes cooked in ghee with cardamom and star anise—until finally, I had my first taste of a perfectly roasted bird in Strasbourg, France.

It tasted like chicken.

CHICKEN BREAKDOWN 101

Once you can break down a chicken, you can use this same technique on any bird.

You will need a sharp boning knife or chef's knife.

Moisten a kitchen towel in the sink, then wring it out so that it is damp but not sopping wet. Lay the damp towel out on your countertop or other clean work surface. Place a cutting board on top of the damp towel. You now have a cutting surface that will not slide around as you work. I recommend this setup every time you are doing a lot of cutting in the kitchen, whether it's meat or vegetables or anything else. It goes a long way toward preventing accidental cuts—to your hands, not the food!

Take the chicken out of the refrigerator and place it on the cutting board, breast side up, with the neck cavity facing you. Pull the flap of skin hanging over the cavity and cut it off. Now you should see the cavity clearly. Using your fingers, feel for the wishbone—it runs to a point up toward the keel bone, while the two tines connect to the wings. Run your knife on the outside of the wishbone to loosen it from the cavity. Using your index finger and thumb, you will now be able to pull it out. Do not worry if it breaks.

Once you have removed the wishbone, take your hand out of the cavity and feel for the keel bone on top, between the breasts. Run your knife down the breast on one side, just to the left or right of the keel bone, exposing it. Using the keel bone and the rib cage as your guide, gently slice down one side until that breast is separated from the rib cage. Keep your knife as close to the keel bone as possible so that you don't waste any meat. The breast meat will still be attached to the wing. Gently pull the breast and wing away from the carcass, exposing the wing joint. Slice through the joint. Now you will have a breast lobe with a wing attached. Repeat the process on the other side.

Once you have removed the wings and breasts, flip the chicken over and look for the "oysters." These are two small muscles, just above where the thighs connect to the back. Put your thumb on one oyster and lift the leg toward you until the large femur bone pops out of its socket. Once it does, you can very easily slide your knife around the oyster and through the gap created where the bone popped out. You will now have a chicken leg quarter (thigh and drumstick). Repeat the process on the other side. Now you have four chicken quarters: two breasts with wings attached and two thighs with drumsticks attached.

If your recipe calls for a whole chicken cut into eight pieces, slice off the wings with just a bit of the breast meat attached. (When I'm cutting chickens up for frying, I like to leave more of the breast meat attached to the wing. It can be a challenge to get large chicken breasts to cook all the way through before the skin burns in the hot oil. This solution creates pieces that are a little more even in size.) To separate the drumstick from the thigh, feel for where the femur attaches to the drumstick and cut straight through the joint.

Save the carcass for stock. (Store it in a large plastic zip-top bag in the freezer if you are not making stock right away.)

CHICKEN BONE STOCK MAKES ABOUT 10 CUPS

The next time you cook a whole chicken, or any pieces of bone-in chicken, save the bones in a plastic zip-top bag in the freezer. I like to add chicken feet for even richer flavor. If they are not available at your grocery store, look for them at an international market. The exact measurements of onion, carrot, and celery do not matter for making stock, nor does the size of the chop.

Bones of 3 chicken carcasses

4 chicken feet (optional)

1 large yellow onion, sliced

4 carrots, roughly chopped

4 celery stalks, roughly chopped

1 tablespoon tomato paste

8 sprigs thyme

2 sprigs tarragon

4 bay leaves

1 tablespoon black peppercorns

1 cup dry white wine, such as sauvignon blanc or Chablis

Preheat the oven to 350°F. Line a sheet pan with parchment.

In a large bowl, combine the chicken bones, chicken feet (if using), onion, carrots, celery, and tomato paste. Mix with your hands to distribute the tomato paste. Transfer these ingredients to the prepared sheet pan and roast for about 20 minutes, until the bones are golden brown and the tomato paste is dark reddish-brown. (If you've just pulled the bones out of the freezer, it might take a few extra minutes.)

Scrape everything off the sheet pan into a large stockpot. Add the thyme, tarragon, bay leaves, black peppercorns, wine, and 1 gallon water. Bring to a boil over high heat. When the liquid boils, turn the heat down to low and let it gently simmer for 2 to 4 hours. Check the stock periodically to make sure that it remains at a very gentle simmer.

Remove the pot from the heat and allow it to cool slightly. Skim off the fat that has risen to the top, then strain and discard the solids. You should have about 10 cups of stock.

If not using the stock immediately, be sure to cool it down to room temperature before refrigerating or freezing. The stock will keep in an airtight container in the refrigerator for up to 5 days. Frozen, the flavor will be best if used within a month. I recommend dividing the stock into smaller portions for freezing (1 or 2 cups each) so that you can easily thaw and use only what you need for a recipe.

SIMPLE HERB AND LEMON ROASTED CHICKEN SERVES 4

I tasted roast chicken for the first time in Strasbourg, France, at the home of my father's colleague. My parents were surprised; our host was delighted. It was my first taste of meat, and simple roast chicken has been a favorite ever since. When I began cooking for myself in college, and eating meat more often, I incorporated several chicken dishes into my repertoire. Even now, roast chicken is my go-to dish for dinner parties. It is easy to cook and very versatile, and while it is in the oven you can actually mix and mingle with your guests. The version I almost always serve is a variation on the one I learned to cook at City Grocery, flavored with garlic, lemon, and rosemary. I brine the chicken so that the flavor penetrates beneath the skin and the bird stays juicy as it roasts. I love the flavor of red pepper flakes, but you can dial them back or omit them altogether if you are not a fan of heat. One 3- to 3½-pound chicken comfortably serves four guests. For a larger party, I'll roast two birds. If you are roasting one chicken for yourself or a couple, you can enjoy the leftovers the next day. This preparation is all about letting the chicken shine, so I recommend splurging on a high-quality, all-natural or free-range bird.

FOR THE BRINE:

½ cup salt

1 lemon, sliced

3 sprigs rosemary

5 or 6 garlic cloves, cut in half lengthwise

1 (3- to 3½-pound) chicken

FOR THE CHICKEN:

5 or 6 garlic cloves, thinly sliced lengthwise

Grated zest of 2 lemons (After zesting, cut the lemons in half and reserve for squeezing over the chicken.)

3 sprigs rosemary, leaves chopped, stems reserved

3 tablespoons olive oil

2 teaspoons kosher salt

1 tablespoon red pepper flakes

1 tablespoon freshly ground black pepper

NOTE: Using a roasting rack allows the air to circulate around the chicken to ensure even cooking. If you don't have one, you can create a "rack" of sorts by lining the bottom of the pan with ¼-inch-thick onion slices so that the chicken does not touch the pan.

Pour 1 gallon water into a large pot or tub, add the salt, lemon, rosemary, and garlic, and stir until the salt is completely dissolved. Lower the chicken into the brine, making sure it is completely submerged. Refrigerate for 2 to 4 hours. Remove the chicken from the brine. Pat it dry with paper towels, removing any particulates that cling to the bird from the brine.

Preheat the oven to 425°F. Place a rack in a roasting pan (see Note).

Using your fingers, gently loosen the skin from the chicken breast. Slide half of the sliced garlic, half of the lemon zest, and about 2 tablespoons of the chopped rosemary under the skin. Using your fingers, spread the garlic, zest, and rosemary around the breast. Squeeze the lemon juice all over the skin and rub it in. Using a sharp knife, poke 6 to 8 small holes in the legs and thighs and stuff them with the remaining garlic slices. Put the remaining zest and the squeezed lemon halves in the cavity, along with the remaining chopped rosemary and stems. Drizzle the olive oil all over the chicken, coating the bird evenly. Sprinkle the salt, black pepper, and red pepper flakes on the outside of the chicken as well as in the cavity.

Tuck the wings behind the back and tie the legs over the cavity with kitchen twine. If you do not have any kitchen twine, turn the chicken so that the cavity is facing you. Pull the flap of skin to the left of the tail and cut a slit in it with the tip of your knife. Pull the right leg across the cavity and carefully thread the end through the slit. Cross the left leg over the cavity and secure it by tucking the end under the right leg. Voilà!

Place the chicken, breast side up, on the rack in the roasting pan. Roast for 45 minutes, or until the internal temperature at the thickest part of the bird measures 165°F on a probe thermometer. (I generally test in two places: where the thigh meets the leg, and at the thickest part of the breast.) Allow the chicken to rest for 15 to 20 minutes before carving and serving. (See Chicken Breakdown 101, page 246, if you need help—this technique works for cooked chicken as well as raw!) One roast chicken yields four generous servings: two breast quarters and two leg quarters. If your guests prefer smaller servings, or if some of them want to mix and match white meat and dark meat, you can cut each breast in half and separate the leg quarters into thighs and drumsticks, yielding a total of eight pieces of meat.

SWEET TEA–BRINED FRIED CHICKEN SERVES 8

In the aftermath of Hurricane Katrina, good folks from all over headed down to the Gulf Coast of Louisiana and Mississippi to help rebuild. Among them was a group of volunteers from the Southern Foodways Alliance that worked for months to help rebuild and reopen Willie Mae's Scotch House, a landmark restaurant in the Treme neighborhood of New Orleans known for its fried chicken. When the hurricane hit and the levees failed, the restaurant's owner and chef, Mrs. Willie Mae Seaton, was eighty-nine years old. (She passed away a decade later.) Willie Mae's Scotch House eventually reopened in 2007 with Seaton's great-granddaughter, Kerry Seaton-Stewart, at the helm. She continues to carry the torch.

In 2009, when John Currence and I opened Snackbar in Oxford, I wanted to put a dish on our Tuesday night special menu to honor the work SFA had done in New Orleans and pay tribute to Mrs. Seaton. This dish remains on our menu and sells out more Tuesdays than not. Make this for a Sunday supper, the quintessential fried chicken occasion in the South, and pay homage to the humble bird and the hard-working people who helped rebuild a city and kept traditions alive.

Seek out small chickens (3 pounds is ideal) for this recipe, as large pieces are hard to cook through evenly. At Snackbar, we serve the fried chicken with a little cup of pepper jelly; I encourage you to do the same. You can find several brands and varieties of pepper jelly at your grocery store. Believe it or not, my favorite pepper jelly recipe is the one on the box of Sure-Jell pectin, and I know several fellow chefs who swear by it as well.

You can halve this recipe, of course, and fry only one chicken. But I feel like if I'm going to fry, I may as well have friends over. I'll serve Stewed Gujarati-Style Black-Eyed Peas (page 49), Succotash (page 40), Collard Green Slaw (page 190), or Crispy Smashed New Potatoes (page 145) alongside. And happily, chicken is one of the few fried foods that makes for delicious leftovers.

FOR THE BRINE:

8 cups sweet tea (store-bought or homemade; if you use store-bought sweet tea, make sure it is not artificially sweetened)

5 garlic cloves, smashed

6 to 8 sprigs thyme, bruised (Slap the sprigs between your hands or with the back of a knife to release oils and flavor.)

2 tablespoons hot sauce

3 bay leaves

1½ tablespoons salt

2 (3- to 3½-pound) chickens, cut into eight pieces each (see page 246)

FOR THE BATTER:

2 cups chickpea flour

1 tablespoon Creole seasoning (store-bought or homemade, page 8)

1½ teaspoons salt

½ teaspoon ground cayenne pepper

2 large eggs

⅓ cup neutral oil, such as peanut or canola

2 tablespoons fresh lemon juice

1½ cups cold club soda

FOR FRYING:

6 to 8 cups neutral oil, such as peanut or canola (I like peanut oil best for frying chicken.)

All-purpose flour or rice flour, for dusting

Stir together the sweet tea, garlic, thyme, hot sauce, bay leaves, and salt in a large pot or tub until the salt is completely dissolved. The brine should be salty-sweet with a nice kick from the hot sauce. Taste before adding the chicken, and add a little more salt or hot sauce if you like the heat. Lower the chicken pieces into the brine, making sure they are completely submerged, and refrigerate the chicken in the brine for at least 4 hours. If there is room in your refrigerator for the large tub of brine, that's great. If not, I've found that the least messy way to do this is to empty out one of your refrigerator drawers, remove the drawer from the refrigerator, and place it on your kitchen counter. Open a 2-gallon zip-top bag and sit it in the drawer. If the bag has a pleated bottom so that it can stand up, all the better. Carefully pour the brine into the open bag, then gently add the chicken pieces. Zip the bag back up and return the drawer to the refrigerator.

Prepare the batter: Mix the chickpea flour, Creole seasoning, salt, and cayenne together in a large bowl. Whisk the eggs, oil, lemon juice, and club soda together in a medium bowl. Slowly pour the wet mixture into the seasoned flour mixture, whisking until you have a smooth, lump-free batter. The batter should be thin enough to just coat the back of a spoon. If it is too thick, add a bit of tap water, 2 tablespoons at a time, to get the right consistency.

Heat the oil to 350°F in a cast-iron skillet, Dutch oven, or electric fryer. If you don't have a deep-fry thermometer, drop in a spoonful of batter to test the temperature. If it sizzles and floats to the top, your oil is ready. If it sinks to the bottom of the pot, the oil still needs to heat up more.

While the oil is heating, set up your frying station. First, remove the chicken pieces from the brine, pat them dry with paper towels, and place them on a large plate or sheet pan. Then, pour a layer of flour into a pie tin or shallow baking dish for dusting. Next to that, pour the batter into another pie tin or baking dish. On the other side of the stove, place a wire rack over a sheet pan. This is where the chicken will drain and rest after it comes out of the oil. Keep a pair of tongs, a slotted spoon, or a spider strainer by the stove for removing the chicken from the oil.

Once the oil has come to temperature, you're ready to begin. Use one hand to handle the chicken, keeping the other hand clean. Take one piece of chicken and dredge it in the flour, turning to coat it lightly and/or using your fingers to sprinkle a light dusting of flour all around the skin. This step helps the batter adhere. Then, dip the chicken in the batter, turning to coat. Gently lower the chicken into the hot oil, being careful not to splash yourself. Repeat with two or three more pieces of chicken so that you have three or four pieces frying at a time. (If the pot is too crowded, it will bring down the temperature of the oil, resulting in soggy chicken that is undercooked on the inside.) After 10 minutes, carefully remove one of the smaller pieces of chicken from the oil. Using a probe thermometer inserted at the thickest part of the meat, check the temperature. If the temperature registers 165°F, that piece of chicken is done. Place the piece on the wire rack to rest and drain. If it is not cooked through, carefully return it to the oil. It may take anywhere from 10 to 15 minutes for each piece of chicken to cook, depending on size and oil temperature. If you find that the skin is burning before the meat is cooked through, your oil is too hot, and you need to reduce the stove heat slightly. When all of the pieces from the first batch are finished, let the oil temperature return to 350°F before repeating the steps for dusting, battering, and frying. Continue frying three or four pieces at a time until all the chicken is cooked.

Allow the fried chicken pieces to rest and drain on the rack for 5 minutes before serving. If you want to wait until all the pieces are fried before serving your guests, you may transfer the drained pieces to a sheet pan in a 200°F oven to keep them warm. Of course, room-temperature fried chicken is completely acceptable for a picnic or other large, informal gathering.

When the fried chicken is completely cool, store any leftovers in a zip-top bag or covered container in the refrigerator. The next day, enjoy it cold (as many Southerners do—especially at picnics or packed in a lunch), at room temperature, or heated back up in the oven.

SWEET TEA

MAKES 1 GALLON

You can find large-format iced tea bags at most supermarkets, near the other tea bags. They are available from several brands, including Lipton and Luzianne.

1 cup granulated sugar

2 gallon-size iced tea

filter bags or ½ cup black tea leaves

Pour 1 gallon water into a large pot, add the sugar, and bring to a boil over high heat. Add the tea bags or tea leaves. Reduce the heat to medium and simmer, uncovered, for 5 minutes. Remove the pot from the heat and allow to steep for 30 minutes. Strain and cool to room temperature before using or storing in the refrigerator.

CHICKEN AND LENTIL PATTIES WITH GREEN CHILES, CASHEWS, AND CILANTRO

MAKES 24 PATTIES

This recipe is very much influenced by Hyderabadi shami kebab, which is a melt-in-your-mouth creation with minced lamb, split chickpeas, shallots, and spices. Whenever there is a party that involves alcoholic beverages in India, the hosts always serve a variety of savory snacks. As an adult, I picked up the same habit. I came up with this version to serve at a cocktail party we were hosting, partly because chicken is cheaper and easier to get in Oxford than lamb and partly because Teresa claims she doesn't like lamb. (Don't tell her that I have seen her put away an entire order of the lamb meatballs, or keftedes, that Tim Hontzas makes at his restaurant, Johnny's, in Homewood, Alabama.)

These snacks are great by themselves, or you can tuck them into a small pita or slider roll with a dollop of Peanut Pesto (page 170). This recipe makes enough patties to serve 8 guests generously as a party snack.

2 teaspoons cumin seeds

12 green cardamom pods

6 star anise pods

4 cinnamon sticks

1½ pounds boneless, skinless chicken thighs, cut into ½-inch pieces

¾ cup red lentils

½ cup raw cashew pieces

3 tablespoons minced ginger

1½ teaspoons ground ginger

1 tablespoon minced garlic

2 teaspoons Kashmiri chili powder or hot paprika

1½ teaspoons ground turmeric

5 small serrano chiles, stemmed and minced, divided

3 small shallots, minced (about ⅔ cup), divided

⅓ cup chopped fresh cilantro leaves and tender stems, divided, plus additional chopped cilantro leaves, for garnish

1 to 1½ teaspoons salt

3 to 4 tablespoons neutral oil, such as peanut or canola, divided

Pita or slider rolls, for serving (optional)

Lime wedges, for garnish

Thinly sliced red onion, for garnish

Toast the cumin seeds in a small, dry pan over medium heat, shaking the pan gently so that the seeds toast evenly and do not burn, about 1 minute. Remove from the heat and, when cool enough to handle, coarsely grind in a spice grinder or coffee grinder, or with a mortar and pestle. Set aside.

Cut an 8-inch square of cheesecloth. Lay the cheesecloth on your counter and place the cardamom pods, star anise, and cinnamon sticks in the center of the cloth. Gather the corners of the square and tie the bundle closed with kitchen twine. Keep one long tail of twine. The idea is that you are using this sachet to flavor the cooking water without adding the spices to the patties themselves.

Tie the long tail of twine to the handle of a large pot and drop the spice sachet in the pot. Combine the chicken, lentils, cashews, turmeric, fresh and ground ginger, garlic, Kashmiri chili powder, and turmeric in the pot. Pour in enough water to cover everything (6 to 8 cups) and bring to a boil over high heat. Reduce the heat to a simmer and continue to cook, uncovered, until all the water has evaporated, the chicken is falling-apart tender, the lentils are fully cooked, and the cashews are very soft, about 1 hour. Remove the pot from the heat and allow the contents to cool completely. Remove and discard the sachet of whole spices.

When the meat mixture has cooled, transfer it to a food processor, along with half the chiles, half the shallots, and half the cilantro, and process until you have a smooth paste. Depending on the size of your food processor, you may need to do this in two batches.

If you do not have a food processor or blender, you may chop all ingredients together as finely as you can. Transfer the mixture to a large bowl and fold in the remaining shallots, chiles, cilantro, and cumin. Taste and add salt as desired.

Divide the mixture into 24 equal portions, each about the size of a golf ball. If you have a 1-ounce scoop, you can use it for portioning. Then, with lightly greased hands, shape the balls into patties about ½ inch thick and place them on a sheet pan. Cover with plastic wrap and chill in the refrigerator for 30 minutes before cooking. This will help the patties hold their shape as they pan-fry.

Remove the patties from the refrigerator. Line a plate with paper towels. Heat 1 tablespoon oil in a large skillet over medium-high heat. When the oil is shimmering, add as many patties as will fit in the skillet without crowding. Cook until golden brown on the bottom, about 3 minutes, then flip and cook for another 3 minutes. Transfer the cooked patties to the prepared plate to drain and cool slightly. Repeat, adding oil as needed and letting it heat up between batches, until all the patties are cooked. Serve warm, in pita or slider rolls if desired, with lime wedges for squeezing, sliced red onion, and a sprinkle of chopped cilantro. If you have any leftovers, make sure they are completely cool before storing them in the refrigerator. They can be reheated for enjoying the next day.

CHICKEN VESUVIO SERVES 6 TO 8

Chicken Vesuvio is a dish that links Italian immigrant communities in Chicago and New Orleans. It originated in Chicago, probably around the 1930s, the brainchild of Italian immigrant cooks. It's a braised chicken dish with vegetables, richly flavored with garlic, herbs, lemon, and white wine.

Chicken à la Grande, a very similar dish with a different name, is a house specialty at Mosca's Restaurant, a legendary hole-in-the-wall in suburban New Orleans. Family patriarch Provino Mosca, an Italian immigrant to New Orleans by way of Chicago, opened Mosca's in 1946 and ran it until his death in 1962. Three-quarters of a century after it opened, Mosca's is still family owned and operated, and still a cult favorite among diners in the know.

I use the Vesuvio name for my version, which incorporates elements of both the Chicago and New Orleans dishes. It is easy to put together, easy to scale up or down, and easy to make and serve out of the same vessel. Plus, it features a bit of dinner theater at the finish.

12 (4- to 5-ounce) bone-in, skin-on chicken thighs, trimmed of excess fat and skin

1½ teaspoons chopped fresh rosemary

Grated zest of 2 lemons (After zesting, cut the lemons in half and reserve for squeezing over the chicken just before serving.)

1½ teaspoons salt, divided

1½ teaspoons freshly ground black pepper, divided

⅓ cup olive oil

1½ pounds small golden, red, or new potatoes, about 2 inches in diameter, cut in half

1½ teaspoons dried oregano

1½ teaspoons dried thyme

15 garlic cloves, cut in half lengthwise

5 bay leaves

1 cup frozen green peas

1½ cups Chicken Bone Stock (page 247) or store-bought unsalted chicken stock

1½ cups dry white wine, such as sauvignon blanc or Chablis

2 tablespoons chopped fresh flat-leaf parsley

Preheat the oven to 400°F.

Pat the chicken thighs dry and season with the rosemary, lemon zest, and 1 teaspoon each salt and pepper.

In a large cast-iron or other ovenproof skillet that can hold the chicken thighs in a single layer, heat the oil over medium heat. (If you do not have a skillet that is large enough to hold all of the chicken at once, don't worry—you can sear it in two batches.) Set a wire rack on a sheet pan near the stove to rest the chicken after it sears. When the oil is shimmering, add the chicken to the skillet, skin side down. Sear until the skin is crispy and golden and some fat begins to render, about 2 minutes. Flip the pieces and sear for 2 more minutes. You're not trying to cook the chicken through at this point; you just want to render a little bit of the fat and put some crisp on the skin to prevent it from getting rubbery. Transfer the chicken to the resting rack. (If searing the chicken in two batches, repeat with the remaining chicken.)

Add the potatoes to the skillet and season with the oregano, thyme, and remaining ½ teaspoon each salt and pepper. Cook, turning as needed, until the potatoes are lightly browned and crisp on all sides, about 4 minutes. Add the garlic, bay leaves, peas, and chicken stock. Lay the chicken thighs on top and transfer the pan to the oven. (If your skillet is not large enough to accommodate everything, transfer everything to a large baking pan.) Cook for 20 minutes, or until the potatoes are soft and a probe thermometer inserted in the thickest part of a chicken thigh registers 165°F.

Carefully remove the skillet or baking pan from the oven. Pour in the white wine, not directly over the chicken but around it, so that it hits the bottom of the hot pan. This will result in a dramatic sizzle and lots of steam. (This is the "Vesuvio" part, so make sure your guests are watching!) Squeeze lemon juice over the top, sprinkle with chopped parsley, and serve.

CHICKEN WINGS WITH SPICY ORANGE MARMALADE GLAZE SERVES 6 TO 8

I consider chicken wings an essential component of watching football. I happen to have a group of male friends, successful professionals all, who get together annually on the Sunday before Labor Day to carry out the great American tradition of Fantasy Football Draft. There is always plenty to drink and eat throughout the day, someone starts arguing that Rush is the best band ever, and the evening concludes with a cookout.

One year, while planning our fantasy draft gathering, we decided to add a chicken wing challenge to the mix. The wings could be fried, baked, or grilled, and the rules were simple: The only ingredient that you were allowed to purchase was the chicken. Everything else for the marinade, seasoning, or sauce had to come from your pantry or refrigerator.

Being the only professional cook in the group, I was disqualified from competition, but I was still expected to bring wings for people to eat. I decided to follow the rules of the challenge. My father, who is a connoisseur of orange marmalade, had just returned to India after his annual summer visit, leaving a jar and a half of marmalade in the fridge. Once I settled on a marmalade glaze, the rest of the spices fell into place. I've since learned that this glaze works for grilled, fried, or baked chicken wings, as well as for other chicken parts—simply prepare the glaze and toss the meat in it immediately after cooking. I've even applied it successfully to duck and quail.

FOR THE WINGS:

¼ cup neutral oil, such as peanut or canola

1½ teaspoons salt

1 tablespoon freshly ground black pepper

1 tablespoon coriander seeds, crushed

Grated zest of 2 oranges

2 pounds chicken wings

FOR THE GLAZE:

1 cup orange marmalade (I like Keiller Dundee Orange Marmalade, which is not too sweet.)

2 tablespoons sambal oelek chili paste or Sriracha

1½ tablespoons soy sauce

2 teaspoons minced ginger

5 whole cloves

1 tablespoon coriander seeds, crushed

2 teaspoons honey or Spiced Honey (page 259)

1 teaspoon chopped fresh rosemary

Salt

Combine the oil, salt, pepper, crushed coriander seeds, and orange zest in a large bowl. Add the chicken wings and toss to coat. Set aside and allow to marinate for 1 hour. (If you have time, marinate overnight in the refrigerator.)

Heat the grill to medium.

To make the glaze, combine the marmalade, sambal oelek, soy sauce, ginger, cloves, coriander seeds, honey, and rosemary in a saucepan with ¼ cup water. Warm slowly over low heat, whisking constantly, until the marmalade melts. Remove from the heat. Taste and add a pinch of salt if desired. Transfer the glaze to a large mixing bowl—you'll toss the wings in this bowl after they cook—and set aside.

Grill the wings for about 10 minutes, turning halfway through. The wings are done when a meat thermometer inserted in the thickest part of the meat (of course, the meat isn't very thick on a wing!) registers 165°F.

Toss the wings in the glaze to coat and serve immediately.

CHICKEN SALAD WITH MANGO CHUTNEY AND PISTACHIOS SERVES 6 TO 8

If you think chicken salad is boring, you haven't had good chicken salad. Here in Oxford, the perfect chicken salad is actually a subject of impassioned debate. Many locals swear by the original recipe of Angelo Mistilis, a local restaurateur who was recognized as the "chicken salad man" long after his retirement. (He passed in 2021.) His version is still sold in half-pint and pint tubs at Lindsey's Chevron gas station on the north side of the downtown Square, alongside sleeves of Ritz and saltine crackers for a do-it-yourself lunch. (Lindsey's is not to be confused with the Four Corners Chevron on the south side of the Square, the home of chicken on a stick. There's a book waiting to be written about chicken and gas stations in our town.)

I've adapted this recipe from my good friend Victoria Pesce Elliott, who lives in Florida. She is lucky enough to have her own mango trees, so she makes her own mango chutney and adds diced fresh mango to her chicken salad when the fruit is in season. At home in Mississippi, I rarely have access to good, fresh mangoes, but luckily store-bought mango chutney works almost as well. (Note that Major Grey's is a style of chutney. Many brands are available; I like Patak's. It is widely available in supermarkets, usually shelved near the relishes and other condiments.) I'm partial to the flavor and texture that toasted, salted pistachios provide, but cashews or almonds would be a good substitute. Serve the chicken salad chilled or at room temperature with crackers, on a sandwich, or atop a bed of lettuce.

¾ cup shelled pistachios

2 teaspoons cumin seeds

1½ tablespoons black peppercorns

1 whole rotisserie chicken, skin and bones removed, meat chopped (about 5 cups; you may, of course, roast your own chicken—see page 248)

½ cup golden raisins, chopped

1 small jalapeño chile, stemmed, seeded, and minced

⅓ cup minced yellow onion

⅓ cup small-diced celery

¼ cup small-diced carrot

½ cup diced fresh mango (optional)

1 cup Major Grey's mango chutney

¾ cup mayonnaise (preferably Duke's)

2 tablespoons Creole or other grainy mustard

2 tablespoons sour cream (optional)

¼ cup chopped fresh mint

¼ cup chopped fresh basil

Salt

Toast the pistachios in a small, dry skillet over medium heat, shaking gently so that they toast evenly and do not burn, 2 to 3 minutes. Remove from the heat and, when cool enough to handle, roughly chop the pistachios. Add the cumin seeds to the same skillet and toast over medium heat, shaking gently so that they toast evenly and do not burn, until fragrant, about 1 minute. Remove from the heat and set aside to cool. Add the black peppercorns to the same skillet and toast over medium heat, shaking gently so that they toast evenly and do not burn, until fragrant, about 1 minute. Remove from the heat. When cool enough to handle, coarsely crack the peppercorns using a mortar and pestle, a rolling pin, or the back of a spoon. Set aside.

In a large bowl, mix together the chopped chicken, raisins, jalapeño, onion, celery, carrot, mango (if using), and pistachios. Set aside.

In a separate small bowl, whisk together the chutney, mayonnaise, mustard, and sour cream (if using). Add the chutney mixture to the chicken mixture and mix well. If you prefer a wetter, creamier chicken salad, you may add an additional ¼ cup mayonnaise. Add the mint, basil, cumin seeds, and crushed peppercorns and mix again. Taste and add salt if desired, up to 1 teaspoon. Let the chicken salad rest for 30 to 40 minutes before serving to allow the flavors to come together. Leftovers will keep well in a covered container in the refrigerator for up to 3 days.

GRILLED CHICKEN THIGHS WITH PEACHES, CHILES, AND SPICED HONEY SERVES 6

Summer is a relatively slow time of year in a college town like Oxford. I'm able to step out of the restaurant more often, so Teresa and I entertain more at home. We love to invite friends over for informal gatherings. Generally, she and I cook a couple of larger dishes and our guests bring side dishes, appetizers, and sometimes dessert. During one of these impromptu dinners, we found ourselves with lots of fresh peaches and chiles that needed to be used. Faced with these ingredients, and fortified with cold beer, I threw together this recipe. It made enough of an impression on Teresa, our friends, and me that I now cook it at least a few times during peach season. I use poblano, Fresno, Anaheim, and jalapeño chiles. Any colorful combination with varying degrees of heat will work.

If good, fresh peaches aren't available where you live, nectarines will work just as well. Look for fruit that is ripe but not mushy, so that it holds its shape on the grill. This is one of those simple summer dishes that stands on the quality of seasonal produce, and it definitely works best on an outdoor grill. The idea is to make something delicious and relatively easy so that you can enjoy time with your guests.

3 tablespoons olive oil, divided

Juice of 2 lemons, divided

3 tablespoons fresh chopped rosemary, divided

½ teaspoon salt, divided

½ teaspoon freshly ground black pepper, divided

12 (4- to 5-ounce) bone-in, skin-on chicken thighs

6 ripe (but not overripe) peaches, peeled if desired (see Note), cut in half, and pitted

1 small red onion, sliced thick enough that they hold their shape on the grill

12 ounces mixed chiles, cut into large enough chunks or rounds that won't fall through the grates

1 recipe Spiced Honey (page 259), for drizzling

½ cup torn fresh mint leaves, for garnish

NOTE: I prefer to peel my peaches, though you can skip this step if you don't mind the skin. Bring a large pot of water to a boil over high heat. Lightly score an X on the bottom of each peach with the tip of a sharp knife. When the water is boiling, carefully drop in the whole peaches. After about 30 seconds, remove the peaches from the water using a slotted spoon. When cool enough to handle, they will be easy to peel.

Combine half each of the olive oil, lemon juice, rosemary, salt, and pepper in a large bowl. Add the chicken thighs and toss to coat evenly. Set aside for 30 minutes to allow the chicken to absorb the flavors.

In a separate medium bowl, combine the remaining olive oil, lemon juice, rosemary, salt, and pepper with the peaches, onions, and chiles and toss well.

Heat the grill to medium.

When the grill is hot, add the peach halves (flat side down), onion slices, and chile pieces. (Place the onions and chiles in a grill basket, if you have one, so they don't fall through the grates.) Grill the peaches, onions, and chiles until they are marked and slightly charred on one side, 2 to 3 minutes. Flip everything and grill for another 2 to 3 minutes. The peaches, onions, and chiles should retain some firmness; you do not want them to feel cooked all the way through. If you did not peel the peaches, the skin will curl up at the edges. Transfer to a serving platter, arranging everything so that the onions and chiles are scattered around the peach halves.

Grill the chicken until a meat thermometer inserted in the thickest part of a thigh registers 165°F, 5 to 7 minutes on each side. Transfer to the serving platter, setting the cooked thighs right on top of the grilled peaches, onions, and chiles. Drizzle some of the spiced honey over the top and garnish with the mint before serving. Bring the remaining honey to the table in a small bowl so that your guests may serve themselves more if desired.

SPICED HONEY

MAKES ABOUT ¾ CUP

You can make this spiced honey while the chicken marinates and the grill heats, or up to a day in advance. It is delicious drizzled on top of biscuits, too.

½ cup honey

1 tablespoon cracked black pepper

1 teaspoon coriander seeds, crushed

1 teaspoon fennel seeds

1 teaspoon salt

Combine all the ingredients in a small saucepan, add ¼ cup water, and bring to a simmer over medium heat. Once the mixture simmers, give it a stir and remove from the heat. If not using right away, transfer to a storage container. Allow to cool completely before covering and storing at room temperature.

Grilled Chicken Thighs with Peaches, Chiles, and Spiced Honey (page 258)

Ahmedabad Street-Style Grilled Chicken (page 262)

AHMEDABAD STREET-STYLE GRILLED CHICKEN SERVES 4

I grew up in Ahmedabad, a city founded six hundred and some odd years ago by Sultan Ahmad Shah I. Like all other Islamic rulers of his age, the first thing he did was build a beautiful mosque, and the city grew up around it. Today, the lanes and alleys around the mosque constitute the city's oldest Muslim neighborhood and have a well-earned reputation for some of the best meat-forward street food in Gujarat. Since I didn't grow up eating meat, I was an adult returning home for a visit when I finally came to appreciate this part of my home city's culinary identity. The street cooks in Ahmedabad halve small chickens and marinate them in yogurt, ginger, garlic, and spices. They grill the meat just inches over coals kept glowing hot by miniature fans. The resulting chicken is slightly blistered and charred on the outside, the skin crispy and smoky. The meat is slightly tangy from the yogurt, subtly spiced, and surprisingly moist. It is cut into four pieces and served wrapped in newsprint, accompanied by slices of red onion and lime and a cilantro sprig. My adaptation, I promise, will make your next outdoor party a hit. The chopped beet in the marinade gives the chicken a beautiful reddish hue.

1 (3- to 3½-pound) chicken, cut into 8 pieces (see page 246), or 4 leg quarters

1 teaspoon salt

½ teaspoon ground turmeric

Juice of 1 lemon

3 cups plain, full-fat yogurt (preferably Greek-style)

1 tablespoon minced garlic

1 tablespoon minced ginger

1½ teaspoons minced serrano chile

1 teaspoon Kashmiri chili powder or hot paprika

1 teaspoon ground cumin

2 teaspoons tandoori masala (I use Spicewalla brand.)

2 teaspoons peeled and minced red beet

3 tablespoons minced fresh cilantro leaves and tender stems

FOR GARNISH:

Sliced red onion

Lime wedges

Chopped fresh cilantro

Chopped fresh green chiles

Prick each chicken piece several times with a fork and toss in a large mixing bowl with the salt, turmeric, and lemon juice. Set aside for 20 minutes.

While the chicken is resting, combine the yogurt, garlic, ginger, serrano, chili powder, cumin, tandoori masala, minced beet, and cilantro in a large bowl. Transfer about a third of the marinade to a smaller bowl and store, covered, in the refrigerator. You will use the reserved marinade for basting the chicken later. Add the chicken to the large bowl of marinade, tossing to coat evenly. Cover and refrigerate for at least 4 hours or up to 12 hours.

When you are ready to begin grilling, remove the chicken from the refrigerator. Heat the grill to medium. Once the grill is hot, remove the chicken pieces from the marinade and place them on the grill. Grill the chicken, flipping once, until a meat thermometer inserted in the thickest part of a breast or thigh registers 130°F, about 4 minutes on each side. Remove from the grill and allow the chicken to rest on a plate or platter for 30 minutes. (If it's an especially hot day, you might want to cover the chicken with aluminum foil and bring it indoors.)

Brush the reserved marinade on the chicken, return the pieces to the grill, and finish cooking for about 3 minutes on each side, until a meat thermometer inserted in the thickest part of a breast or thigh registers 165°F. This two-step grilling gives the chicken a nicely charred crust.

Serve hot off the grill garnished with sliced red onions, lime wedges, chopped cilantro, and/or chopped fresh green chiles.

MOROCCAN CHICKEN STEW SERVES 6 TO 8

Rafik Said was my first friend in France. Rafik's father, a dentist, and his mother, a teacher, had moved to Strasbourg from Morocco in the late 1960s. Mrs. Said took my mother and me to Maghrebi markets where we could buy spices, tea, nuts, and dried fruits like dates and figs that I had grown up eating in India. In this far corner of eastern France, a family from India and a family from Morocco bonded over shared stories of family life, immigration, and food.

One of the dishes that made an impression on me was Mrs. Said's chicken tagine. It was rich yet light, with hints of sweetness from figs and tartness from preserved lemon. Green olives added a salty note, and tomatoes balanced the acid. Then, of course, there were the spices: cinnamon, cumin, coriander, and star anise. Even though many of the flavors were new to me, the dish immediately reminded me of the stews I had grown up eating. I have traveled back to France a few times as an adult, and I realize now that couscous and tagine are as much a part of French cuisine as pommes dauphinoise and coq au vin.

This recipe adapts that tagine from my memory for a Dutch oven. It serves a large family or a dinner party and fills your home with the fragrance of warm spices.

12 boneless, skinless chicken thighs

Salt

Freshly ground black pepper

4 tablespoons olive oil, divided

3 cups diced yellow onion

2 tablespoons minced garlic

4 cups diced ripe tomatoes or 2 (28-ounce) cans diced tomatoes, drained

1 (28-ounce) can crushed tomatoes

1 cinnamon stick

1½ cups chopped dried figs

1½ cups green olives, such as Castelvetrano or picholine

1 lemon, sliced into ¼-inch rounds, plus grated zest of 2 lemons

1½ tablespoons Moroccan Seasoning (page 264)

1½ teaspoons red pepper flakes

1 generous pinch saffron

4 cups Chicken Bone Stock (page 247) or store-bought unsalted chicken stock

1½ cups pecans, toasted and chopped

Crusty bread or naan, for serving

Season the chicken thighs generously with salt and pepper and set aside at room temperature for 20 minutes.

Heat 2 tablespoons oil in a large Dutch oven over medium-high heat. When the oil is shimmering, add half the chicken thighs. Cook until the flesh begins to turn brown and some of the fat starts to render, about 2 minutes. Flip the pieces and cook for 2 more minutes. You're not trying to cook the chicken through at this point; you just want to render a little bit of the fat and brown the meat. Remove from the heat and set aside on a plate. Repeat with the remaining chicken thighs.

Add the remaining 2 tablespoons oil to the Dutch oven and sauté the onions until they start to brown, about 5 minutes. Add the garlic and sauté for an additional 3 minutes. Add the diced and crushed tomatoes, lower the heat to medium, and cook until almost all the water has cooked out of the tomatoes, about 20 minutes. Add the cinnamon stick, figs, olives, lemon slices, Moroccan seasoning, red pepper flakes, and saffron. Stir and cook until the spices are fragrant, 3 to 4 minutes. Add the stock and the browned chicken thighs and bring to a simmer.

Turn the heat down to low, cover, and cook until

RECIPE CONTINUES

the chicken is falling-apart tender, about 40 minutes. Carefully lift the cover and stir in the pecans and lemon zest. Season with salt and pepper to taste. Cover and let the stew stand for 15 to 20 minutes before serving. Ladle into bowls and serve with crusty bread or naan.

NOTE: If you like, you can cook this in the oven. Follow the recipe until the stew comes to a simmer. Then, instead of cooking it on the stove, cover and cook in a 325°F oven for 1 to 1½ hours. Add the pecans and lemon zest after the stew comes out of the oven. This method is especially convenient if you need to cook something else on the stove, or if you want to do a little cleanup before dinner.

MOROCCAN SEASONING

MAKES A GENEROUS ½ CUP

1 tablespoon coriander seeds

1 tablespoon cumin seeds

1 tablespoon fennel seeds

1 tablespoon garlic powder

1 tablespoon dry English mustard powder

1 tablespoon salt

1 tablespoon freshly cracked black pepper

1½ teaspoons crushed dried rosemary

1½ teaspoons ground cayenne pepper

1 teaspoon ground turmeric

½ teaspoon ground cardamom

½ teaspoon ground cinnamon

¼ teaspoon freshly grated nutmeg

Toast the coriander seeds in a small, dry pan over medium heat for about 1 minute. Add the cumin seeds and fennel seeds and toast, shaking the pan gently so that the seeds toast evenly and do not burn, until both spices are fragrant, about 1 more minute. Remove from the heat and, when cool enough to handle, grind in a spice grinder or coffee grinder, or with a mortar and pestle. Transfer to a small bowl, add all the remaining ingredients, and mix well. Store in a tightly covered container at room temperature for up to 1 month.

DELUXE
LE CREUSET

CHICKEN CAFREAL SERVES 6 TO 8

Unlike other parts of India, Goa, on the southwestern coast, was a Portuguese-occupied territory for over four hundred years, until its liberation in 1961. That Iberian influence shows up not only in architecture and religious practices but in all other aspects of life, including art, music, and food. Goan cuisine is distinct, with layers of influence from Portugal, other former Portuguese colonies like Mozambique, and the surrounding Konkan coast region of India. While vindaloo may be the best known of Goan dishes, my favorite is the more humble chicken cafreal. It is a great dish to make for company—an easy-to-assemble crowd pleaser with a vibrant green color from the marinade and tons of bright flavor. It can be cooked on a stovetop, as is traditionally done, or just as easily grilled outside.

Since you will be blending the marinade ingredients in a food processor, it is fine to roughly chop the ginger, jalapeños, and shallots. You can also use this marinade for fish, shrimp, or pork. Or try tossing it with roasted cauliflower or roasted potatoes.

I like to serve this dish with Potato Raita (page 147), Whole Grilled Okra (page 60), or Summer Pea Salad (page 42).

2 bunches cilantro, including stems

⅓ cup chopped ginger

2 small jalapeño chiles, stemmed and chopped

6 to 8 garlic cloves, peeled

4 small shallots, chopped (¾ to 1 cup)

½ cup plus 2 to 4 tablespoons olive oil, divided

Grated zest and juice of 2 limes

2 teaspoons garam masala (store-bought or homemade, page 8)

1 to 2 teaspoons salt

½ teaspoon ground turmeric

2 (3- to 3½-pound) chickens, quartered (see page 246) and skinned, or 8 leg quarters, skinned

To make the marinade, combine the cilantro, ginger, jalapeños, garlic, shallots, ½ cup olive oil, lime zest and juice, garam masala, 1 teaspoon salt, and turmeric in a food processor or blender and process to a smooth paste. Taste and add additional salt if desired.

Put the chicken pieces in a large bowl, add the marinade, and toss well. Cover the bowl and allow the chicken to marinate in the refrigerator for at least 2 hours or up to 6 hours.

About 20 minutes before you are ready to cook the chicken, remove it from the fridge. Give everything a good stir, cover the bowl again, and set aside at room temperature. Letting the chicken come to room temperature rather than cooking it straight from the refrigerator helps it cook evenly.

Heat 2 tablespoons olive oil in a cast-iron skillet or other heavy-bottomed pan over medium-high heat. When the oil is shimmering, gently lower the chicken pieces into the skillet smooth side down (the side the skin was on). Do not crowd the pan. Depending on the size of your skillet, you may need to cook the chicken in two batches. Cook the chicken on one side for 4 minutes. Using tongs, turn each piece and cook for another 4 to 5 minutes, until a probe thermometer inserted in the thickest part of a thigh registers 165°F. Transfer the cooked chicken to a serving platter. If cooking a second batch, add 2 more tablespoons of oil and allow it to heat to shimmering before adding the rest of the chicken. Serve immediately.

SEON'S CHICKEN RAMEN SERVES 2 TO 4

My friend Seon Woen grew up in Seoul, South Korea. I met him my sophomore year of college at the University of Kentucky, when he sublet a room in my apartment for a semester. For the first two months, Seon complained about how nothing in Lexington measured up to Seoul, especially the food. When, in my ignorance, I suggested that we could go try out a new sushi place in Georgetown, he almost punched me. He proceeded to educate me on the troubled history of Korean-Japanese relations. As a peace offering, I offered to make us ramen. At that time, my idea of ramen was to follow the directions on a pack of instant noodles and doctor the finished product with some Maggi Hot and Sweet sauce and a dash of Tabasco.

You should have seen Seon's face. He told me he would have preferred to eat at the sushi restaurant than touch the abomination I had put in front of him. I told him that if he thought he could do a better job with those cheap packs of noodles, I would drive him the seventy-five miles to Louisville and treat him to a proper meal at one of the state's only Korean restaurants. The next day, Seon came home with a bag full of groceries and made the best bowl of ramen I'd ever had. The following weekend, I drove him to Louisville.

Though I've adapted his method into my own recipe over the years, I still think of Seon when I make ramen. This makes an easy, flavorful, and comforting weeknight dinner for a couple or a small family.

2 teaspoons rice vinegar

1 teaspoon brown sugar

3 tablespoons soy sauce, divided

3 tablespoons gochujang paste or Sriracha, divided

2 tablespoons neutral oil, such as peanut or canola, divided

4 boneless, skinless chicken thighs, cut into thin strips

8 cups Chicken Bone Stock (page 247) or store-bought unsalted chicken stock

1 bunch scallions, thinly sliced

½ cup thinly sliced bok choy or green cabbage

½ cup thinly sliced carrots

½ cup thinly sliced mushrooms

1 serrano chile, stemmed and thinly sliced

2-inch piece ginger, sliced into very thin matchsticks

3 packages dried instant ramen noodles, such as Maruchan (discard seasoning packets)

Combine the rice vinegar, sugar, and 1 tablespoon each of soy sauce, gochujang, and oil in a bowl. Add the chicken strips, toss to coat with the marinade, and set aside for 30 minutes.

Heat the remaining 1 tablespoon oil in a Dutch oven or other wide, heavy-bottomed pot over medium-high heat. When the oil is shimmering, remove the chicken strips from the marinade, shaking off excess liquid as you transfer them to the pot. Sear the chicken strips for 1 to 2 minutes on each side. Remove the chicken and set aside on a plate.

Add the chicken stock, scallions, bok choy, carrots, mushrooms, chile, and ginger, turn the heat up to high, and bring to a boil. Stir in the seared chicken and the remaining 2 tablespoons each soy sauce and gochujang. Turn the heat down to medium and simmer, uncovered, for 5 minutes. Add the ramen and cook until the noodles are cooked through, 2 to 3 minutes. Serve hot.

CHAPTER THIRTEEN

PORK AND LAMB

Working at City Grocery, I quickly started learning about grilling, roasting, and braising meats.

Every fall, I worked with the guest chefs at the Southern Foodways Alliance Symposium in Oxford. I met some of the best culinary minds in the country and learned to cook regional dishes. I began to see a common theme, especially in the dishes served family-style: They gathered friends and strangers alike around a communal table to celebrate what was available that season. These ideas were not very different from the ones I had grown up with.

Hogs have been raised in the South since Spanish explorers left hogs on the barrier islands of what is now Georgia. (Ossabaw Island hogs are their descendants.) Relatively inexpensive and easy to raise, they have fed Southerners of all races and classes for centuries. They have figured into major cultural and culinary events, from late-fall hog killings to celebratory barbecues.

When I first met Teresa's father, I was afraid that I would not be welcome in the family. I quickly realized how wrong I had been. We bonded over stories of family gatherings in western Kentucky and western India, stories of grandmothers churning butter and putting up pickles. We bonded over corn and okra and whiskey. We soon understood that we had a lot in common. To celebrate, he took me to Starnes Bar-B-Q in Paducah and we broke bread together—pulled pork sandwiches, to be exact.

Ever since I started eating meat, I have always been a fan of lamb. It also happens to be just as widely appreciated as pork and has long been a part of the Southern diet. Lamb is raised throughout the South and eaten on holidays and special occasions with gusto. Given that lamb has a smaller environmental footprint than beef, I hope that these recipes inspire you to cook and eat more of it.

Many of the recipes in this chapter make a generous 8, 10, or even 12 servings. You can absolutely cut them in half to suit your needs. My feeling is that if you're making a hearty stew, you might as well invite friends over to share it.

GRILLED PORK TENDERLOIN WITH TANDOORI SPICES SERVES 4 TO 6

If you are anything like me, chances are you have had plenty of tandoori chicken but rarely any tandoori pork. Most Indian restaurants choose not to serve beef or pork, especially if their owners, clientele, or both are predominately Hindu and/or Muslim. It turns out that the lean pork tenderloins benefit from a yogurt marinade, just like chicken breasts do.

For the best results, score the tenderloins so that they absorb the marinade, and marinate them in the refrigerator for 6 to 8 hours before grilling them. If you don't have a grill, the sear-and-roast method outlined at the end of the recipe works almost as well. After the tenderloins have rested, I slice them and serve them with Kashmiri-Style Collards (page 195) and either Potato Raita (page 147) or Sweet Potato and Peanut Salad (page 161).

This is an excellent main dish for a dinner party, and the leftovers make great sandwiches. You can scale it up for a larger party or down to just one tenderloin for a couple.

- 1 cup plain, full-fat yogurt (preferably Greek-style)
- 2¼ teaspoons tandoori masala (I use Spicewalla brand.)
- 1 teaspoon salt
- ½ teaspoon Kashmiri chili powder or hot paprika
- ¼ teaspoon ground cayenne pepper
- 1 teaspoon honey
- ½ teaspoon fresh lemon juice
- 1½ teaspoons minced garlic
- 1 tablespoon minced ginger
- 2 pork tenderloins, silverskin and excess fat trimmed

Combine the yogurt, tandoori masala, salt, chili powder, cayenne, honey, lemon juice, garlic, and ginger in a medium bowl and mix well. Taste for salt and adjust if necessary. Score the pork tenderloins a few times with a sharp knife to absorb the marinade. Add the pork to the marinade and make sure it is completely coated. Cover and refrigerate for 6 to 8 hours.

Remove the pork from the refrigerator 30 minutes before you are ready to begin cooking. Heat the grill to high.

Shake the excess marinade off the pork and lay the tenderloins on the grill. Cook on each side for 4 minutes, letting the meat take on an uneven char. The pork is done when a meat thermometer inserted in the thickest part of the tenderloin registers 145°F. When done, transfer the tenderloins to a platter and allow to rest for 6 to 8 minutes before slicing and serving.

If you do not have a grill, preheat the oven to 375°F. Heat a skillet over medium-high heat and sear the tenderloins on all sides. (Depending on the size of your skillet, you may need to sear one tenderloin at a time.) Transfer the seared tenderloins to a large sheet pan. Bake for 8 to 10 minutes, or until a meat thermometer inserted in the thickest part of the tenderloin registers 145°F. Allow the pork to rest for 6 to 8 minutes before slicing and serving.

CONFIT PORK RIBS WITH MEXICAN ADOBO PASTE SERVES 8

I love barbecue ribs. Unfortunately, I do not have a smoker at home—you probably don't, either. So if I want really good ribs, I have to make a pilgrimage to Memphis or come up with a creative way to make them myself.

The idea of doing the confit treatment at home first came to me when I watched Ben Barker make confit lamb ribs for a Southern Foodways Alliance symposium in Oxford years ago. I've made those lamb ribs many times since, mostly for events and festivals. Eventually, I crossed over into pork ribs, and decided to try the confit technique in my home kitchen. I wanted an assertive seasoning and experimented with the spice blend until I came up with this version of an adobo paste. It builds on the elements of a Mexican adobo but is decidedly not traditional, layering in some of the flavors of a Memphis dry rub and rounding things out with orange zest and brown sugar.

I marinate these overnight for the ribs to really absorb all the flavors, then cook them submerged in a combination of lard and olive oil for 4 to 5 hours, until the meat is falling-off-the-bone tender. If you like, you can add a layer of flavor by giving the ribs a quick turn on the grill after they've cooked and rested.

There's a good chance your grocery store sells lard. If you don't see it near the oils, it may be in the Latino foods aisle and labeled "manteca." It's also great for pie crusts, cookies, and frying. If you can't find it, use additional olive oil.

Serve these at your next party with Collard Green Slaw (page 190) or Cabbage, Kale, Carrot, and Peanut Salad (page 186)—and plenty of paper towels or napkins!

FOR THE MARINADE:

12 medium dried chiles, such as guajillo or New Mexico, stemmed

2 tablespoons cumin seeds

1½ tablespoons salt

1 teaspoon dried oregano

1 teaspoon ground cinnamon

1 teaspoon ground allspice

½ teaspoon ground cloves

1 yellow or white onion, diced (about 1¼ cups)

8 garlic cloves, peeled

½ cup apple cider vinegar

3 tablespoons olive oil

Grated zest and juice of 3 oranges

¼ cup brown sugar

FOR THE RIBS:

4 slabs baby back ribs

3 cups lard, melted

6 cups olive oil

Thinly sliced red onion, for garnish

Chopped fresh cilantro leaves, for garnish

Lime wedges, for squeezing

Toast the dried chiles in a small, dry pan over medium heat until fragrant. Remove the chiles and set aside. In the same pan, toast the cumin seeds over medium heat, shaking the pan gently so that the seeds toast evenly and do not burn, about 1 minute. Remove from the heat. When cool enough to handle, grind the chiles and cumin seeds in a spice grinder or coffee grinder, or with a mortar and pestle. You should have a generous ½ cup of toasted chile-cumin mixture.

Transfer the chile-cumin mixture to a food processor or blender and add the salt, oregano, cinnamon, allspice, cloves, onion, garlic, cider vinegar, oil, orange zest and juice, and brown sugar. Blend until smooth.

Place the ribs in a roasting pan large enough to hold them (cut the racks in half if necessary).

Pour the marinade over the ribs, making sure that it covers the meat completely on both sides. Cover the pan with plastic wrap and refrigerate for 6 to 7 hours or overnight. There is no need to turn the ribs during marinating as long as they are completely submerged in the marinade.

RECIPE CONTINUES

When ready to cook, preheat the oven to 275°F. While the oven is heating up, pour off the excess marinade that has collected at the bottom of the roasting pan. Combine the melted lard and olive oil in a large bowl and mix well. Pour this mixture over the ribs, making sure you have enough fat to submerge the ribs completely. Cover the pan tightly with aluminum foil, slide it into the oven, and cook for 4 hours.

After 4 hours of cooking, the ribs should be falling-off-the-bone tender. Allow them to rest in the fat for 30 minutes before carefully removing them.

While the ribs rest, heat the grill to medium. Carefully transfer the ribs to the hot grill and cook for 1 to 2 minutes on each side, just to impart some char and extra flavor. Do not skip the resting step, or they will fall apart on the grill.

Transfer the ribs to a serving platter and serve with thinly sliced red onion, a sprinkle of cilantro, and lime wedges for your guests to squeeze on their ribs as desired.

PORK COUNTRY CAPTAIN SERVES 6

Country captain is an iconic dish of the South Carolina–Georgia Lowcountry with direct links to India. Thin cutlets of meat, usually chicken, are pan-seared and then simmered in a tomato sauce flavored with curry powder. The dish traces its roots to a time when Savannah, Charleston, and other Southern ports were the entry points for spices imported from the East Indies. From there, black pepper, cinnamon, nutmeg, ginger, cardamom, and other spices made their way into Southern cuisine. To me, country captain is the most clearly Indian of Southern dishes. Every time I make this dish, I am reminded that even across hemispheres, we have so much in common. We only need to look in the spice cabinet and on the stove.

My version of country captain uses pork as the meat. If you prefer the more traditional chicken, use a similar quantity of boneless breast cutlets or boneless thighs, pounded thin. Serve over steamed aromatic rice or Grits Upma (page 140).

1¼ cups all-purpose flour

3 teaspoons freshly ground black pepper, divided

2 teaspoons salt, divided

¼ cup ghee (store-bought or homemade, page 9)

12 (2- to 3-ounce) boneless pork chops, pounded to an even thickness of about ¼ inch (You might see these labeled as pork cutlets.)

2 tablespoons unsalted butter

¼ cup chopped bacon

2 cups minced yellow onion

2 cups diced red and yellow bell pepper (1 large red and 1 large yellow pepper)

1⅓ cups diced carrots

4 garlic cloves, thinly sliced

2 tablespoons minced ginger

2 dried chiles de árbol, stemmed and broken in half

1 (28-ounce) can crushed tomatoes

1⅓ cups diced fresh tomatoes

½ cup dried currants, raisins, or dried cranberries

½ cup Chicken Bone Stock (page 247) or store-bought unsalted chicken stock

2 teaspoons curry powder

1½ teaspoons garam masala (store-bought or homemade, page 8)

½ teaspoon Kashmiri chili powder or hot paprika

Steamed rice or Grits Upma (page 140), for serving

2 tablespoons chopped fresh flat-leaf parsley

¼ cup slivered almonds, toasted

Combine the all-purpose flour with 2 teaspoons black pepper and 1 teaspoon salt in a shallow plate or pie tin; set aside.

Heat the ghee over medium-high heat in a Dutch oven or large, high-sided skillet with a lid. Line a platter with paper towels. When the oil is shimmering, lightly dust the pork chops in the seasoned flour and, working in batches, sear them for 20 to 30 seconds on each side. (The meat will cook most of the way through and finish later in the sauce.) Shingle them on the prepared platter and set aside.

Wipe the Dutch oven or skillet clean. Add the butter and let it melt over medium-high heat. Add the bacon and cook until it starts to brown, about 3 minutes. Add the onions and cook, stirring occasionally, for 7 to 8 minutes, or until they are very soft. Add the bell peppers, carrots, garlic, ginger, and dried chiles and cook until the vegetables are tender, 6 to 7 minutes. Add the crushed and diced tomatoes. Lower the heat to medium, cover, and cook until the tomatoes start to break down and thicken, about 20 minutes. Stir in the currants, stock, curry powder, garam masala, chili powder, and remaining 1 teaspoon each salt and pepper. Simmer until the currants are plump. Gently add the seared pork to the sauce and simmer for an additional 6 to 7 minutes, until the meat is cooked through.

To serve, place a serving of rice or grits on each plate. Top with two pieces of meat and a scoop of sauce. Garnish each serving with chopped parsley and toasted slivered almonds.

If you have leftovers, allow them to cool completely before storing, covered, in the refrigerator for up to 2 days.

TRINIDAD PORK PELAU SERVES 8 TO 10

We often forget about the American South's long association with the Caribbean, forged first in the era of Spanish exploration, and then by the atrocities of the transatlantic slave trade. It may be that, today, we prefer not to think of the cruelty and human toll of that time. Instead, Americans are more likely to think of the Caribbean as a vacation paradise, largely disconnected from history, culture, and cuisine.

However, when we look at the foods we eat, we cannot but help realize just how much the South and the Caribbean have in common. Pork came to our tables from pigs brought by Spanish explorers, rice from Africa and the Far East, okra from Africa, and sugar from India. These elements and more formed the building blocks of a creolized Southern cuisine.

One such dish is Trinidadian pelau, a filling, one-pot meal that serves a crowd. It is a first cousin to Lowcountry purloo. Pelau is most often made with chicken, but I find this caramelized pork version to be more flavorful and more soulful. Sweet, spicy, and rich, it is a one-pot meal that pairs well with rum cocktails, soca music, and the company of good friends.

FOR THE MARINADE:

4 pounds boneless pork shoulder, cut into 2-inch cubes

3 tablespoons fresh lime juice

1 teaspoon Worcestershire sauce

1 teaspoon ketchup

1 tablespoon minced garlic

2 teaspoons minced ginger

1 medium yellow or white onion, minced (about 1¼ cups)

1 large tomato, minced (about 1 cup)

¼ cup chopped scallions

¼ cup fresh thyme leaves

3 tablespoons chopped fresh cilantro leaves and tender stems

1 habanero pepper, seeded and minced

1 tablespoon salt

1½ teaspoons curry powder

1½ teaspoons ground allspice

FOR THE PELAU:

2 tablespoons neutral oil, such as peanut or canola

2 tablespoons light brown sugar

2 cups fresh or frozen pigeon peas

1 large carrot, diced (a scant ½ cup)

2 (13.5-ounce) cans full-fat coconut milk

3 cups brown rice, washed in 3 changes of cold tap water and drained

NOTES: If your grocery store sells pork stew meat already cut into pieces, you can certainly use that. If you want a hit of acid to cut the richness, serve the pelau with a little bowl of your favorite pickles on the table for guests to help themselves.

Rinse the pork under cold running water and pat dry. Combine all the marinade ingredients in a large bowl and stir to mix well. Add the pork to the marinade and stir to coat. Refrigerate for 30 to 40 minutes.

Heat the oil in a Dutch oven or other wide, heavy-bottomed pot over medium heat. When the oil is shimmering, add the brown sugar and cook until it caramelizes, 6 to 7 minutes. The sugar will melt and begin to bubble. Keep an eye on it and stir frequently so that it does not burn. Add the pork with all of the marinade. Stir thoroughly to coat the pork evenly in the caramelized sugar. Cover and cook for 8 to 10 minutes. The pork will begin to release water and take on a stewy consistency. Remove the lid, increase the heat to medium-high, and cook, stirring frequently, until most of the liquid has evaporated, 6 to 7 minutes. Turn the heat back down to medium and stir in the peas, carrots, and coconut milk. Simmer, uncovered, for 5 minutes. Add the rice and 6 cups water. Stir to mix well, turn the heat up to high, and bring to a boil. When the mixture boils, turn the heat down to low, cover, and cook until the peas are soft, the rice is cooked, and the pork is cooked but not falling apart, 35 to 40 minutes. Serve hot.

If you have leftovers, allow them to cool completely before storing, covered, in the refrigerator for up to 2 days.

PORK INDAD SERVES 6

Most Indians do not eat pork. The exceptions are clustered along the southwestern coast of the subcontinent, where the Portuguese established colonies and converted residents to Catholicism as far back as the 1400s. Pork vindaloo, a curry most closely associated with the states of Goa and Kerala, has a well-deserved international reputation as one of India's great dishes.

Halfway between the Goan capital of Panjim and the Kerala port of Kochi lies the less-touristed city of Mangalore. Like Goa and Kerala, Mangalore was influenced by Portuguese occupation and trade. This pork indad, which rivals any vindaloo I've had, is served at Christmas in the homes of Mangalorean Catholics. Once you make this dish on a cold winter night, you will return to it again and again. It is a warm, comforting dish that needs only rice or flatbread to make a meal.

- 2 pounds pork shoulder, cut into 1-inch cubes
- 2 tablespoons minced ginger
- 3 tablespoons minced garlic
- 1 tablespoon salt, divided
- 5 dried chiles de árbol, stemmed
- 5 dried guajillo chiles, stemmed
- 2 tablespoons black peppercorns
- 2 cinnamon sticks, broken into pieces
- 2 teaspoons cumin seeds
- 2 teaspoons poppy seeds
- ½ teaspoon ground turmeric
- 2 yellow or white onions, minced
- 2 tablespoons raisins
- 2 tablespoons tamarind concentrate
- 5 tablespoons apple cider vinegar
- ½ teaspoon ground turmeric
- 3 tablespoons neutral oil, such as peanut or canola
- 1 teaspoon light brown sugar
- ¼ cup chopped fresh mint leaves, for garnish
- Steamed rice, for serving

Rinse the pork under cold running water and pat dry. Season with the ginger, garlic, and ½ tablespoon salt. Set aside for 30 minutes.

Meanwhile, put the dried chiles in a bowl of warm water and allow them to soak until soft, about 10 minutes.

Toast the black peppercorns and cinnamon stick pieces in a small, dry skillet over medium heat. After 1 minute, add the cumin seeds and poppy seeds. Continue to toast, shaking the pan gently so that the seeds toast evenly and do not burn, until all of the spices are fragrant, 1 to 2 more minutes. Remove from the heat. When cool enough to handle, grind all the spices together in a spice grinder or coffee grinder, or with a mortar and pestle. Set aside.

Drain the chiles and put them in a food processor, along with the onions, raisins, tamarind concentrate, vinegar, turmeric, and ground spices. Blend into a smooth paste and set aside.

Heat the oil in a Dutch oven or other wide, heavy-bottomed pot over medium heat. When the oil is shimmering, add the seasoned pork. Most of the ginger and garlic will fall off the pork and into the pot. Cook, stirring often, so that the ginger and garlic do not stick to the bottom of the pot and burn. Continue cooking until the pork is browned on all sides. Increase the heat to high, cover, and cook for 10 minutes. (You no longer have to worry about the garlic and ginger burning because the pork will begin to release liquid at this stage.) Uncover the pot and lower the heat to medium. Cook, stirring occasionally, for an additional 8 to

RECIPE CONTINUES

10 minutes, until the liquid released from the pork has evaporated and the fat begins to render out.

Add the chili-onion-spice paste, stir to mix well, and cook for about 10 minutes, until the mixture darkens in color and becomes thicker. Add 2 cups water. Scrape up any bits stuck to the bottom of the pan and add the sugar and remaining ½ tablespoon salt. Cover, reduce the heat to low, and simmer for 30 minutes. Uncover the pot, raise the heat to medium, and cook until some of the excess water evaporates and you have fork-tender pork in a thick, reddish gravy.

Garnish with the chopped mint and serve over steamed rice.

If you have leftovers, allow them to cool completely before storing, covered, in the refrigerator for up to 2 days.

NOTES: Pork stew meat will work as well and saves you the step of cubing the meat. If you like pork belly and your butcher has it available, you can use 1½ pounds shoulder meat and ½ pound cubed raw pork belly. This dish calls for tamarind concentrate, which you may also see labeled as tamarind paste. Made from the tropical tamarind fruit, the paste has a fruity-sour flavor. You can find it at many international markets, including Indian, Latino, or Caribbean grocery stores, or you can order it online.

BRAISED PORK SHANKS WITH COCONUT MILK AND MALABAR SPICE SERVES 8

There is something magical about taking a tough, ungainly-looking piece of meat and cooking it slowly so that you end up with a soul-warming, tender, and richly flavorful meal to feed a large group. And you don't have to stand over the stove for hours.

Traditionally, when one thinks of braising, it is the French technique and flavors—coq au vin, daube, and boeuf bourguignon—that come to mind. I was the same way until I met chef Asha Gomez and tasted her food. Asha and I are members of Brown in the South, a group of chefs of South Asian descent now living and cooking in the American South.

An Atlantan by way of Kerala, Asha's cooking, especially her touch with spices, is transcendent. When I created this dish, I was inspired by the sort of spice profile with which Asha cooks. The recipe depends on the freshly toasted and ground Malabar spice blend (page 284)—there is no prepackaged substitute.

I start this braise on the stove and then transfer it to the oven. But if you are adept with a slow cooker or Instant Pot, this recipe is a good candidate for adaptation to either of those methods. Grits Upma (page 140) or Khichadi (page 21) would make an excellent accompaniment, as would a simple pot of steamed aromatic white rice.

- 8 pork shanks (often sold as pork osso buco)
- 1 tablespoon salt, divided
- 3 tablespoons Malabar Spice (page 284), divided
- 3 tablespoons coconut oil, divided
- 2 teaspoons brown mustard seeds
- 2 teaspoons cracked black pepper
- 2 sprigs curry leaves, plus more for garnish (optional)
- 3 small red onions, thinly sliced
- ¼ cup minced ginger
- 2 tablespoons tomato paste
- 4 cups diced fresh tomatoes
- 8 cups Chicken Bone Stock (page 247) or store-bought unsalted chicken stock
- 2 tablespoons tamarind concentrate
- 2 (13.5-ounce) cans full-fat coconut milk
- Unsweetened shredded dried coconut, for garnish (optional)
- Flash-fried curry leaves, for garnish (optional; see Note)

NOTE: To flash-fry curry leaves for garnish, heat neutral oil in a small skillet over medium heat and add the leaves. Cook, stirring, for about 10 seconds. Remove from the heat. You can do this while the sauce is having its final simmer.

Put the pork shanks in a large bowl and season with ½ tablespoon salt and 1 tablespoon Malabar spice. Cover and refrigerate for 30 minutes.

Preheat the oven to 325°F.

Heat 1½ tablespoons oil in a Dutch oven or other wide, heavy-bottomed pot over high heat. Sear the seasoned shanks, turning with tongs until nicely browned on all sides, 6 to 8 minutes total. Transfer the shanks to a platter. Lower the heat to medium and add the remaining 1½ tablespoons oil to the pot. Once the oil is shimmering, add the mustard seeds and cook until they start popping, about 30 seconds. Add the black pepper and curry leaves and cook, stirring, until they are very fragrant, about 30 seconds. Add the onions and ginger and cook until the onions are soft and translucent, 6 to 7 minutes. Add the tomato paste and cook, stirring frequently, for 2 to 3 minutes. The tomato paste will become several shades darker. Watch closely and be careful not to let it burn. Stir in the diced tomatoes and remaining 2 tablespoons Malabar spice.

Turn the heat down to medium-low, cover, and cook for 5 to 6 minutes, until the tomatoes start to break down. Add the chicken stock, increase the heat to medium-high, and bring to a boil. Return the pork shanks to the pot and stir in the tamarind paste and

RECIPE CONTINUES

remaining ½ tablespoon salt. Cover the pot and transfer it to the oven.

After 1 hour, remove the pot from the oven and stir in the coconut milk. Cover and return the pot to the oven for 30 to 40 minutes, or until the pork is falling-off-the-bone tender.

Carefully transfer the shanks to a serving platter. Return the sauce to the stove and bring to a simmer over medium heat. Reduce the heat to low and simmer for 10 minutes, skimming off any fat that rises to the top. If you like, you can blend the sauce with an immersion blender until smooth. (This step is optional and a matter of personal preference. I blend the sauce at the restaurant and leave it chunky at home.) Pour the sauce over the shanks. Garnish with a sprinkle of shredded coconut and flash-fried curry leaves, if desired, and serve hot. If it seems too messy to pour the sauce over the shanks on the serving platter, you can place a serving of meat on each guest's plate, spoon the sauce on top, and garnish individual servings with coconut and curry leaves.

If you have leftovers, allow them to cool completely before storing, covered, in the refrigerator for up to 2 days.

MALABAR SPICE

MAKES ABOUT ¾ CUP

Try using Malabar spice in place of garam masala for a slightly different flavor profile. It is especially good sprinkled on fish, shrimp, or cauliflower.

- ¼ cup coriander seeds
- 1½ tablespoons cumin seeds
- 2 teaspoons fennel seeds
- 2 teaspoons black peppercorns
- 1 teaspoon fenugreek seeds
- ½ teaspoon brown mustard seeds
- 1 star anise pod
- 5 whole cloves
- 1 cinnamon stick, broken into pieces
- 2 sprigs curry leaves
- 2 tablespoons unsweetened dried shredded coconut
- 1 teaspoon ground ginger
- 1 teaspoon ground turmeric
- 1 teaspoon ground cayenne pepper

Toast the coriander seeds, cumin seeds, fennel seeds, peppercorns, fenugreek seeds, mustard seeds, star anise, cloves, cinnamon stick, curry leaves, and dried coconut together in a small, dry skillet over medium heat, shaking the pan gently so that the spices toast evenly and do not burn. Heat until all the spices are fragrant, about 3 minutes. Remove from the heat. When cool enough to handle, grind to a fine powder in a spice grinder or coffee grinder, or with a mortar and pestle. Add the ginger, turmeric, and cayenne and mix well. Allow the mixture to cool completely before storing in an airtight container at room temperature. Use within 1 month for best flavor.

LAMB KHEEMA SERVES 6 TO 8

Where I live, it can be a little tricky to find specialty cuts of lamb in the grocery stores, but ground lamb is reliably available. Perhaps it's the same where you are. If so, you're in luck: You can make kheema any time you like. The term can apply to any loose ground meat, but lamb or goat kheema are by far the most common at restaurants and street vendors across India. Think of it as you would picadillo, or the filling for a sloppy joe.

Once you have mastered the art of kheema-making—which will take you no more than an hour—try incorporating it into quesadillas, scrambled eggs, omelets, hand pies, and shepherd's pie. Eat it on soft buns, sloppy joe style, like they do on the streets in Mumbai, or use it for a pizza topping with some paneer and feta. Kheema is so versatile that you will have no problem using all of it.

1 tablespoon cumin seeds

3 small onions, roughly chopped (about 4 cups)

2 tablespoons neutral oil, such as peanut or canola, or ghee (store-bought or homemade, page 9)

2 tablespoons minced ginger

1 tablespoon minced garlic

1 small jalapeño chile, stemmed and minced

2 tablespoons tomato paste

1 cup plain, full-fat yogurt (preferably Greek-style)

3 green cardamom pods, crushed, or 1 teaspoon cardamom powder

1½ tablespoons garam masala (store-bought or homemade, page 8)

1 tablespoon Kashmiri chili powder or hot paprika

2 teaspoons salt

½ teaspoon ground turmeric

2 pounds ground lamb

1½ tablespoons chopped fresh mint leaves, for garnish

1½ tablespoons chopped fresh cilantro, for garnish

NOTE: Caramelized onion is the foundation of the kheema flavor, so have patience with this step. It may take as long as 30 minutes. Look for most of the liquid to cook out and for the onions to take on a caramel-brown color. They will break down to more of a paste consistency than individual pieces.

Toast the cumin seeds in a small, dry pan over medium heat, shaking the pan gently so that the seeds toast evenly and do not burn, about 1 minute. Remove from the heat and, when cool enough to handle, crush with a mortar and pestle or coarsely grind in a spice grinder or coffee grinder. Set aside.

Put the onions in a food processor and process until very finely chopped. If you do not have a food processor, you can achieve a similar texture by grating the onions. (If grating, begin with the 3 small onions whole rather than chopped.)

Heat the oil or ghee in a large skillet over medium heat until shimmering. Add the onion and cook until caramelized, 20 to 30 minutes. Be patient and do not rush this step, as you want the richness of the caramelized onions to bring a depth of flavor to the meat mixture. Stir the onions frequently as they cook. If they are sticking, you can add a tiny bit of water and stir to scrape up any brown bits from the bottom of the pot. If the sticking is persistent, turn the heat down slightly. The onions will turn completely brown and begin to break down. If you taste a bite, it will have some sweetness.

When the onions are fully caramelized, stir in the ginger and garlic and cook for 5 to 6 minutes. Add the jalapeño and tomato paste and cook, stirring to incorporate the tomato paste, for another 5 to 6 minutes, until the tomato paste gets several shades darker. Add the yogurt, cardamom, garam masala, chili powder, salt, and turmeric and cook, stirring often, until all the water has cooked out of the yogurt. The contents of the pot should be a very fragrant, golden-brown paste at this point. Stir in the ground lamb and cook, breaking up the meat with a wooden spoon or spatula, until it is cooked all the way through, about 10 minutes. Garnish with the chopped mint and cilantro.

GROUND LAMB (KOFTA) KEBAB, TWO WAYS

Mrs. Fatima Ali was an Ahmedabad restaurateur and the mother of my good childhood friend Mumtaz. She served me my first lamb kebab, which I ate without shame. It was succulent and utterly delicious, loaded with ginger, chiles, and cardamom. For a long time, it remained my standard for judging all kofta kebabs. And it cemented my assumption that kebabs were an Indian invention.

Many years later, my Turkish friend Gokhan Karahan invited Teresa and me over to have dinner with his mother. That night, Mrs. Karahan treated us to an elaborate Turkish feast with seemingly endless mezze. Among the dishes was lamb kebab. I recognized the shape and texture right away, but the flavors were unlike anything I'd had before. While I was used to kebabs being chile- and spice-forward, this version was mild and subtle, seasoned with fresh parsley, garlic, and just a hint of Urfa pepper.

Kebabs are made for grilling and taste best when cooked that way. If you do not have a grill, you can cook them in a grill pan or on a stovetop griddle. Alternatively, you could form the meat into patties rather than kebabs and cook them in a cast-iron skillet. As different as they are, I find Mrs. Ali's and Mrs. Karahan's kofta kebabs equally delicious. Try each recipe and see which you prefer.

MRS. KARAHAN'S RECIPE

MAKES ABOUT 18 KEBABS, SERVES 6 TO 8

- ½ cup shelled pistachios
- 1 tablespoon cumin seeds
- 2 pounds ground lamb
- 1 large egg yolk
- ¼ cup grated yellow or white onion
- ¼ cup chopped fresh flat-leaf parsley
- 3 tablespoons minced garlic
- 2 tablespoons chopped fresh mint leaves
- 2 teaspoons salt
- 1 teaspoon smoked paprika
- ½ teaspoon ground cinnamon
- 1 teaspoon neutral oil, such as peanut or canola
- Olive oil, for brushing

Heat the grill to medium.

Toast the pistachios in a small, dry skillet over medium heat for 1 to 2 minutes. Add the cumin seeds and toast, shaking the pan gently so that the nuts and seeds toast evenly and do not burn, until both are fragrant, about 1 more minute. When cool enough to handle, grind the pistachios and cumin seeds to a coarse powder in a food processor, in a spice grinder or coffee grinder, or with a mortar and pestle.

Transfer the pistachio-cumin mixture to a large bowl and add the lamb, egg yolk, onion, parsley, garlic, mint, salt, paprika, and cinnamon. Knead with your hands until everything is mixed very well. Or, if you prefer, combine all the ingredients in the bowl of a stand mixer fitted with a paddle attachment. Mix on the lowest speed until well combined, about 3 minutes.

Heat the neutral oil in a small skillet over medium heat. When the oil is shimmering, break off a small piece of the meat mixture and cook it until cooked through. Remove from the heat and allow to cool slightly before tasting to check for seasonings. If you think the meat needs more salt (or any of the other spices), add them to the bowl as desired and mix again to incorporate. (This step is helpful the first time you make the kebabs. Once you learn how you like them, you can skip it.)

Using lightly greased hands, form the meat mixture into portions about the size of a golf ball. Thread a skewer through each ball and use your hands to form the meat into a sausage shape 5 to 6 inches long. (If using wooden skewers, soak them in water for 15 to 20 minutes first so that they do not catch fire on the grill.) Repeat until you have used all of the meat mixture. You will have about 18 kebabs. Lightly brush each one with olive oil to keep them from sticking to the grill.

Grill the kebabs for 2 to 3 minutes on each side. If you find that the outside of the kebab is burning before the meat is cooked through on the inside, your grill is too hot. Lower the temperature or shift the kebabs to a less hot part of the grill.

Slide the kebabs off the skewers and onto a serving platter.

MRS. ALI'S RECIPE

MAKES ABOUT 18 KEBABS, SERVES 6 TO 8

3 tablespoons chickpea flour

2 pounds ground lamb

½ cup grated yellow or white onion

¼ cup chopped fresh cilantro leaves and tender stems

2 tablespoons minced ginger

2 tablespoons minced garlic

2 teaspoons salt

2 teaspoons freshly ground black pepper

2 teaspoons garam masala (store-bought or homemade, page 8)

1 teaspoon ground cayenne pepper

½ teaspoon freshly grated nutmeg

½ teaspoon ground turmeric

1 teaspoon neutral oil, such as peanut or canola

Olive oil, for brushing

Heat the grill to medium.

Toast the chickpea flour in a small, dry skillet over medium-low heat until fragrant, about 1 minute. Remove from the heat and set aside until cool enough to handle.

Transfer the toasted chickpea flour to a large bowl and add the lamb, onion, cilantro, ginger, garlic, salt, pepper, garam masala, cayenne, nutmeg, and turmeric. Knead with your hands until everything is mixed very well. Or, if you prefer, combine all the ingredients in the bowl of a stand mixer fitted with a paddle attachment. Mix on the lowest speed until well combined, about 3 minutes.

Heat the neutral oil in a small skillet over medium heat. When the oil is shimmering, break off a small piece of the meat mixture and cook it until cooked through. Remove from the heat and allow to cool slightly before tasting to check for seasonings. If you think the meat needs more salt (or any of the other spices), add them to the bowl as desired and mix again to incorporate. (This step is helpful the first time you make the kebabs. Once you learn how you like them, you can skip it.)

Using lightly greased hands, form the meat mixture into portions about the size of a golf ball. Thread a skewer through each ball and use your hands to form the meat into a sausage shape 5 to 6 inches long. (If using wooden skewers, soak them in water for 15 to 20 minutes first so that they do not catch fire on the grill.) Repeat until you have used all of the meat mixture. You will have about 18 kebabs. Lightly brush each one with olive oil to keep them from sticking to the grill.

Grill the kebabs for 2 to 3 minutes on each side. If you find that the outside of the kebab is burning before the meat is cooked through on the inside, your grill is too hot. Lower the temperature or shift the kebabs to a less hot part of the grill.

Slide the kebabs off the skewers and onto a serving platter.

NOTE: Serve kebabs with flatbread, like naan or pita. I like Mrs. Karahan's Recipe with Turkish Tomato Salad (page 92), and Mrs. Ali's Recipe with Peanut Pesto (page 170).

RED CHILE AND YOGURT–BRAISED LAMB SHOULDER (Laal Maas) SERVES 10 TO 12

A year after we were married, Teresa and I traveled to India. It was my first trip back in sixteen years and her first trip to India. We both felt like we would need a couple days of "vacation" time after completing our packed itinerary of family obligations. I booked us a room at the Shiv Niwas Palace Hotel, overlooking Lake Pichola in the sixteenth-century royal city of Udaipur.

In my enthusiasm to make sure Teresa had as authentic a travel experience as possible, I booked a Hindustan Ambassador car to drive us the 150 miles or so from Ahmedabad to Udaipur. Between the antique automobile, the roads, and the traffic etiquette of India, the trip was a four-and-a-half-hour game of chicken. Needless to say, we didn't feel very good when we arrived at our beautiful hotel.

I had booked us a dinner for two on the ramparts of the palace, overlooking the lake. I envisioned a romantic meal, sipping our gin and tonics as the sun set over the lake, with the temple bells echoing in the hills. Instead, Teresa became ill as soon as we checked in and retired to our room for the evening. Our table for two became a table for one.

While my wife sipped warm Coca-Cola in our suite, I made the ultimate sacrifice and dined alone. The centerpiece of the meal was laal maas, the signature lamb curry of Rajasthan.

I felt terrible that I was unable to share this dish with my wife, so I had the chef send me his recipe. The next year, when I made it for our anniversary, I learned that Teresa is not a big fan of lamb. Nearly twenty years later, we are still happily married—and she has come to enjoy lamb, including this dish, a little more.

As you'll see, this recipe makes a large quantity. You could scale it down for a smaller family (or a romantic dinner, like the one I botched), but it's special enough to deserve a table full of hungry friends. Serve it with Makki Ki Roti (page 139) or naan.

- 5 pounds boneless lamb shoulder, cut into 2-inch cubes
- 2 tablespoons salt, divided
- 10 medium dried guajillo or New Mexico chiles, stemmed
- ¼ cup minced ginger
- ¼ cup minced garlic
- 1½ tablespoons coriander seeds
- 1½ tablespoons cumin seeds
- 4 black cardamom pods
- 6 green cardamom pods
- 1 cinnamon stick, broken into pieces
- 2 cups plain, full-fat yogurt (preferably Greek-style)
- 1 tablespoon Kashmiri chili powder or hot paprika
- 1 teaspoon freshly grated nutmeg
- ¼ cup plus 2 teaspoons of ghee (store-bought or homemade, page 9), divided
- 4 or 5 small yellow onions, thinly sliced
- 5 tablespoons tomato paste
- 5 bay leaves

Season the lamb with 1 tablespoon salt in a large bowl and set aside.

Soak the dried chiles in a bowl of warm water until soft, about 10 minutes. Drain the chiles and purée them in a food processor or blender.

Combine the minced ginger and garlic in a small bowl; set aside.

Toast the coriander, cumin, both cardamoms, and cinnamon together in a small, dry skillet over medium heat until fragrant, about 2 minutes, shaking gently so that everything toasts evenly and does not burn. When the spices are cool enough to handle, grind them in a spice grinder or coffee grinder, or with a mortar and pestle. Whisk the toasted spice powder with the yogurt in a medium bowl.

Transfer half the spiced yogurt mixture to a small bowl, cover, and store in the refrigerator. You will use this later when you are cooking the sauce for the lamb. To the other half of the spiced yogurt, add the chile

RECIPE CONTINUES

purée, Kashmiri chili powder, nutmeg, and half of the ginger-garlic mixture. Stir to combine very well. Pour the yogurt mixture over the lamb and stir to coat the meat completely. Cover the bowl with plastic wrap and allow to marinate in the refrigerator for at least 4 hours, or overnight if possible. Cover the remaining ginger-garlic mixture with plastic wrap and refrigerate.

When ready to cook, preheat the oven to 300°F. Remove the marinated lamb, reserved ginger-garlic mixture, and reserved spiced yogurt from the refrigerator.

Heat ¼ cup ghee in a large Dutch oven or other wide, heavy-bottomed pot over medium heat. When the oil is shimmering, add the sliced onions and a pinch of salt. Cook, stirring often, until the onions just start to caramelize, 12 to 15 minutes. Add the ginger-garlic mixture and cook for 5 minutes. Add the tomato paste and cook, stirring often, until it thickens and turns several shades darker, about 5 minutes. Add the spiced yogurt, lower the heat, and cook for 10 to 12 minutes, stirring often. If the tomato paste begins to stick to the bottom of the pot, deglaze with a teaspoon or two of water and stir to scrape up any stuck bits so that they do not burn. (If this is a problem, you may also want to reduce the heat further.) Continue to cook until all the water has cooked out of the onions and yogurt and you have a uniform, red-orange paste, about 5 more minutes.

Add the lamb with all of the marinade and stir to combine everything well. Add the remaining 1 tablespoon salt and cook until the newly added yogurt is cooked through, 5 to 6 minutes. Stir in the bay leaves and enough water to just cover the lamb. Bring to a simmer, cover the pot, and transfer it to the oven. Cook for 1 hour to 1 hour 15 minutes, until the lamb is fork-tender.

When the lamb is finished cooking, remove the pot from the oven and return it to the stove over low heat. Fold a piece of aluminum foil to make a small, shallow bowl. Light a piece of lump charcoal directly on a second burner of your stovetop and heat until it is glowing red. Uncover the pot and place the foil bowl directly on top of the cooked lamb. Using tongs, transfer the hot piece of charcoal onto the foil and spoon the remaining 2 teaspoons ghee on top of it. This will create a cloud of smoke. Cover the pot, turn off the heat, and allow it to smoke for 3 to 4 minutes.

Remove the lid. Discard the foil and burnt charcoal before serving the lamb.

If you have leftovers, allow them to cool completely before storing, covered, in the refrigerator for up to 2 days.

NOTES: Begin preparing the ingredients up to a day in advance of when you want to serve the laal maas, as the lamb needs to marinate for at least 4 hours or preferably overnight. The quick-smoking technique at the end is a hallmark of true Rajasthani laal maas. You could skip it if it sounds intimidating to you. But I promise it is not difficult, and the flavor it imparts is well worth the extra step.

LAMB NECK WITH TOMATOES AND OLIVES

SERVES 8 TO 10

This recipe is a tip of the hat to my friend Rebecca Wilcomb, a New Orleans–based chef with Italian roots. She cooked a similar dish at a pop-up in Oxford a few years ago. I couldn't get that dish out of my head, so I created my own version. Invite some friends over, open a bottle of red wine, put some Louis Prima on the stereo, and try it for yourself. I recommend serving it over polenta.

4 pounds bone-in lamb neck or shanks, or 3 to 3½ pounds boneless lamb shoulder (If you have a butcher who can cut the necks or shanks into steaks, have them do so.)

1 tablespoon salt

1 tablespoon freshly ground black pepper

⅓ cup olive oil

2 large leeks, whites and light green parts, sliced into half-moons, washed, and drained

2 fennel bulbs, diced

4 medium carrots (about 1 pound), peeled and diced

8 garlic cloves, sliced

2 large tomatoes, diced

1 cup canned crushed tomatoes

1 cup red wine, such as Chianti or Côtes du Rhône

4 cups Chicken Bone Stock (page 247) or store-bought unsalted chicken stock

1 cup mixed green and black olives, pitted (do not use canned)

2 tablespoons minced fresh rosemary leaves

2 teaspoons red pepper flakes

Cooked polenta or grits, for serving

Preheat the oven to 300°F.

Season the lamb generously with the salt and pepper and set aside for 30 minutes.

Heat the olive oil in a Dutch oven or other wide, heavy-bottomed pot over medium-high heat. When the oil is shimmering, add the lamb pieces and cook, turning until you get a nice sear all around the outside, 2 to 3 minutes. Depending on the size of your pot, you will probably need to sear the lamb in two or three batches so that you do not crowd the pot. Transfer the seared lamb to a plate. Add the leeks, fennel, carrots, and garlic and cook until very soft, 10 to 12 minutes. Add the diced tomatoes and cook for a couple of minutes to cook some of the water out, then add the crushed tomatoes and lower the heat to medium. Cover and cook until the tomatoes are broken down and most of the water has cooked out of them, 8 to 10 minutes.

Add the wine, raise the heat to high, and cook until the liquid is reduced by half, about 10 minutes. Add the stock, seared lamb, olives, rosemary, and red pepper flakes and bring to a boil. Cover the pot and transfer it to the oven. Cook for 1½ to 2 hours, until the lamb is falling-off-the-bone tender. (Whole, bone-in necks will take longer than steaks. Shoulder will cook a bit more quickly.)

If you like, skim the fat off the surface before serving. Serve the lamb over polenta or grits, spooning additional sauce over each portion.

If you have leftovers, allow them to cool completely before storing, covered, in the refrigerator for up to 2 days.

NOTE: There is a good chance that your local grocery store or butcher does not carry lamb neck. Ours doesn't. I am able to source it from our friends at Home Place Pastures, who raise and process excellent pigs, cattle, and sheep about thirty miles north of Oxford in Como, Mississippi. If there's a lamb purveyor at your local farmers' market, ask if they will do this specialty cut for you. Chances are, they'll be happy to oblige. If you can't get lamb neck, don't despair. You can also make this recipe with easily available lamb shoulder or shanks.

LEBANESE LAMB AND WHITE BEAN STEW

SERVES 8 TO 10

A couple of years ago, we hosted a summer dinner series at Snackbar called Mississippi Mondays. I invited young chefs from around the state whose cooking I admire to join me in the kitchen. We planned menus that highlighted Mississippi ingredients, and the dinners raised funds for Good Food for Oxford Schools, a non-profit that promotes healthy eating in our local public school system.

One of our guest chefs was Alex Eaton, who owns the restaurants Manship and Aplos in Jackson. Chef Alex is of Lebanese descent, so we planned a Lebanese-inspired lamb stew in his honor. Our friends at Home Place Pastures in nearby Como, Mississippi, supplied us with beautiful lamb shoulders. The meal was a hit.

This stew would obviously make a great dish for a winter evening, but it is surprisingly light enough to be appropriate any time of the year. Serve it with some crusty bread for sopping up the flavorful broth, a simple green salad, and perhaps a bottle or two of Lebanese wine.

2 cups dried white beans, such as cannellini or great northern, or 3 (15.5-ounce) cans white beans, rinsed and drained

3 pounds lamb shoulder, cut into 2-inch cubes

1 tablespoon salt, divided

1 tablespoon freshly ground black pepper, divided

2 teaspoons cumin seeds

1 teaspoon fennel seeds

¼ cup olive oil

1 medium onion, diced (1 to 1¼ cups)

2 celery stalks, diced (about ¾ cup)

3 carrots, peeled and diced (about 1 cup)

6 to 8 garlic cloves, thinly sliced

¼ cup tomato paste

8 to 10 cups Chicken Bone Stock (page 247) or store-bought unsalted chicken stock

1 cinnamon stick

1 tablespoon chopped fresh rosemary leaves

2 teaspoons ground paprika

1 teaspoon ground allspice

2 tablespoons pomegranate molasses

NOTES: This is the rare recipe where canned beans work well. If your butcher or grocery store sells lamb stew meat, by all means use it and save yourself the step of cubing the meat. Pomegranate molasses adds a pleasantly tart flavor and just a hint of sweetness to the stew. If your supermarket does not carry it, you can find it at Middle Eastern or international grocery stores or order it online. Besides this stew, I love using pomegranate molasses in salad dressings.

If using dried beans, put them in a bowl and add enough water to cover them by 1 to 2 inches. Cover the bowl with a kitchen towel or plate and let the beans soak for at least 4 hours or overnight at room temperature. When ready to begin cooking, drain the beans, rinse them, and drain again. Set aside.

Season the lamb with ½ tablespoon each salt and pepper and set aside for 30 minutes.

Toast the cumin seeds and fennel seeds in a small, dry pan over medium heat, shaking the pan gently so that the seeds toast evenly and do not burn, about 1 minute. Remove from the heat and, when cool enough to handle, grind in a spice grinder or coffee grinder, or with a mortar and pestle. Set aside.

Heat the oil in a large Dutch oven or other wide, heavy-bottomed pot over medium-high heat. When the oil is shimmering, add the lamb and cook, turning the pieces until they are browned on all sides. (Depending on the size of your pot, you may need to brown the lamb in two batches so that you do not crowd the pot.) Transfer the browned lamb to a plate. Add the onion, celery, carrots, and garlic and cook, stirring occasionally, until very soft, 8 to 10 minutes. Add the tomato paste and cook until it turns several shades darker, about 5 minutes. If using soaked dried beans, add them now, along with 8 cups stock. Stir, turn the heat up to high, and bring to a boil. Turn off the heat, cover, and allow to stand for 15 minutes to cook the beans.

After 15 minutes, turn the heat back to medium.

Return the lamb to the pot and stir in the toasted spices, cinnamon stick, rosemary, paprika, and allspice. Bring the stew to a simmer, then reduce the heat to low and cover. Simmer for 1 hour, or until the beans are cooked through and the lamb is fork-tender. Check the stew periodically to make sure there is enough liquid. If the stew seems too dry at any point, add more stock (or water) ½ cup at a time, to reach the desired consistency.

If using canned beans, add them at this point and simmer for 8 to 10 minutes. Once the beans and lamb are cooked through, stir in the pomegranate molasses and the remaining ½ tablespoon each salt and pepper. Taste and adjust the seasonings, then ladle the stew into bowls.

Allow the stew to cool completely before covering and storing leftovers in the refrigerator for up to 2 days.

WHAT SHOULD I MAKE?

A Recipe Finder by Occasion

Rather than menus, I've organized recipe suggestions by occasion.

BRUNCH

VEGETARIAN OPTIONS

PICNIC OR SUMMER LUNCH

COCKTAIL PARTY

GRILL AND CHILL

Whole Grilled Okra (page 60)

Succotash (page 40)

Monsoon Grilled Corn (page 120)

Grilled Chicken Thighs with Peaches, Chiles, and Spiced Honey (page 258)

Ahmedabad Street-Style Grilled Chicken (page 262)

Grilled Shrimp with Mango Chutney Glaze (page 211)

Grilled Pork Tenderloin with Tandoori Spices (page 273)

Coal-Roasted Sweet Potatoes (page 155)

WEEKNIGHT QUICK FIXES

Chicken Cafreal (page 267)

Bombay Toasties (page 148)

Stir-Fried Shrimp with Black Pepper and Coriander (page 213)

Lamb Kheema (page 286)

Catfish Parmesan (page 242)

Maque Choux (page 133)

Skillet-Fried Corn and Okra (page 131)

Seon's Chicken Ramen (page 269)

ONE-POT DINNERS

Collard Greens Garni (page 189)

Lebanese Lamb and White Bean Stew (page 294)

Trinidad Pork Pelau (page 279)

Moussaka (page 116)

Khichadi (page 21)

Sunday "Everything" Dal (page 43)

Shrimp with Okra and Coconut Milk (page 217)

DINNER FOR A CROWD

Rice Pilaf with Chicken, Raisins, and Cashews (page 27)

Jambalaya (page 30)

Lebanese Lamb, Okra, and Tomato Stew (Bamia) (page 78)

Stewed Gujarati-Style Black-Eyed Peas (page 49)

Saag-Style Collards (page 193)

Lamb Neck with Tomatoes and Olives (page 293)

Moroccan Chicken Stew (page 263)

Chicken Vesuvio (page 254)

Not Your Mama's Cornbread (page 137)

Mom's Rice "Pudding" (page 37)

COOL-WEATHER SUPPER

Mustard Green and Field Pea Minestra (page 199)

Afghan-Style Spinach with Dill and Cilantro (page 187)

Shrimp Recheado (page 221)

Kung Pao Catfish (page 240)

Pork Indad (page 281)

Red Chile and Yogurt–Braised Lamb Shoulder (Laal Maas) (page 290)

Stewed Lima Beans with Winter Spices (page 57)

For Further Reading (and Cooking)

Ben and Karen Barker, *Not Afraid of Flavor: Recipes from Magnolia Grill*

Floyd Cardoz, *One Spice, Two Spice: American Food, Indian Flavors*

Ashley Christensen, *Poole's: Recipes and Stories from a Modern Diner*

Asha Gomez, *My Two Souths: Blending the Flavors of India into a Southern Kitchen*

Jessica B. Harris, *Sky Juice and Flying Fish: Traditional Caribbean Cooking* (I also love *Beyond Gumbo: Creole Fusion Food from the Atlantic Rim*, but *Sky Juice* was the first book of Harris's that I read, so it's special to me.)

Karen Hess, *The Carolina Rice Kitchen: The African Connection*

Madhur Jaffrey, *An Invitation to Indian Cooking*

Raji Jallepalli, *Raji Cuisine: Indian Flavors, French Passion*

Niloufer Ichaporia King, *My Bombay Kitchen: Traditional and Modern Parsi Home Cooking*

Edward Lee, *Smoke and Pickles: Recipes and Stories from a New Southern Kitchen*

Bill Neal, *Bill Neal's Southern Cooking*

Todd Richards, *Soul: A Chef's Culinary Evolution in 150 Recipes*

David Shields, *Southern Provisions: The Creation and Revival of a Cuisine*

Chris Smith, *The Whole Okra: A Seed to Stem Celebration*

John Martin Taylor, *Hoppin' John's Lowcountry Cooking: Recipes and Ruminations from Charleston and the Carolina Coastal Plain*

ACKNOWLEDGMENTS

Nothing happens in a vacuum. I would not have had any stories to tell without all the people and places that have been a part of my journey. The journey began with the Ancestors and will continue long after I am gone.

Kumar, Kashmira, Smita: Thank you for teaching me how to think, read, tell stories, and appreciate all the small things that make a big picture. To all the clans—Bhatts, Pattanis, Parasharyas, Vaidyas, Mehtas, Vyas, Shuklas—y'all made growing up very special and allowed the children to flourish and express themselves. I am eternally grateful to be a part of your legacy.

My wife Teresa: Your patience, your grace, your love, and your never-ending encouragement make me do things I never thought I could. You are the best.

John Currence: Without you there would be no career, no cookbook, no stories to tell. Thank you for being a great boss, a better mentor, and an even better friend. I don't have enough space here to tell you everything, so we will do it with a glass of bourbon and a bucket of fried chicken.

Rushir: Your fearlessness and drive to pursue your dreams is a true talent and a trait that makes me happy and hopeful for the future.

My Brown in the South family: Meherwan, Cheetie, Maneet, Asha, Samatha, Farhan, Sunny Bhai, Chandra, Stacey, Mikey, Rajkot Paul, Danny Bhai, Sir James—you guys give me so much joy and laughter.

John T. Edge: Thank you for pushing me and convincing me that I should tell my story. Your friendship, scholarship, and guidance are responsible for making me who I am.

My Southern Foodways Alliance family: There are too many of you to list here individually, but please know that I am truly humbled and thankful for everything all of you have done for me over the years. Your support of my work means the world to me.

The city of Oxford: You took me in, made me a part of the community, and supported me through thick and thin.

The city of Ahmedabad: You raised me to be an open-minded, adventurous eater and taught me that there was a world beyond.

City Grocery Restaurant Group: What can I say? Where would I be without y'all? Working with every one of you has been a privilege.

Sara Camp: I can't believe this is done. I don't know anyone else who would have taken on the task to go through my scribbles word by word, line by line, and done it better. You took me and this book on as a project despite having two full-time jobs. You are Superwoman. I hope you are proud of what we have created.

Osayi: You looked at my half-baked idea of an introduction at that hilltop in Sewanee and helped me mold it into an idea that sold a book. You saw something I didn't know I had. This book would have been a non-starter without you.

Dr. Jessica B. Harris: For over twenty years you have taught me and have been a friend, a mentor, a sounding board, and a steadying influence. I hope I can make you proud.

Dr. Patricia Wilson and Chef Bruce Ozga: You two taught me that there was a lot more to being a chef than cooking. You taught me how to organize, how to write recipes, and how to communicate with coworkers and colleagues. Thank you!

Bess Currence: You continued to ask me when I was going to write. You continued telling me that I could do it. Looks like you were right.

Melanie Tortoroli: You went to bat for me after our meeting at Emma's Torch and landed this book. Your attention to details, your belief that I had it in me to finish this, and your timely encouragement has made this seem like a breeze. Thank you! I hope we get a chance to work together again.

Angie Mosier: You have managed to turn words into the most beautiful pictures I have ever seen. You are a pro's pro. The absolute best.

David Black and Melissa: What can I say? You two are the most generous, selfless, beautiful people I know. Saying "thank you" doesn't do justice to how Teresa and I feel about all you have done to get us here.

Big ups to all the folks who tested recipes and gave feedback. Without your help, there would be no recipes. I am especially indebted to Michael Koury, Stacey Ballis, Shannon Kinsella, Chandra Ram, Cheetie Kumar, Melissa Hall, and the Sunday Supper Club.

A special shout-out to the Bill Neal Crew: the late, great Johnny Apple, Ben Barker, the late Karen Barker, Robert Stehling, Bill Smith, John Currence. That fateful August night in 2003 at the Beard House, you made me realize how closely connected the place I grew up in and the place I call home are. It was on that evening that I knew I was a Southern chef and that I wanted to do everything I could to carry on your legacy.

Bollingers, Hoffmisters, Halls, and Pauls: Thank you for being amazing, supportive in-laws and sharing your Southern stories with me.

In memory of chefs Floyd Cardoz and Raji Jallepalli: My journey would have ended before it started if it wasn't for the path you paved.

INDEX

Note: Page references in *italics* indicate photographs.